WHEN I WAS ELENA

WHEN I WAS ELENA

ELLEN URBANI HILTEBRAND

THE PERMANENT PRESS
Sag Harbor, NY 11963

Library of Congress Cataloging-in-Publication Data

Hiltebrand, Ellen, 1969–
    When I was Elena / Ellen Hiltebrand.
      p.   cm.
    ISBN 1-57962-124-4 (cloth)
    1. Hiltebrand, Ellen, 1969– 2. Americans—Guatemala—Biography.
  3. Indians of Central America—Guatemala—Biography. 4. Teachers—
  Guatemala–Biography. I. Title.

CT598.H55A3 2006
920.72089'9707281–dc22
[B]   2005056137

Printed in The United States of America.

To Frank Hiltebrand, who became my husband.
To Keith McDonough, who became my brother.
To Paul Montanchez, who became my friend.

Although your stories are not told here,
the impact of your presence looms large in my life.

— *Mil de gracias* —

AUTHOR'S NOTE

Although these stories are true, the details have been ascribed in such a way as to fictionalize certain events, locations, and participants to ensure the personal integrity and security of the individuals involved. The names have all been changed, because the names are not mine to disclose. To borrow the words of a master: "If the reader prefers, this book may be regarded as fiction. But there is always the chance that such a book of fiction may throw some light on what has been written as fact." (Ernest Hemingway, Preface, *A Moveable Feast*.)

*"The true worth of a race must be measured
by the character of its womanhood."*

— Mary McLeod Bethune

Prologue. Elena's Story

*T*he nicest thing anyone ever said to me came cloaked in an insult which, while essentially inaccurate, proved astute in its initial perceptiveness: "We all thought you'd fail." They all thought I'd fail. In saying it, writing it, even now, years after the fact, a familiar sensation echoes from the place where my backbone connects to my tailbone. A prickly primitive emotion grows there and threatens to burst, charging up my spine and spreading through the vertebrae across my back. A dog cornered, I imagine my hair prepared to rise, hackle-like, from my skin while I bare my teeth and growl, "I will not fail!" Yet my hair lies flat and my lips are closed serenely, with only the slightest hint of a coy smile pulling at the corners. Because, in reflection, I resolve to recognize that they were right. Of course they thought I would fail. Everyone did. Truth be told, I may have occasionally entertained the thought myself.

Few times in my life have I ever looked so entirely out of place. A sorority girl, fresh from college in the refined Deep South, with her Laura Ashley dresses and long, be-ribboned tresses, should be hosting tea at the country club. One expects to see a girl like that having her nails done. Laws of congruence dictate that this girl will shop at Saks, sip at mint juleps, and appreciate the opera. So then, watching her wield a hoe—chopping into the coarse Guatemalan soil, ducking from the dirt kicked up by her novice swings—seems as natural as watching a champion racehorse pull a plow. Witnessing the blood drizzling down the handle of the hoe, watching the sanguine fluid pour from the blisters cropping up along her creamy palms to water the earth, who could be blamed for thinking: "This will never work. She will surely fail."

The day of the hoe and the blisters is the day the Americans with whom I trained christened me The China Doll, believing my soft skin more worthy of caresses than interaction with the elements. The fact that they embraced me anyway, accepted me as one of them in spite of the belief that I would not last, speaks well of their appreciation of my intentions. Nonetheless, the men placed bets—

"I'll give her three days,"

"No, one week,"

"Five bucks says she lasts two months!"

—turning my struggle into a game, wondering aloud how long I would persist before retreating for the comfort of home. They thought I didn't know; I heard every word.

The Guatemalan trainers, in their love of all which reeks of Americana, chose instead to refer to me as Barbie. "*Pobrecita,*" they cooed as I walked in from the field that day, dragging the barbaric hoe behind me. "Poor little thing, you." Ignoring the blood streaming from my hands, for blood and grave injury are things to which they are impervious, the short, round, brown women with smiles for faces reached their hands toward my head, saying: "*Amorcita,* little love, it appears a horrible and unfortunate thing has occurred. There is land in your hair." Picking with their gnarled fingers, the women rid my scalp of small stones, branches, clumps of dirt, and one kernel of corn. The mess from my head ground into the floor under their feet as they circled me in the dining hall, brushing my hair, adjusting my ribbons, cleaning me up. "*Ya, mira,*" they said, shaking their heads up and down, smiling at each other with gold-plated teeth that glimmered from mouths otherwise full of decay. "The Barbie is better," they said, shoving me toward the door with bruised hands, an aching spirit, a battered ego—but good hair. "What a pity she won't last," they lamented behind me. "She is so nice to look at."

Had we known the truth when we began, likely none of us would have stuck it out. By the end, over two years later, our little corps of American trainees would be culled by more than half: the weaker (?), the smarter (?), having fled for home. The head count, at the end, included a few beaten, four raped, another kidnapped. One dead. Some stalked, many shot at, even more chased from their homes. One fled under the cover of night, secreted away by the Marines, a bounty on his head. Of the group of us who lasted, every one fell sick enough to require swift medical intervention, every one fell victim to the thieves who hid behind the mask of the neighbor's child or the helpful bus assistant. Laughable, in light of the statistics, that on that long-ago day someone bet money on the fact that a little dirt in my hair would be enough to scare me away. Even more ironic: The bettors beat me home.

1. Elena's Story, Spring 1992

*D*arkness hugged tight to the ground and night loomed hot and dry over the site where the bus deposited me on the side of the highway. The scrub brush scratched at my ankles with spiny tentacles of welcome as a trio of lizards followed the fading fumes of the bus down the lonely two-lane road. The succulent and tropical Guatemala I expected, this was not. *National Geographic* lied. The broad-leafed, dew-dripping rain forest images peeking out from the glossy pages of the magazine with headlines coaxing, "Guatemala, Land of Lushness," existed in some place other than the country beneath my feet. My toes touched turf crossed by cowboy boots on the heels of gunslingers who defended their honor, their women, and their drunken opinions with loaded pistols and lewd gestures toward what they apparently presumed were well-endowed genitalia. The Wild West turned crude. Even in the pitch dark of the unlit night, the smell of sage and dust badgered me with each breath—a constant reminder that no tropical paradise would be found here.

Having visited this town whose name I couldn't pronounce once, the month before, I knew the mountain range must still be there, to my left, a ghostly apparition loitering long enough for my eyes to adjust to the black night. As it claimed its shape, other, more diminutive monuments began asserting their position at the base of the towering giant. A cactus. An iguana. The bus stop (an elementary lean-to with one slumbering drunk prostrate just outside its range of coverage). All hugged the base of the mountain on the opposite side of the road. A broken kiosk stood sentinel next door. The specter of the leathery woman who manned it during the day stared me down; echoes of her pitch ("Coca-Cola! Coca, Coca, Coca-Cola!") mixed with the cry of an owl, and together they screamed at abandoned me while darkness engulfed me thick in her exhaust-laced embrace.

Loneliness, that age-old companion of night, almost brushed past me when, with an arrogant brace of my chin, I reminded myself, "You've visited here once before." But just as swiftly, my mind spewed forth images of the faces and places I met on that one brief visit: a vision of eyes, noses, and mouths swirling together to create a spiraling, incarnate mass. The phantasm loomed large, reminding me that I remembered not a single name, nor the path to the house I could rent for eighty *quetzales* a month. So loneliness, that sly denizen of caves in the spirit, quickly drifted back and clutched me deep within her grasp.

The weight of her crushed me and, seeking relief from the sudden pressure, I let loose the bags which, evenly distributed, had provided me with some semblance of equilibrium. Slowly uncurling my fingers from the strap stretched taut between my two hands, I let the largest duffel bag crash to the ground first. Purchased on a hazy Alabama summer day during my final trip to say goodbye to my college boyfriend, this duffel distressed me. Initially valuing aesthetics at least as highly as function, I lamented my inability to locate a royal blue duffel to match my new backpack, and had settled for black. At least, I rationalized at the time, the color matched the backpack's straps. Halfway through packing the thing, however, my obsession had turned instead to its inadequate size.

The belly of the bag longed to burst. The seams groaned. With the contents of a life, or a life to be, stuffed within its limited space, the zipper screamed for reinforcement, and in its voice I heard echoes of my father's words. His insistent command, "Take this, take this, take this," rolled through my memory, playing a strong bass note to the faint soprano of the cicadas and the persistent screech of a hidden owl. As clearly as if he stood beside me now I saw his frame outlined in my bedroom door the night before I stepped onto a plane and out of his life for years.

"Take this," he insisted, pressing a thick new roll of duct tape into my hands.

"Dad," I whined, arching an eyebrow and rolling my eyes at the already overstuffed bags lining the bedroom floor, "there's no room."

"Find room," he commanded in the exacting father-bred tone which ultimately indicated that if you didn't, he would. "Duct tape is important."

He quizzed me the morning before I left: "You have the tape?"

I extended my arm for his inspection. Lacking a place to squeeze the roll into the capacity-breached bags, I wore my father's duct tape like a bracelet into my new world.

The detested duffel now wore it too, cinched tight around its length in a zigzagging zebra fashion, a blessed reprieve for the soon-to-explode casing. Like the bag, lying forlornly along the side of the lonely road on this lonely night, I found some comfort in the silver-tinged lines of my father's duct tape which reflected speckled shafts of moonlight through the dissipating cloud of dust onto my shoes.

Slouching my left side, I let gravity have the second bag, relieving the place where the strap carved a raw, red line into my shoulder's skin. It crashed down with a frightening clatter. The contents smashed together as the bag fell, striking the ground and the peace of the night with an alarming chorus of metal upon metal. Apparently stunned, even the cicadas acquiesced, obliging the racket with their silence.

I damned this duffel too. Purchased hastily in a panic-driven moment when its larger twin refused to accommodate all my belongings, the original contents of this duffel had long since been farmed out to other bags. It now sheltered a full set of dishes, pots, and pans, and the sound of them crashing together chastised me. The bag spoke to me of my disobedience. It resonated with the voice of my mother.

"Take this," she had said, silhouetted in the doorframe recently vacated by my father. A tiny woman, her presence loomed large and soft, and she purposefully extended her arms to me. Between her two hands, which smelled faintly yet perpetually of raw garlic, she balanced a gift.

"Take this, take this, take this," she coaxed, placing the heavy-duty, no-stick, antiburn, handle-guaranteed-not-to-fall-off frying pan on top of the bursting duffel.

"Mom," I whined, arching an eyebrow and rolling my eyes for a second time at the piles of items about to be left behind for lack of space, "there's no room."

"Try to find room," she urged. "A frying pan is important."

I never found room. Of all the items I packed that night, sure I could never find a comparable product in Guatemala, at least 25 percent could be purchased in local *tiendas*. Another 25 percent sat on community market tables, poking out from between piles of stolen-and-available-for-resale sunglasses and assorted unfinished clay statues of the Virgin. But a good, hard-working frying pan did not exist in this country. As I

13

stared down at the duffel full of tin pans which would soon turn black from the fire, wear thin, and disintegrate, I questioned the judgment involved in leaving behind this gift from my mother.

Of course, I brought along many others. In fact, as I let fall to the ground the rope bag of hammocks and the backpack full of clothes and toilet paper, I decided the stubbornness inherited from my mother may have had the most direct impact on my current predicament. "Stick-to-it've-ness" would have been her preferred means of couching the phrase, but determination, loyalty, and stubbornness all hide within the same definition in my book. So when my hardheaded Irish mother married my hot-blooded Italian father, borne within me were the genes which meant that once thought up, an idea must unfailingly be carried through to its ultimate conclusion. Thus, when my parents first raised doubts about the sanity of a single young woman teaching abroad, the seed of the idea became so cemented within me that it plotted a virtual road map to this very spot where I now stood, forsaken, on the side of a highway in the Guatemalan desert.

This place: The physical geography I ran to in a calculated attempt to alter the emotional landscape I fled from. Traditional. Ordinary. Wholesome. Reasonable. Mere words, yes, but they bore for me the weight of a conviction: a decree that image and social standing counted for more than honesty, more than a *true* life. Words that could trap you within the confines of your own backyard. My friends were planning weddings and picking china, choosing between the man of their dreams and the man with the trust fund, compromising the life they imagined for the one with the best 401K plan and six weeks' vacation. But I could have been Virginia Woolf's young Clarissa Dalloway, confronting the crossroads no one recognized: life with Richard (the sane, stable choice) or passion with Sally (the daring decision). I craved the cliché of the road less traveled, for it had suddenly become far too easy to see how the sensible life resulted in padding your pocket with a rock and walking placidly to a mundane death at the bottom of an anonymous river.

To this point, my life glistened with a veneer of shiny accolades and unquestionable accomplishment. Yet in the surface beneath I had little faith. I sensed acquaintance only with the mirage of me; feared the essence might not match up, were it there at all. I came to Guatemala to find me—all the vast possibilities of me—and save them from the gradual eroding decay of disuse. A trial not by fire but by cultural rift. If the substance of me was not buoyant enough to rise here, perhaps I was already lost to myself.

Lost, frankly, is how I felt. The month before when I visited this town for a few hours, I lingered long enough to put money down on a house, buy a popsicle, and catch the next bus out of town. Now I have forgotten where the house is. A month ago I drew a map in my mind which every day since has been chinked at and erroneously erased by the learning curve of acclimatization. There should be stairs breaching the precipice to my right, leading to San Marquesa de Trójillonada, the town in the valley below. Well, perhaps not stairs, per se, although the intent showed: Some cracked cement blocks embedded into the earth started the path from the road, and ended not quite halfway to their destination—at a point some distance beyond where I'm sure I myself would have sacrificed my body to the pure exhaustion of the effort. Stairlike carvings in the parched soil completed the downward dive into town, a multitude of etched impressions worn thin by the footfalls of a community. Leaving my bags behind, I searched for the staircase, peering over the hillside where cement blocks consorted with boulders, where every ten feet a rock formation masqueraded as steps. Their voices finally led me to its location; a small group of singers hovered in the night at the bottom of the stairs on the edge of the town.

I stood there awhile, staring down into my future, watching the group grow. My hands, finally free of the bags they ferociously clutched from bandits and beggars on the four-hour bus trip, moved maternally across the protruding belly of my dress. Courage must be gathered before moving from this limbo space. Gently, I eased the puppy Calixta out from inside my clothes where she'd been cinched conspiratorially above my waistband for the long, pregnant bus trip from the capital. Calixta would allow me to move forward for myself without moving forward alone.

Navigating a stairwell in darkness is never easy. Navigating a hand-made quasi-stairwell while balancing all your worldly possessions in four about-to-burst bags and simultaneously dragging one newly-awakened puppy on an improvised leash of two knotted shoelaces and one hair ribbon is, as I came to discover, essentially impossible. Once, visiting our new home in Virginia, my uncle walked off the top riser, thinking he turned into the bathroom, and incurred a few broken ribs, one shattered elbow, and a dislocated knee and collarbone. His damaged body haunted my steps. We proceeded gingerly. Each move required precision, analysis, and a good deal of contortion as the angle of the stairs conformed more to the lay of the land than to technical proportions. Some cantered off to the side rather than hover directly below; others required a leap, both of faith and of body, to land on the far-flung subsequent tread. As the unmistakable chorus of "Oh How I Love Jesus" wafted from the crowd below, my plodding gait acquired a cadence. We were almost there.

One step to level land. One chance to make a first impression on my new neighbors upon whom we snuck while their backs were turned.

Evidence how one misstep changes everything.

I remember the frog, landing on the overburdened duffel suspended between my extended forearms. I remember the sensation of shoelaces and ribbon lashing my ankles and knees together, turning my body into a living catapult. I remember the noise when Calixta's mandible gorged the frog, ripped the bag, rained my kitchenware upon the unsuspecting townsfolk. I remember the silence that followed the death of the last rolling pot lid, as everyone circled to stare in holy awe at my upended pink panties in the pile of self and stuff tangled on the ground.

I try to forget that on my first day in town, I crashed, and flashed, the annual Evangelical revival.

* * *

Oddly, my soap disappeared first. Very few items the general populous might consider theft-worthy accompanied me on my Latin American trek: Gortex hiking boots, a waterproof watch, a hand-me-down 35mm camera, a U.S. passport. The fact that someone stole my Crabtree & Evelyn Spring Rain Body Bar—instead of those far more worthwhile goods!—within less than twenty-four hours might have amused me were I not blinded with indignation at the intrusion into my personal space.

In retrospect, what did I expect? My house reeked of luxury: concrete walls and floor, a tin roof, a bed with a Sealy mattress, two rooms (three counting the one stuffed top to bottom with drying corn kernels). A door with a lock, a little front porch. My own *pila* in the yard for collecting water and washing clothes. And attached behind the house, not a latrine, but a bathroom. An intact, viable bathroom. The toilet, a beautiful porcelain model, required simple assistance from a bucket of water tossed into its bowl to function perfectly. (This in contrast to the filthy thrones in the capital's airport lounge; the things deposited there float, waterlogged, then coagulate.) Beside my toilet a showerhead graced the wall, useful at night when the water barreled into town sometime after sundown. Its arrival time being somewhat unpredictable, I learned to leave the *pila* faucet in a perpetual state of "open." Every evening as the curtain of night fell, sounds greeted me: mules' hooves on cobblestone, the soft scamper of sandals past my door, the collective crackle of supper fires, and the hungry clatter of spoons. Finally, the glorious racket—water, trickling at first, then splashing, ranting against the deep stone walls of the *pila*. The noise, a nightly taskmaster, bid me run to my bathroom and bathe. Soap on the clothes first, then clothes off and soap on me. Move fast enough, and the first few spurts burst warm from the pipe daily boiled by the beat . . . beat . . . beating of the sun. Too soon, hot transitioned to cold. Frosty drips slapped my skin, stung, but like a penitent child I stood rapt in the icy embrace, savoring the short-lived attention. Quickly it ended. A twenty-three and three-quarters hour drought ensued. With luck, the yellow plastic tub in which I stood performing the cleansing ritual captured sufficient bathwater for subsequent toilet-flushing reuse. I'd towel myself, pee, bask in the habitual pleasure of my makeshift boudoir.

But in the beginning, uninitiated still, the inherent splendor of my bathroom eluded me, and I merely lamented the theft of the soap. The ensuing discovery of two long black hairs—clearly Guatemalan!—in my hairbrush fanned my fury. Not only had I been robbed on my first day in town, but my beauty products had been vandalized. Worse, those two hairs bode a dire possibility. Lice might have gained a launch pad to my hair. Of all the things worth fearing in Guatemala—burglars, snakes, earthquakes, cholera—I arrived truly dreading only two. Lice and chickens.

Persistent childhood memories served as the source of both paranoias. Lice invaded my head once as a little girl. After hanging our heads over the sink for mom to scald and scrub, my sisters and I sat crying in a line on the floor before the living room sofa while dad systematically scraped the eggs from our scalps with a nit comb. With thick red hair hanging to my waist now, the mere thought of dragging a nit comb through it all made my eyes smart and my skin prickle. The chicken issue—significantly more anxiety provoking than the fear of lice—developed directly from the day at my uncle's farm when someone thought it would do the suburban kids good to see a chicken slaughtered. The death, although lengthy and brutal due to poor knife

17

preparation, held my attention but nothing more. However, the rampaging headless beast charging directly at me, spewing blood (from where? the head is gone!) and flapping its unmanned wings left six-year-old me unglued. My sister's need to cap the event by chasing me through the barnyard, swinging and twirling the head in the air by that strange rooster-skin-flap-thing like a perverse party favor forever sealed my fate as a fearer-of-chickens.

Unless a chicken stormed the building, I naively assumed the day could not get worse.

I decided to boil the infested hairbrush.

Boiling supposedly solves a multitude of problems. Primarily, it stifles amoebas, giardia and the brain worms that savage their way from feces to river to pipe to faucet to cup to feasting on your inside parts. Surely boiling would kill nit eggs in a brush. Know, though, that the decision to boil the water is not one I arrived at easily. The thermometer screamed 118°F in the April shade of the jacaranda tree. Waves of heat ricocheted off the metal roof and radiated back from the cement floor to create a palpable band of heatstroke potential inside the house. A lifetime fan of bare feet, I slunk outside in sneakers to keep from burning my soles on the sandy soil. Cali, inspired I suppose by the roasting her fur and fanny took on all solid surfaces, climbed into a hammock of her own accord. I swayed her on the front porch, feeding her air; her tongue dangled through the cloth mesh, slurping the breeze.

I couldn't even bring myself to boil our drinking water, opting instead to squirt bleach into the *pila* receptacle, judging the mixture adequately cleansed when it exuded the fresh smell and taste of a community swimming pool. So the decision to boil the brush betrayed my alarm. It also involved inordinate effort. I owned a two burner cook-stove, but needed to purchase the gas *tambo* to fuel it.

Cali and I set forth for the store at a languorous pace. The heat crept upon our backs; it weighed us down. Its heft bowed my shoulders, plastered me with sweat. I pitied our scorched lungs, the air pumping in too hot and back out still warm. For Cali's part, her tongue never entered her mouth, strung like a snake from her lips to dry above the burning pavement. As we walked, she left a trail of sloughed fur, an accelerated shed reaction, in our wake. Even the trees, mostly palms, stood listlessly erect beneath the midday glare with drooping leaves that begged for solace. These sentinels to the sun lined the street, pointed out our path, but threw us no shade. By their presence alone the pretty palms—decorative, sexy even—hammered home the message: In Guatemala, beauty serves little purpose.

Yet I searched for beauty, for joy. Something to which I could cling when the heat wanted to smother me and my belongings decided to depart with some stranger. Something beautiful to tie me to this place and justify my staying when my stomach growled, my muscles ached, and my bones screamed for the simple luxuries of home that I never before recognized. In that moment, I settled on the street. All the town streets (and by all I refer to the two streets coming into town, the two streets going out, and the two connecting them down the middle) were made of cobblestones. I liked the cobblestone streets. Cobblestones are quaint—not filthy, cracked, broken, muddy, or shifting. Cobblestones are stable. Cobblestones pave the streets of Europe and other places I've never been to but always wanted to visit. Cobblestones click-clack under the wooden clogs of imagined children in Hans Brinker stories, and decorate the otherwise boring roads in the colorful pictures hidden within my favorite book of childhood fairy tales. Cobblestones speak of things special, of magic. The word alone rolls off the tongue in a masterful way.

Cobblestones, too, equal richness. There is one, and only one, surefire way to determine the affluence of a community in Guatemala, and the trick is in keeping your eyes to the ground. The surfaces of the streets share all the secrets. Woe is the village whose roads consist of footpaths between outbuildings, trails of matted-down grass or trampled sand. These are the truly impoverished. The next class, the terrifically poor, peer from holes in their mud huts onto dirt roads rutted and ravaged by floods, earthquakes, age. Moderately more affluent, the plain-old-poor traverse roads of dirt minus the ruts—worn flat and kept flat by increased traffic and the occasional vehicle. Gravel is the domain of the poor-but-pretending-not-to-be; asphalt the exclusive right of the poor middle class. Cobblestone—well, cobblestone is for the chosen few. And my neighbors considered themselves nothing if not chosen.

I would soon learn a seemingly baseless yet monumentally important rule of genetics: the definition of chosen. Everything in a Guatemalan's life—his facial features, his worldly station, the size of his perpetually divided plot of land—depends on the flavor of the blood roiling through the veins of his ancestors. Indigenous counts for nothing. *Mezclado*, "mixed," counts for something. But pure, unadulterated, straight-from-the-Spanish, my-grandfather's-grandfather-was-a-Conquistador ("and I will prove it if you want to fight about it!") Ladino counts for everything. The people of San Marquesa de Trójillonada, with no documentation or even any record past the lifeline of their most recently deceased relative, believe with all the fervor of the newly converted that they are 100% uncontaminated European. Ladinos extraordinaire. This good fortune of breeding manifests in myriad ways ranging from the subtle to the unabashedly overt. Farmers live banished in the outlying provinces—only the shopkeepers, the tailors, the men of business dwell in San Marq. When venturing out, these people of education and culture stand shoulders erect (and in this heat, I admit, *that* I admire them for) and stare down the bridge of their noses at any and everyone, daring the frightened souls they encounter to question the flat, squat, Mayan-predisposed arch of their proboscises. Finally, without exception and under no circumstances, will a San Marq-ian condescend to share his row on a bus with an Indian. In these parts, Indians stand on buses full of empty seats. San Marq epitomizes, in short, a lovely and heat-ravaged bastion of bigotry; a hamlet of Aryan sentimentality in a country of mixed breeds.

Were they not so nice to me (were I not white, were I not blue eyed) I might have hated it. Under other less harsh circumstances, I would have self-righteously despised it. The Northern-born, Southern-bred youth in me (really, I was a virtual adolescent still) straddled the fence of convenience. I dated the handsome black boy when it was high school hip and my friends did the same, and joined the exclusive all-white college sorority when they did that, too. I walked past a burning cross once in Tuscaloosa, deriding the action with carefully crafted intellectualisms at luncheon while passing the silver creamer. But I never joined the protest. I turned my back on the good'ole SAE boys when they booed the African American homecoming queen and waved that God-awful Confederate flag. But I didn't change my seat; kept close to the crowd. Now, it bothered me not one bit to be able to walk to the *tienda* for my gas *tambo* instead of having to wait for the weekly market to purchase goods, as would have been the case had I lived in many other more indigenous towns.

After stopping only twice to rest, to breathe, on the arduous two-block walk to the *tienda*, we arrived at our destination just as the heat overtook us. Cali promptly barfed on the threshold. Yet even in the presumptuous towns, barf, shit, blood, and litter are left to lie where they land. We stepped over the steaming pile of slobber into the store.

20

In tiny towns, *tiendas* function as the life force of a community: grocery, apothecary, diner, hardware store, bar, and meeting hall. This one served all purposes, simultaneously, that Sunday. But the gentle shopkeeper, bless his heart, promptly identified me as his neediest customer. He immediately handed me an orange popsicle; I immediately placed it in Cali's mouth. Oblivious to the stares of the customers whose own mangy dogs survived wildly chained to trees, she curled on the floor to suck her sweet. I faded onto the counter and paid for a second, for me.

Together we sucked and sucked, energy only for sucking. Sucking and smiling through orange lips and frozen teeth into the eyes of the shopkeeper who beamed and nodded in time with my suckling of the treat. We squared off over the counter, me leaning upon it for strength, him moving in closer to observe. Had I been standing straight, I would have dwarfed him; at 5'3", I towered above everyone. But my lean brought us face to face, mine innocent, his wizened. A few months before we met, the lines had started appearing on his face, when he wrapped his only daughter in a blanket and carried her to the one hospital in the country where they had a spitting chance of making his kidney function in her disintegrating body. His sallow eyes bore the effects of the surgery, his wrinkled brow marked endless nights waiting for hope. The furrow from tears foretold the failure. His daughter lay dying on the other side of the shop wall, in his house's adjacent bedroom, and he had paternal love to spare on me.

Slowly, cautiously, he reached out and patted my hair. Everyone touched my hair. Even in the States, the ultrared hue garnered copious attention. But here, everyone—every single living being—needed to touch it, feel it, smell it, pull it, comment on it, and lay a yanking claim to it. A little girl once shyly wondered if my hair was "made in the United States," and realizing that technically, in the conception summer of 1968, it had been, I answered yes. My hair never permitted me to be invisible; it drew too many into its mystical embrace. In the Central American world of all black and all straight, curly and red harked as a portentous phenomenon.

But the shopkeeper patted where everyone else tugged. Not out of curiosity, not motivated by alarm. He patted with kindness until I finished the pop, and then asked, "*¿Ya?*" The word meant all of this:

"Are you feeling better?"

"Is that enough?"

"Wasn't that delicious?"

"Are you happy?"

"Do you like me?"

"How about another popsicle?"

Before I answered, he produced two more pops—cherry this time—and with pursed lips and a jerk of his chin toward where Cali lay, charmingly indicated he expected one to be given to the dog. When I bent to offer her the cool confection, and pluck the chewed remains of the first stick from her gummy forearm, the crew of rebels in the corner sprung to life.

"¡A la gran puta! ¿Qué hace ésta gringa aca?" [Son of a bitch! What's that fucking white girl doing in here?]

The shopkeeper, sweet man, leapt to action, castigating the creeps while I hovered beside the relative safety of the counter. He hit the plumpest man on the head with a towel, knocking his cowboy hat to the floor while I pretended to ignore the commotion and diverted my eyes. An array of shelved items, startling in their diversity, captured my attention beneath the murky glass case of the counter. Nails, scissors, single aspirins in a long row, playing cards sporting naked women, firecrackers, a box of bullets, buxom truck-flap-lady stickers. But most were profoundly religious: rosaries, Mass cards, candles graced by the Holy Mother's glowing face, miniature versions of all the saints—the two Marys (Mary the beatific and Mary the whore), Joseph, Bernadette, Francis with his untamed pets. And a multitude of crosses. Jesus in every shape and form dying again, bleeding chipped plastic blood, suffering plaintively beside a full and dusty box of outdated and unwanted condoms.

From the edges of the counter to the ceiling corners stretched parade banners, and little flags strung from plastic streamers advertising the national beer, Gallo (read: Rooster), with namesake images of prancing cocks strutting from one end of the room to the other. A room full of cocks—the ones on the walls and the ones in the corner—and now the shopkeeper beckoned me to a chair at the cowed table of chastised men. Cali repositioned with me, curled beneath my chair, growled until the inebriants all backed off by two feet. She didn't like the smell of them and neither did I. To a man, they craved a bath not coming.

They congregated here to drink off their hangovers, still staggering in from Saturday night on Sunday afternoon. Their clothes stuck to them with a paste of weekday sweat, late night love, and face-down-in-the-pavement weekend grime. Clothes salvaged from another decade, another place, another man's closet—striped shirts with plaid pants, women's leisurewear bottoms with uniform tops, frilly tuxedo formals with bicycle shorts. All American discards, given to Goodwill or church charities, and reappearing as *Ropa Americana*, "American Clothes," dumped by the truckload twice a week in larger towns to be sold for a few *quetzales* per item. The fat man, the one who got whacked, donned a T-shirt with the word "Baby" emblazoned across the front above an arrow which pointed down over his protruding belly.

"Good afternoon, gentlemen," I said in perfectly studied Spanish. They all nodded their heads; the oldest among them, propped against the window frame, lost his balance and toppled to the floor. Knowing now that I could understand their crude comments, they stared in stunned silence and said nothing.

The shopkeeper's wife spilled half a bowl of soup broth on the floor in her haste to bring me something to eat. Then she flitted about for a few seconds, getting the presentation just right. She flicked a fly, folded the torn and quartered piece of a paper napkin—waste not, want not—and tucked it beneath the bowl. After blowing on the spoon and polishing it clean on the hem of her dress, she placed it daintily in my right hand and stood back to watch me eat. The shopkeeper brought me a *tamarindo* juice (yes, he guaranteed me, the water had been boiled) extracted from the seed pods of the tree that hung heavily pregnant through the window to my right. Everyone watched and waited. They gauged my constitution from the way I handled the food.

Minutes passed, endless hours of stifled questions, soaring expectations, and cultural concerns. Finally, the newly erected elderly drunk cleared his throat. Sloshed enough to have loosened inhibitions and sober enough to recognize the import of the occasion, his age allowed him the authority to broach the silence.

"Don Gustavo saw a vision of God at the revival," he said quietly, reverentially. "God whispered a message in his left ear." Everyone ahhed in awe. (Don Gustavo lost the hearing in his left ear from mumps at age seven. Who but God could he have heard on that side?) "God told him that cars from the United States are the best." Now he looked directly at me. "So I think I will start to save for a Ford. What do you think about that?"

I passed test one; I ate the soup. Test two: an intelligent answer.

"Fords are good," I replied to the affirmative nods, glances, and collective hmmms of the group.

The big fat man saw his chance, seized the moment. "What does this mean?" he asked, pointing to the word "Baby" on his shirt.

The truth, clearly, would be too much to bear. He would be ridiculed, and I would be the cause of his humiliation. Too quickly the three pistols on the tabletop (it is downright rude to imbibe among friends with hidden weapons) might spring to action. Men have lost toes, if not lives, with lesser provocation. I fished for an appropriate, albeit false, answer.

"It means powerful," I said loudly, so all could hear.

He eyed the word "Powerful," spelled B-A-B-Y across the front of his shirt, with the arrow pointing down toward his swelling crotch, then smirked at me with a lascivious two-toothed grin.

* * *

The shopkeeper insisted his son would carry the gas *tambo* to my house *en un rato*, "in a little while," which I had already learned meant "in a few hours, if we remember to get around to it, otherwise stop by to visit and remind us again in a few days and we can probably get it to you by the end of the week, as long as it is still in stock, which it might not be by then; actually, it probably definitely won't be, so we'll order it for you from the supplier, who unfortunately is on strike right now, but don't worry, it won't last too long, just, um, *un rato* or so."

No reason to rush home now. No excuse for hurrying.

This would take some getting used to.

I ran at life, sped through it. Filled my datebook, loaded my dance card, never said no, and initiated projects like a philanthropist possessed of the need to see my name in print, in lights, in esteem. I loved to eavesdrop on intimate discussions only to find myself and my endeavors to be the topic of conversation. I projected my persona like a sail that's full and awe-inspiring when the wind blows, but mimics a plain old piece of cloth when the current dies down. In the private spaces, I feared losing control; who would I be without the command that comes with perpetual preoccupation? So I amassed credentials and accumulated certificates, building my life (or at least its trappings) to a roaring crescendo until the moment I slammed—SMACK! and bruised my nose—on the plodding pace that was Central America.

Who is a calendar-crammer who loses track of the days? A powerwalker who strolls? A busybody who idles? Who would I be, what would I do, where would I go with nothing to hurry home for?

24

In a family of overachievers, it can be hard to discern whether the world with its collective circles of friends likes you for you, for the essence of you, or simply enjoys the vicarious success you epitomize. Truth be told, I had no idea how many of my peers gravitated to me because I was the cheerleader, the club president, the A-student, the person to know. Asked something personal and important—whom I loved or what I dreamed for—I imagine a number would be so focused on the superficial as to be unable to formulate an answer. Their expectations of me, my expectations of myself, could sometimes be stiflingly small despite being larger than life.

And Guatemalans expected no less from me. They labeled me by the place I came from, the government I grew up in, and the color of my skin. Either they loved me for it or they hated me for it, with no in-between. A Yankee pied piper, I might march along with an enthralled audience of dozens, all wanting to talk to and touch me, and still from some hidden place in a far-off field the shrieks could stalk me: "Go home, stupid white bitch!" The men who tried to hurt me, to fuck me, to wrap their hands around my throat and steal the privilege they envied me for stood in stark contrast to the two adorable community emissaries who once asked if I'd be willing to bear them an heir so the town could have its own white baby. Their motives swelled from different desires, yet any way you look at it they all expected to get a piece of me.

But there were a few, women all, who wanted me not as a trophy prize or for bragging rights. They ignored my reputation, my background and my qualifications. They sought me out because they sincerely liked me. Liked me just because I walked through the door, not because of what I could do for them. They found me, settled on me for no reason, and let me find and get settled with myself in their company. Our spirits all met midway, our collective consciousness bumped into each other from afar, that odd "don't I know you from somewhere?, haven't we met before?" mystique that allowed us to step across some cultural divide to touch each others' hands, eat each others' food, and immerse ourselves comfortably into each others' spaces.

It happened initially when I got sick on the way home from a popsicle pit stop one sweltering afternoon. Before anyone else thought to, Lupe arrived and helped. The first thing she did for me was to hold back my hair while I vomited cold orange-red sugar and hot bile onto those lovely cobblestones beside her front gate. Then she ushered me inside to her favorite lawn chair, turned her fan upon me, and became my friend. The vomit played matchmaker and Lupe made me her bosom buddy.

We talked about nothing necessarily that first day. Just chatted. Pretended and in the pretending made real the idea that our lives were not separated by years and customs and lines drawn by politicians on barren patches of land; pretended that in real life we were neighbors which now, in fact, we were.

Lupe looked fortyish, acted fiftyish, wouldn't live to be sixtyish; but by birthright she's thirtyish and looking forward to a life done living. She peers in the mirror and sees the next decade, she listens to her voice and hears an elderly echo. She's met her man, had her kids, and is slowly adjusting to the idea that in terms of excitement, her life is finished. "Thirty feels very old," she said to me one day. "You are lucky still to be young."

But I'm getting ahead.

On that first day I started with this: "You live in a lovely town."

She launched into a description of its capsulated history, beginning with the church. "A crew of carpenters has worked every day since it fell to rebuild it. Don't you admire their work on . . ."

I had especially admired the church flanking the town square, or rather the face of the church, for a face is all that stood. Look behind the façade—peer through the door or peek around the corner of the front wall—and the remaining walls and roof squat in a pile of debris littered with pews, altars, and other blessed church attire. Something out of a World War II movie that makes you think you should scream for help and start digging for survivors.

". . . because after the church fell during the last earthquake, they've worked so hard to repair it," she concluded.

I think I have misunderstood. The last big earthquake was almost two decades ago. The most recent small shake was maybe two weeks ago. "A little tiny tremor did all that damage?" I asked incredulously.

"No," she reiterated, "the last *big* earthquake," and she shook her hands viciously in front of her to simulate the violent rocking, actually causing her chair to bounce a bit and the joints to rattle.

I know my history. Guatemala wiggles all the time on the back of a creeping tectonic plate. No one pays the motion any mind. But a big one hit in '76; the kind that makes the nightly news. I'll bet my father watched it from his overstuffed La-Z-Boy while I parked my bike, the blue one with the basket and the training wheels, in the garage and ran inside to wash my hands for Wednesday's meatloaf dinner. Maybe he saw my church crumble.

Then this occurs to me: They have been rebuilding, every day, for sixteen years, and have erected one wall. At this rate they'll just be getting the roof on when the next big one hits in a hundred years and the whole thing will topple to the ground again.

"My first daughter was born in the year of the earthquake," Lupe continued, "and my second was born when Canela had her litter."

Canela is a mutt who runs with a pack of town dogs who all escaped their chains and meager food scraps to flourish on a diet of recycled feces and survive in the open-air arcade of speeding buses and blistering sun. From the day she learned to walk, Canela likely wore a strapping stud straddled on her back, stuck to her end to end propagating the scabby species. Canela and all the other weary female dogs ceaselessly suckled, birthed, or gestated a litter.

Through the wide-open front door, I eyed Canela's current pack of pups nesting beneath the back left tire of a parked pickup truck and pointing wondered, "You have an infant?"

"Ay, Mary Mother of God, help me, no!" Lupe screeched while making the sign of the cross and clapping her hands together in front of her face. "My parts are too dried up for that!" Her privates may be dry but her hands are not. The only young thing about her, her hands do not work for a living. Lupe is well-off, but of course I already knew that because she owns a fan.

"Not that litter," she continued, jerking her chin toward the one outside, "the *other* one," referring to the time ages ago when Canela birthed a puppy—one of fourteen—with two heads. (Some interpreted the delivery as a sinister omen, but Lupe, who knew her own baby would arrive that day, decided to decipher the message in a more practical way. She viewed it as a sign of intellectual potential doubled.)

So Lupe meant to say that her second daughter came into the world on the tail of Canela's remarkable litter, not Canela's regular litter. This is how dates are determined here. One daughter's age is in sync with the earthquake, the other's with a two-headed anomaly of nature.

"Enough about my boring life," Lupe said. "I want to know all about you. You are a missionary?"

"God, no," I said, startled.

"Of course you are," she reprimanded. "You came to us at the revival."

I'm thinking that I didn't actually come to the revival—rather, I fell into it, but I don't want to stir her memory. So I said, "No, I don't work for a church. I'm in the Peace Corps."

"Right. Like I said, you're with a peace group so you are a missionary."

"No, I'm not with a peace group, I'm with the Peace Corps."

"If you are a missionary it doesn't make any difference to me which peace group you are with," she explained.

I tried a new tack. "I apologize if my Spanish is not good and I am causing myself not to be clear. I am not a missionary. I work for the U.S. government."

"The White House?!"

Well, yes, sort of. So I nodded.

"The White House sent you?"

Still sort of. I nodded again.

"And your parents, your father, they sent you?"

I wouldn't actually put it that way myself, but at least my folks had adjusted to the idea by this time. I continued to nod.

She smiled broadly. "I am very proud to meet you. My house is your house. Our town is honored to host you."

Guatemalans can be very formal people, so her tone, while effusive, did not surprise me. I told her I also felt proud and honored to be here.

She invited me to stay for dinner. I accepted.

Glad to have cleared up the missionary question so succinctly, I looked forward to being properly introduced to her family who arrived home together shortly thereafter. Lupe's husband, the mayor, her daughters, the students—she spied them coming up the road at sundown and—that quick!—scooped me up, rushed me through the door, and stood hugging me in a tight embrace outside the garden gate. So that all could hear, so that all could see, she raised her voice and with a grand flourish of her arms pronounced:

"I would like to introduce you all to Elena, the daughter of the President of the United States of America, sent to us by her father George Bush from the White House, as a missionary of peace!"

The gossip flew through town at a lightning pace that defied all other movement in this part of the world. Before the last man arrived home for his evening meal, the whole community learned my new identity. I set Lupe straight rather quickly, but outside of her family the misunderstanding proved impossible to entirely clear up. I insisted my father never ran for, let alone occupied, the office of president. (I complicated the tale, I know, by showing to anyone who would look the only photograph I brought with me of my father, unfortunately shot at a party moments after he doffed a tricolored clown wig to entertain a group of children. I explained to them that it was false hair, but people remained baffled. "How strange; I thought he would have looked more like you," they repeated over and over.) In spite of the authenticity of the freak-haired picture, most persisted in believing the president sired me; they thought that by denying my true roots I demonstrated great modesty. They trusted me more for my humble nature. They needed me to be someone I wasn't for the sense of privilege it bestowed on them, and as privilege is such a rare commodity, I complied.

For all I know, time is still told in that town from the year the American president's daughter moved to San Marq.

* * *

Did I not prefer my solitude to the melancholy of her home, I might have passed every night in the comfort of Lupe's house. But the girls, sixteen and fourteen, wore pointy noses like pecking beaks, with angular faces that pierced and poked me aside as opposed to inviting in friendship. Their general malaise and teenage angst built a barrier which even my most probing questions failed to breach. Shrugs, hmms, and uh-huhs rounded out their emotive repertoire. At the dinner table they played bookends to Lupe, looking dazed and suddenly mute, and her husband who oozed off the edges of his chair like a lump of fresh clay. The few meals I shared there resounded with the clatter of my own voice and his occasional questions, always about life in the United States and American culture. They clung to those answers, all four of them. Their eyes drifted to the skies in fierce contemplation of my remarks. Their profound desire to be elsewhere weighed heavily upon them and smothered me.

Chicken always topped the menu. Roasted chicken, baked chicken, fried chicken, and—on the night I stopped dining there—chicken feet soup. Now, I must preface this tale by mentioning that I had been warned never to turn down food. To do so is a grave insult to people who have so little food to share. (Which is why I ate any and everything and wound up with all sorts of parasite-borne diseases which, at that time, I wasn't yet aware grew within me.) But I couldn't eat the feet; I couldn't even look at them. It appeared as if some top-heavy hen tripped on the rim of the dish and landed upside down in my bowl, the floating feet the only evidence of the swollen carcass hovering within the cloudy broth. The wrinkled-skinned, rigor mortised toes with their scratchy little nails still wore evidence of the last thing the chicken stepped on cooked to a crisp on the bottom of its unfortunate appendages.

"I am very, very sorry," I said as I carried my bowl back to the stove and returned its contents to the cookpot. I had to remove the feet from my sight. I felt spew in my mouth. I swear a toe wiggled in my direction.

"I'm not accustomed," I said vaguely by way of excuse as I sat back down at the table.

"Not accustomed to soup?" Lupe asked.

"Not accustomed to the chicken," I elaborated.

"You were accustomed to the chicken yesterday," she said.

"Yes, but yesterday it was a different part of the chicken. Today it's the feet part, and I'm not accustomed to eating feet."

"You've never eaten feet before?" Lupe confirmed, and I shook my head.

Then, wonder of wonder, a daughter spoke. "What do they do with the feet in the United States if you don't eat them?" she asked.

Here I made a fatal mistake which, in my defense, erupted from my mouth quite spontaneously, perhaps spurred on by the startling sound of the girl's voice. "I think they make dog food from the feet," I said innocently enough.

That Lupe served me dog food for dinner spread through the town in a more lagging way than the story of my parentage, but it nonetheless made the rounds. Everyone tittered about it wherever Lupe went, turning her "blunder" into a jingle-like mantra: dog food to the gringa . . . dog food to the gringa . . . dog food to the gringa. And what bothered me most is this: It had to be her own family spreading the tale of her foible, belittling her through their own cruel design. So I immediately started vacating her house before the family returned from work and school. We built the rest of our relationship around more private moments.

Alone, Lupe threw open the curtains of her world to me and filled her hours with my presence to such an extent that I grieved the plodding spiral of her days before my appearance whipped them into a flurry. I occupied her time and imagination. She clutched my hand—laced her fingers through mine and grasped my palm tight between both of hers, forcing us to walk so close together that our hips bounced in union with each other. In this way she led me through town, pointed out the history, showed me her chicken farm, filled my ears with gossip, told me her stories, laughed at mine, continued to cook for and feed me, introduced me to important people, threw me parties, watched over and cared for me. On those days we spent apart, when I taught at the local school, I sometimes spied her on my way to and from work: strolling toward her farm, rocking on the patio, peering from her window. Not a joyful stroll; a reluctant one. Not a vigorous rocking; a tedious one. Never peering in purposeful anticipation, her eyes always shielded regret. Separated, I glimpsed her life as it was without the hobby of me.

The other women in town referred to Lupe as the chicken lady—the one with the farm and the chicken-parts business, the one they bought scraps from, the one they admired. She had a house, not a hut, a refrigerator and a fan with electricity to run it, a *muchacha* to clean her laundry and other belongings. The clothes she bought at shops in the capital, never at *Ropa Americana*, covered her square, stocky frame in a practical, modest, and fairly modern fashion. But Lupe only tolerated her station with a dull annoyance and bland visage. Her dissatisfaction suggested she had once aspired to more lofty endeavors but somehow the persistence of the decades drained her of the motivation to achieve them. Even at her most joyful—and we met often with great joy—offhand comments belied her insidious disappointment:

"These children are not the ones I thought I would have."

"Marriage? After some years it is just a convenience."

"My father once was very proud of me."

"You do not know what I could have been."

Who is the darling she meant to be, then? I imagine the girl Lupe planning the life of the woman she would become; I suspect she fancied herself a future full of vivid, colorful splashes: romance, adventure, intrigue. Eyeing her present trappings—limp, brown clothes; manly, unstyled hair; unkissed lips—I wonder where that girl went and what intruded to veer the woman's fate in this other direction. I wonder if she has forgotten entirely who she intended to be, or if the girl Lupe might be hiding beneath this woman's skirt, weeping with equal parts irony and fury for the woman she did not become, lamenting the one who exists instead. I notice the picture frames full of people from twenty years ago, the plants outside flourishing but the one inside dying a slow death in its pot on the sill. How I yearn to know more of this unhappy woman whom others so unwittingly admire.

Then my novel emergency brought us closer.

Cali stepped on a scorpion.

Animals and people step on scorpions all the time. Scorpions scuttle across the desert sand with the same ferocity of purpose witnessed in Alabama's red fire ants. Even *idiotas* born bereft of much higher brain functioning learn through rote and stinging experience to tamp their shoes and flail their clothes before donning them in the morning. No one hops into bed without peeking first through the sheets. And blessed is the man who lives his entire lifetime without ever rising from the latrine to belatedly discover a scorpion newly settled into the crotch of his trousers. (Oh, the sound that accompanies that encounter!) Healthy adults, horses, and cattle live to bear the scars of a scorpion sting; children and large dogs are touch-and-go; puppies, cats, and infants die a convulsing, foam-mouthed death.

Since Guatemalans consider puppies an entirely expendable commodity, Cali's impending death mattered to no one but me. Me and Lupe, that is. My terror brought an excited flush to her cheeks and a rush of pleasure absent from her reality, tempered with a touch of empathy for my sadness. She appreciated my fear, but also relished the opportunity to play a part in the rescue.

Quickly we organized an anti-venom militia. Lupe rushed to summon the mayor, who could drive, the business of the municipalidad secondary to the life of the gringa's dog. While they shuttered their house and revved their pickup, I plunked Cali into the *pila*. Whether the water assisted at all, who knows? I had no idea what else to do. I sang to her, kissed her head. When I discovered she could float, I ran to gather Benadryl, gagging her with one pill and shoving the other into my sock along with five *quetzales* for later use. Jorge the mayor drove; Lupe sat silently on the seat beside him. I cradled Cali in my lap in the bed of the truck as we sped toward the capital.

The air tore around the cab of the vehicle, engulfing Cali and me in the dead-calm center of a wind-whipped storm. I spread my skirt as much as possible across the gyrating metal base of the truck, then cushioned Cali on the makeshift gurney of my extended legs. Her weight hurt. I seemed to have been shrinking in direct proportion to her growth—as she gained five pounds, I lost them—and now this enormous pup stretched to almost half my size. Funny that only months ago, when I first found her, she fit in the palm of my hand. A hunchbacked Italian man sold her to me, the progeny of the German shepherds who guarded his cheese factory on the outskirts of Guatemala City. He weaned her from teat onto ricotta cheese in an unprotected kennel in the dead of winter; I took her too early, but treated her better. She slept with me, shared my food, sat through schoolhouse days with me, and house-trained within a day at six weeks of age. (Granted, I found some poop piles under the holiday tree, but she can't be blamed for that—she knew to poop beneath trees; I had the audacity to erect one inside!) This smart, gentle, beloved girl drifted from me now; her head lolled back and her eyes, black marbles, bounced in their sockets.

The road sped by hard beneath us; we took the turns fast. Jorge spared no energy surging toward the vet and each time he hit a rock, a pothole, or the brakes my head would crack hard on the glass partition that separated us, the outsiders, from them, the insiders. Each wallop bid Lupe open the sliding window to inquire as to the health of my head— "Yes, I'm fine"—and the health of the dog—"No, she's not"—before quickly shutting us out in the road dust that threatened her complexion. I looked in on her as we drove. She sat upright, hands folded in her lap, never moving unless my skull pounded on the glass. This woman who checked on me each of the dozen times my head crashed against the window never once said a word to her husband. Cali moaned and was more demonstrative than Lupe and her spouse.

The vet had little to offer us—diagnosed a blood infection and fever from the wound, paralysis from the venom, and said Cali would die. In his white patched coat with the frazzled hem, in his cramped office in the back room of someone's untidy home, I surely irritated him by insisting there must be something I could do. He had better things to do than fret over a dying dog, and I frustrated him by holding her so close.

"Here is what you do," he said sarcastically. "To prevent her brain from boiling, keep her cold in the desert. To combat paralysis, give her vitamins that are not sold in our pharmacies. And to build her strength, feed her protein in this country that does not have enough for its own children."

I handed him my money and began to cry. He watched for a moment as my tears soaked into the downy fur on Cali's belly as I scooped her up and slung her body across my shoulders. Then he returned the money to me, pushing it back gently across the exam table with one finger, as if to stay as far away as possible, separating himself from my misunderstood tragedy. Softly, he said, "I can do nothing for you. It is better just for you to go."

Lupe killed the first of her sacrificial chickens as soon as we returned home that night. While I plucked, boiled, and tore the flesh from its carcass, Lupe arranged with the gentle shopkeeper to rent me space in his freezer where each evening I could place one bag of water for the next day's ice. I stopped taking my Peace Corps-issued multivitamins, feeding them instead to the dog, two at night, two in the morning. Between noon and three o'clock, the hottest hours, I floated Cali in my chlorinated drinking water in the *pila* to keep her cool, the bag of ice tied to her head with a long, thick, sport sock. Every night Lupe arrived with a dead chicken, which I prechewed and mixed with some *queso fresco*, "soft cheese," a ricotta-like return to the food that had once nourished her so well. Combined with raw egg, the mixture slid easily down the back of her throat when Cali ceased to be able to swallow.

Oh—she got so skinny! Her backbone and ribs protruded so far that her course, straight hair curled in little burls around the bones. She wilted before me and seemed so sad, so I devised a course to coax her from her coma. Bearing her body bowed around my neck, like Christ with his little lost lamb, we moved in unison through the altered routine of my days. On the way to school, I waded in the river, teasing her with a swim. On the way home I plucked ripe mangos from the tree in the yard, painting her lips with their juice, begging her to lick. Every evening I piggybacked her a mile down the highway with Lupe to her chicken farm to witness the slaughter of Cali's protein-rich dinner. Before retreating to my protected perch on the low limb of a nearby citrus tree, I settled Cali on the ground near the chopping block, waiting for the night when the surprise of the slaying might rouse her to snap at the hen's shuddering body. Blatantly ignoring my newfangled vegetarian sentiments, I watched as Lupe graciously traded the life of her animals for the salvage of mine.

We were well into the third week of this massacre when Lupe paused before chopping off the seventeenth head. She held the knife poised in the air, ready to arc down over the extended throat, while I concentrated my attention everywhere but there. The orange blossoms scented the air with the sweet ripe flavor of their fruit, and the dusky breeze carried the faint sound of the river which I struggled to hear over the horrified squawking of the condemned. Then suddenly, instead of severing the feathered skull, Lupe rooted the knife in the wood and planted her hands on her hips, oblivious to the frenetic flapping of the upside-down fowl suspended by its claws in her left hand. She stared in my direction—not into my eyes, but over my shoulder toward the sky behind my back—and said with no particular emphasis, "There is another man I should have married.

"He is very poor," she continued immediately, "but very handsome, still. I saw him again for the first time yesterday, at a soccer game, and I still love him." As she spoke, she righted the chicken, cradled it in her arms, stroked its feathers to calm it down. "He still loves me, too. He asked me to come away and be with him." The rush of her words flooded past me as if I didn't exist, aimed instead, I imagine, for the girl of her youth who called to her from the forsaken past. Her eyes shifted and stared at the ground, covered in the dried blood of the butchered birds. Her voice hushed. "Sixteen years ago, for what I thought at the time were good reasons, I picked the wrong life. Now I get to choose between my own happiness and the stability of my family."

I gasped a quiet breath, and she noticed me again. "What would you do?" she inquired.

I fumbled, tried to be honest. "I cannot make your choice," I said. "As for me, I hope I will try to pick happiness when I first have the opportunity to choose."

At that moment, the chicken brazenly tried to make its escape, but she threw it upon the block and sliced its neck with the knife. Distracted, she made a sloppy cut, and the thick warm blood pulsed from its neck as the animal struggled in her grip. Quickly, with two strong hands, she strangled its cries and snapped its neck.

"Yes, there will always be something to regret," she said, then rubbed the blood off her palms and turned toward home.

2. Lupe's Story

The thing about Elena is that she reminds me of the me I meant to be. I was a beautiful girl too, once, full of all the energy for life that she now has. Just as everyone wants to be near her, and be counted as her friend, there was a time when they felt that way about me also. But oh, what years and events have passed since then! So much has changed and that person is so lost to me now that even the remembering is a difficult thing. The me I thought I would grow to be is like an almost-forgotten character from some childish tale; I have a dusty recollection of such a person once occupying my thoughts, but all the old identifying details have long ago disappeared.

I once asked Elena why she came here—and not just for the reasons of having an adventure or doing something good, which were her first answers, but the real *why*. She said after some thought that she came to Guatemala to have a "defining moment." Of this thing, a defining moment, we talked at length. Elena had the idea that of all the things that happen to us, after many, many years there are only a few things left that we remember clearly. A few moments or a few events that come to mind as clearly as if they had happened only yesterday, when in truth it may be almost a full lifetime ago that they occurred. In her opinion, we remember them so clearly because they are defining moments, a time when something happened to us, or we did or said a certain thing, or responded to a challenge in such a way that defines who we most truly are.

"For example," Elena said, "I only have one memory from when I was a baby. And the truth is, it probably isn't even something I truly recall as I would have been too young. It's probably just a story that was told to me—but that's not the point; the point is, this is the story I *remember*. I was sitting in my highchair, and threw my spoon onto the floor. One of my parents said, 'No,' and handed the spoon back to me. Again, I threw the spoon onto the floor, and they said, 'No,' and handed the spoon back to me. The third time I threw it down—obviously thinking this was a fun game—my father slapped my hand, only a two-fingered swat that wasn't intended to hurt me, but nonetheless, according to my mother, it obviously stung much more than he meant. Tears welled in my eyes, but instead of crying out, I turned and glared at him. My parents say it was a rather amazing thing to see, this little baby refusing to let even one tear fall, instead defiantly staring down the person she believed had wronged her.

"That one memory—or that story I've made a memory of—so clearly defines me! It is not necessarily the most flattering definition of me, but it is *me*. And alone, it says more about me than a year's worth of typical interactions might otherwise say. So, Lupe, the long answer to your question of why I came here is this: I'm looking for new challenges, chances for something to happen that I will remember forever, opportunities to redefine myself with stories that will become memories I can always look back on and say: This is who I truly am; this is the core of who I can be."

I have thought often since that conversation with Elena of my definition of myself. I have much free time to think about how I grew to be the woman I am now, this woman I didn't expect to wind up being, and about the choices I made that took me each time further in this direction. There are three times in my life, three memories, three stories, that have stuck more firmly in my mind than any others. If Elena is right, these must be the ones I have held onto for a reason. These must be my defining moments.

So I will tell them to you now, in the order that they occurred, and we will see what you think of the truths they say about me.

I have always been part of an important family, first the one I was born into and then the one I married into. My father made much money from his concrete factory, and we lived in the biggest house in our desert town surrounded by the sand that brought him his business. Ours was the tallest house in the town, with a porch along the roof where we could sit in the shade of evening and look down on all the less wealthy people who moved out into the streets with the cooling of the night. Nighttime is when the regular townspeople come out to visit and to do business that the heat of the sun during daytime prevents, and when I was young my mother always made certain I was inside during those hours so as not to be bothered and molested by encounters with the working class. So at night I sat on the porch watching the streets and during the day I attended academy, all the way through to the secondary level, which is further than even most men get to go. The academy bus came for me and the other businessmen's children every morning and drove us quickly past the public school that met under a palm-covered pavilion on the edge of town, and picked us up again in the afternoon for the long drive back home from the factory property that housed our school, where the thick concrete walls and the ceiling fans helped to keep us cool even on the most hot days.

Academy students wore uniforms, which is how you could tell we belonged in the academy and not just the regular school. The girls wore blue and gray striped dresses with crisp white shirts underneath, and the boys wore blue pants, white shirts, and gray vests. A man from a store in the capital came out every holiday season to measure us, and when the new school year started after Christmas we all had new uniforms in larger sizes to wear. My old things got given away, to clothe orphans . . . but that is not important to the story I am telling. This is all just information to help with your understanding. Here is my first defining moment:

It was the first day of school, the first day I attended the primary level of the academy, and after helping me dress in my new uniform my mother lifted from a shoebox a pair of new black shoes, which the servants had polished to make even shinier than when they were purchased, with expensive wooden soles and a solid gold buckle on each strap, and she slipped them onto my feet. Then she tied into my hair a thick silk ribbon that changed colors when the sun hit its folds, the most beautiful ribbon I had ever seen, and she also attached at my collar her jade brooch. At any other time I would have been pleased with these new things, but even so young, on my first day of school, I knew what these things would mean. I tried to untie the ribbon and kick off the shoes, saying, "I don't want to wear these things to school. No one else will be wearing these things. They'll all make fun of me for looking different."

Very quickly my mother spun me around to look at myself in the tall mirror in her room, and tightly tied the ribbon back into my hair. "Lupe, you *are* different!" she said angrily. "You are better than every other child in that school; you come from a better family, and none of them can ever hope to be as good as you. Therefore, you deserve to have better things, and to wear them proudly! Do not forget who you are."

But I was right. None of the other girls had silk ribbons or gold buckles or jewelry of any kind, and they whispered and pointed and left me to sit alone on the seat on the bus. So the next day, while I waited to be picked up, I took off the ribbon and the pin, hid them in my pocket, and smudged some of the road dust onto my shoes. I thought it would be better than the day before, but still I was left alone in my seat, only on the second day no one whispered or paid any attention to me at all, and it was in fact worse than the day before. So on the third day I climbed onto the bus with my pretty things in place, but when I sat down I took the ribbon from my hair and said aloud: "I am tired of wearing this ribbon. If anyone would like to come get it, you may wear it throughout the day." And soon a girl with plain hair came and sat beside me, and she told me her name and where she lived while I tied her hair back in a ponytail with my ribbon, and we were both happy. I did the same thing every day after that, picking something new to let someone borrow, and soon everyone wanted to be chosen by me and kept their thoughts on me all throughout the day. This, then, is my first clear-as-if-it-happened-yesterday memory: Of how on the third day I started to hand out some of my most prized possessions, one each day to the person who treated me best, and how this brought me much attention and made me the most popular of all the academy girls.

Memory number two happened years later, while I was still a girl, but an older one. I would have been in the secondary level at school, and my best friend of many years was Isabel Garcia, the daughter of one of my father's foremen. We ate our lunch together every day, and talked of the weddings we would one day have and how our children would grow up to be lifelong friends, and even though her father was not at all as important in the business as my father was, still my family included her in all our gatherings on the holidays and other special occasions because she meant so much to me. So in this year of which I am thinking, the most exciting thing to happen is that *el presidente* planned a trip to our town to tour the factory and also view the site for the dam the government planned to build nearby. Everyone was full of anticipation of this visit, and the mayor decided to award to one of the academy girls the honor of presenting to *el presidente* the key to our city. Although all of us were eager for this honor, none of the others could have wanted it as much as I and my parents wanted this—for me to address *el presidente* as the city representative! The academy leaders decided on an essay contest to determine the representative, with each girl writing five hundred words on the theme "Guatemala's Youth: A Vision for the Future," which would then be read before a panel of instructors who would vote on the winner. Isabel and I worked very hard on these essays, and spent much time practicing our speeches before the mirror in my mother's bedroom. Isabel is a very good reader, but I was certain my ideas on labor and class, subjects my father addressed with me often, would win more favor. Eight girls competed, and I can still remember the churning in my stomach when at the end of the day the principal came on the loudspeaker and announced that the winner was . . . Isabel.

I threw up on the bus ride home, thinking of what my father would say, and of the great disappointment I would be to my parents who had put all of their expectations on me. I was already crying when I arrived there, and despite turning the lock on my bedroom door, my father pounded on it and insisted I let him in. Though I put my face down on the pillow, I could still see them, my mother and my father, standing there with their arms crossed at the end of my bed, with their mouths clenched tightly, staring at me full of anger. They had heard the news, and my father said, "Shit! What has happened?"

It is because I was embarrassed, and because I wanted to have won so badly—I *deserved* to have won!—that without thought I lied and told him that Isabel cheated and stole her ideas from other people's work! I wanted it to be true so much, for her to be wrong and me to be right, that it felt true, these things I said about her, and I found myself angry at this deception of hers that I had invented only a few moments before. My father cursed loudly and slammed the door behind him, and my mother brought me cookies and said that everything would be okay. All through that night I could hear the far-off sound of men's voices rising in his office, and in the morning when I returned to class the principal announced there had been an error, and in fact I had won and would be addressing *el presidente* on behalf of the city. At lunchtime Isabel, in tears, tried to pull me aside, and said, "You know it isn't fair, you know I won, you can't let them do this to me!"

She was right, of course, but I wanted to meet *el presidente* so badly that even I was beginning to believe otherwise, and I said: "I don't know any such thing. It is out of my control, and you should not be such a sore loser." After that, my best friend never spoke another word to me, not once, and I found it easiest just to stop thinking of her and act as if I did not care. After all, I got to meet *el presidente*, and my father was proud.

The third memory . . . of the third memory I need time to think, to put my thoughts in some order. The third memory is the one that hurts the most, but it is also the one that could, perhaps, be changed. We will see.

* * *

Always as a child, when I thought forward to the adult I would become, I planned to be a rich woman with a husband who loved me more than any other, with children who would be grateful for all the kindnesses I showed them, the mother of a big family of much status that everyone in the community would look at with great admiration and think, "If only I had that for myself."

These years later, whenever I suddenly recall that childish idea, which is happening more and more, I realize that *I* am the one who is on reflection thinking, "If only I had that for myself." So I just try most of the time not think on this subject at all, but that is suddenly becoming harder and harder to do.

I once asked Elena if, when she made the choice, she planned to marry for love or marry for money. She did not even have to think about it before she said with a good deal of sincerity: "For love of course! Money comes and money goes, Lupe; everyone knows that. While money definitely can make your life easier, it cannot make you happy. So what is the worth of a fortune if you are miserable?" Then she laughed and added, "Besides—I can make my own money; I don't need a husband for that!" And I believed her, I truly did, and that was the whole difference between us, right there. She had the courage I used to like to think I had but now know I never really did. She does not make her decisions based on the risks of things, but instead on the rewards. She has an independent type of mind, whereas I have always given more consideration to what others told me to do and that is why she is living the excitement I missed. Oh, it is true, her choices startle and sometimes scare me, but I can say—looking back with great regret—that I do think they are the wiser ones to make. I married for money. She will marry for love. And because of this difference, more than any other, she may get the happiness I have always only chased. But still, wishing it were otherwise for myself cannot make it so! Not now; not after all this time. It is too late. I am who I am. Those are the choices available only to the young. I should not even think anymore on these foolish thoughts. I am no longer a youthful girl. I have squandered my chances.

Besides, I am not Elena! I care too much for the opinions of others to be as free as she is. She does what she wants without thinking of how it will appear—too much sometimes, if you ask me! There are limits to what people will endure! Why, there was the whole incident in the orange grove, which I did not witness but I heard about, as everybody did, that made everyone (except me) certain for awhile that she was a witch, and even still there likely are people who continue to think so. How she could not have thought better than to pick up the body of a dead rattlesnake, and, shaking its tail, approach the group of workmen while remarking on the fascinating noise it made, I do not know! Even without her red flying-about hair and odd blue eyes, shaking the body of a dead snake at people is enough to scare the bravest of men, who ran from her straight home to their wives, who all then claimed to have bad dreams in succession and oversee regular cat fights on their patios—proof of witchcraft. They claimed her status as an outsider gave her more potent powers, and I only convinced them of her innocence by pointing out that she does not drink alcohol, ever, and a real witch can only keep from going crazy by consuming regular amounts of *aguardiente.*

Then there was the time Elena went to the post office to retrieve a package sent to her from the United States and got into an argument with the postmaster over the fee he decided she should pay to get back the sneakers he had removed from her box and was holding behind the counter. Of course she would not pay the fee, as he assumed she would not (this is what he was counting on, that the shoes would have to be left behind with him, for his wife), but Elena surprised him greatly by grabbing a pair of scissors off his desk and chopping the sneakers into many pieces before he had time to stop her. She then left without them, yelling, "Fine, if you want the sneakers so badly, you can keep them!" It took seven free chickens and a bottle of rum for me to convince the postmaster's wife not to kill Elena, for the woman truly wanted those sneakers and looked forward to wearing them every day from the moment her husband removed them from the package.

This is what Elena did not understand as I did: A reputation is an important thing, sometimes a woman's only important thing. I warned her that she should be more careful with hers. Still, even though I shook my finger at her and gave her these warnings in a stern manner, privately I did take some pleasure from her courage and had much fun imagining over and over the look of surprise and amazement she could bring to the face of even the most serious person. It is as if all the things I wished I could do and say over the years, but could not, were finally happening. For in truth I did not like the postman's wife either, and had injured her many times in my mind, and then Elena came and made it happen in real life! For that reason we were a perfect match—Elena could do those things I wished to be able to do, and I could defend her actions against the townspeople's wrongful thoughts. She is lucky she was an outsider; everyone is more forgiving of strangers, cripples, and idiots. It is people like me, people for whom everyone has the highest expectations, who are not allowed to behave in ways that are unanticipated. For someone like me, there would be no defense, ever, and so I am left to carry my burdens silently.

This is what you should remember if you wonder, when I am done with my story, why it is I did not leave my husband. Maybe you will not even think I should have married him to start with. But if those are your thoughts I think that you do not know of the responsibilities that come with high position and social status. I think you have not been the daughter of an important man whose powerful image is what helps him succeed in his business. I think you have not been the wife of the mayor, whom everyone looks to for the example of what is best in the community. I think you must not know what it is to feel that your only pleasure for many years has been thinking of the high thoughts people have of you and knowing that to them you are someone more special than who you really are. You do not know how quickly that one pleasure would disappear if I left my husband and my children, so you cannot judge me!

And who is to say any new pleasures would enter my life to replace that one I would lose if I made that choice? At a certain point, holding on to what you have can be the safest option. It can become the only option. Besides, I am used to my life. I have stopped expecting more.

From the start, my marriage was never one of anything more than convenience to me, and I am used to the fact that my children are a disappointment. That is perhaps my own fault, my disappointing daughters. I was vain in those years when I was pregnant with them, when I was young and my looks were more important, and it may be that I did not eat enough during my pregnancies and that is why my daughters were born desiring everything and wanting always more than anyone can give. Especially me. It is as if they were born with their mouths wide open, and they can never be filled enough, and they always want, want, want—some new toy, or some greater privilege, or some more space—

and I have never had the patience or the energy for their cravings. Even when they were little girls they were not frequently satisfied, and their father would do for them anything they requested. I remember the time he drove his new pickup to the capital to buy them beds, beautiful wooden beds with cotton mattresses and butterflies painted across the board at the head, but when he arrived home, and put them together in the room the girls shared, one said she would have preferred a bed with a canopy top. The other then insisted that she too wanted a canopy bed, and soon they were both crying and refusing to even sit upon their beautiful new beds. And what did my husband do? He said they were good and wonderful girls who deserved whatever they wanted, and he loaded those perfect beds into his truck, took them back to the store, and returned later that night with two canopy beds.

True, this is only one story, but it is the normal way of things, the normal pattern of our whole lives, and not an unusual story. The girls appreciate nothing, want everything, and their father acts as if he has nothing better to do than to give it to them. He once said to me, when I complained to him of his actions, "Who am I to give my love to if not to them?" but with him I found it hard to distinguish love from competition for favor. Anything they wanted he would do, every privilege that existed he was sure they deserved, and any slight or wrong they ever encountered he would step in and fight to fix whether there was any merit to their injury or not . . .

Well, stated that way, this is sounding a lot like the stories I've been telling you about myself, isn't it? Hmm. So, if I am to be honest, maybe the greatest problem with my children is that they remind me too much of the spoiled child I once was. Maybe they are just the result of the worst parts of me and their faults are my own failures. But I would not even know now how to begin to behave with them differently, which proves again that some changes would come so late in life that in the end they cannot come at all.

Which is how it is with my husband, too, I suppose.

He was never who I wanted to be with, he is only who I was convinced I should marry. They said he would be an important man, and that I would be an important woman if I married him, and so it happened. But everything about him, every day, reminded me that he was not the man I had wanted to choose. His smell was not the smell of the man I had grown to love. His gifts did not inspire me, and the words he spoke of love sounded only dull to me. From the very first night, and every time after, his hands on me always made me cringe, so that once I had finally done my duty and provided him with two children I took a bed in the sewing room, where I turned my back to him until finally he stopped knocking and asking to enter. It is not his fault that he was not the husband I wanted, but after some time it became impossible not to hold it against him. The most awful insult was when, on our fifth anniversary, after I would have thought he understood the way our marriage was going to work, he took me to his orchard and showed to me my gift: a swimming pool he built for me where a stand of orange trees had previously grown.

"I used to watch you," he said, "before we were married. Before I had the courage to ask for your hand, I sometimes followed you in the evening, down to the river, and stood in the shadows as you swam beneath the moon to the other side. I have never seen you look so strong and beautiful and happy as when you dove into the water, and it is what convinced me that I would do whatever it took to marry you.

"It has been a long time," he continued sadly, "since you have looked that happy, so I built you this pool with the hope that some of that pleasure might come back to you."

I could have spit nails at him, I was so furious—how dare he!—and I vowed at that moment never to set foot in his horrid pool, not once.

He fills and empties it every day now, to irrigate his fields.

I have never even dipped so much as a toe in it.

* * *

I once was loved by a man I did not marry. I am loved by him still! It is to him I swam when my limbs were still young and strong and crossing a river was but a simple passage. I would swim to no one else ever again—for him alone would I slip into the cool water and let it wash over my body. To swim to or for anyone else, to fulfill my own pleasure or theirs, would be the final betrayal of this man I betrayed in every other way already. It is the only thing left that I will not do.

When I came of the age to marry, my father found a man whose potential he admired, a young man who worked hard and invested wisely. Already at a youthful age he owned an orchard where he grew oranges and secured an export license of great value. Even better, the man had political ambitions that inspired my father greatly, and so it was arranged that Jorge came to call on me every Friday night with my parents' blessing. He was a nice-enough man, and has continued to be so every day of the sixteen years I have been married to him. But he never stirred in me what he stirred in my father, and he also likely suffered from the fact that at that point in my life I had tired of all the important decisions about myself being made on my behalf by others. My mother even picked out the clothes I wore on our dates, and if my girlfriends did not approve of her choices I let them rearrange my accessories while I sat on the edge of the bed like a dress-up doll. No one ever even asked what I thought, or if they did I must only have nodded my assent without thinking and they took this to mean I would do whatever I was told. Jorge ordered my dinners and decided where we would go on our dates, and I went along because I did not know how to be any different.

One day, he took me to a soccer game, and there I fell in love, but not with Jorge. I fell in love with the goalkeeper.

I cannot say what it is that first caused in me such a great attraction: whether it was this man's build that was strong and tall, or his presence that was swift and fierce, or the cutting look in his eyes or the respect he commanded or the way every other man seemed small and feeble and faded from view when he took the field. I only know that I could not keep my eyes from turning to him, and that he met my gaze and held it, and that lying to Jorge about returning home with my girlfriends felt natural, and lying to my girlfriends about returning home with Jorge felt natural too, and waiting beneath the stands for the soccer player seemed like something I was simply destined to do.

This, then, is the third memory.

As you can guess, he was not a rich man. He did not own an orchard or a car or possess the means to buy them. He was not destined to be the mayor or an army official or anyone else with goals of the kind that would impress my father or bring my mother peace. He was a farmer's son who worked with a hoe and could not afford shoes for his feet or a horse for his plow, yet he was the most special man I have ever known and when I was with him my heart was full.

He knew nothing of the things I knew; all the regular topics I knew to discuss, such as the books I read and the social causes I supported, were ones I could not share with him. And of his labors in the field, the rotation of the crops and the structure of the seeds, I was unschooled and also uninterested. So we found our own diversions, together, and focused on those. Staring up at the black sky, we traced the pattern of the stars with our fingertips, giving each design a physical shape and every shape a story that became for us a history and also a future. With our hands clasped together we raced through moonlit cornfields, and there chased down every sound and every creature, imagining them to be great demons we could defeat together. Under cover of night we hunted for berries, sucked juice from cacti, ran in the rain, drew designs on each others' palms with hay, and kissed long and hard and deep before parting at the first hint of morning's dawn. He would walk me to the river, and I would swim my way home.

My mother was suspicious from the start, when I returned home alone that first day from the soccer game, something I would never have normally done. That we managed to have three whole weeks together before being caught only proves how strongly she believed I would never disappoint her. The irony, though, is that in the end it was not her suspicions but my own carelessness that ruined it for us. I left my bicycle in the yard, at the bottom of the stairs, in too much of a hurry and too eager for night to fall to be bothered with storing it away. Usually the servants picked up those things I left lying about, but on that day they had departed early without my knowing so that later, when I tiptoed out the back door and ran down the stairs, I kicked the bike over with a disturbing clatter. Though I crouched there on the stairs a moment and waited to be sure no one awoke, in my excitement I did not wait long enough, and that is how it came to be that my father followed me, discovered me moving toward the river, and, sensing my purpose, dragged me home.

What a horrible argument came about that night! For the first time, I defended myself, and my attitude shocked and scared them. At first they were only full of questions: "What have you done? Have you forgotten who you are?" Against those sorts of inquiries and insults I could be strong, and true to the man I loved, but I had more trouble finding answers when my mother pressed me by asking, "What can he possibly give to you? What can you ever expect from a man like that?" When she saw that this is where I was weak it was there that she focused her attention. "We always expected better from you than this," she said, "and you are entitled to expect more from yourself, from your own life! You have a reputation and responsibilities to uphold. What in the world would people think if someone such as you were seen with a farm boy, if you associated with a *laborer*?"

47

"What about what I think?" I yelled. "Why don't you ask me how I feel or what I want?"

She yelled back: "A young woman cannot possibly know what is best for herself! You must rely on your parents and then your husband to make such choices for you, and then you adapt. That is the role you were born to! Look at me, that is what I did, and I have a fine life."

"But are you happy?" I asked her.

She said: "What is happiness? Is the beggar in the street happy? Is the farmer's wife who works all day happy? All of my necessities are provided for. That is enough. Happiness does not put a roof over your head. Happiness does not feed your children. Do not fool yourself into thinking that people will flock to you and want to be your friend and care for your opinion just because of your happy mood. Happiness has nothing to do with it! Do you like your fancy clothes or do you want to wear discards from the United States? Do you like riding in the car or would you prefer to be on the bus with the filthy Indians? Do not talk to me about happiness when privilege is your right! No child of mine—and no one who wants to continue to call herself my daughter, or inherit my things, or enjoy the continued privileges of this family—will make a decision of which I do not approve, especially not one based on some stupid idea of happiness. You do not even know what happiness is, or what it costs! You will marry Jorge; it will be arranged in the morning."

Then she left, and I thought about what she said. I considered all that I would have to give up for love. And what I decided is this: Under the circumstances, getting what I wanted would be to lose too much, so either way my chance for happiness was gone. Then it was just a matter of doing what was easiest. So I let my mother convince me to repeat her life and I was married to Jorge by the end of the month, living with him in an expensive house my father bought for us in a town some distance away.

But it was not so simple to forget what I gave up. Every night since then, without fail, I have seen the love I betrayed in my dreams, my nightmares, the ones that haunt me, and he is wandering back and forth along the riverbed, searching for me, turning toward each ripple in the smooth surface, spinning every time a fish leaps or a toad jumps from one rock to another. In a hushed voice, scared of waking the neighbors or of calling attention to our meeting, he speaks my name softly but surely into the dusk. Over and over he asks, "Lupe, are you there?" He

48

imagines many things while he paces and waits for me; he imagines me injured or delayed or drowned, but never, never, does he imagine I simply have chosen not to return. He continues to search for me, to plead, "Lupe, Lupe . . ." And this is what I have awakened to, every morning, for sixteen years, the sound of his voice begging, calling to me from all those years back, "Lupe, Lupe, where have you gone?"

* * *

Recently, the girls decided to attend a soccer game, some all-star reunion match between the greatest players from our *departamento* and that of Zacapa. Jorge offered to drive them, but could not stay for the game as he had a meeting to attend, and so because I had no other plans he insisted I accompany them for the day.

It was a hot, blue-sky day and the stands were packed with fans. I searched for a seat, but we were late after the long drive and all the spaces were taken, so we sat down in the grass along the sidelines, near the goal. And there he was. Still the goalkeeper with the same strong, tall build and swift, fierce presence. Every other man seemed again to be small and feeble, fading from view when he took the field. And when I caught his eye, like the first time, I was again unable to escape it. It was as if sixteen years had disappeared in an afternoon.

I sent the girls off with their friends for a cola at the end of the game, and was alone when he came to me after the final score. What in the world does one say at such a time? I tried to find the words to make an apology—how does one apologize for having done what I did?—but he stopped me with a hand on my lips and said: "Lupe, I loved you then, and I love you still. And over the space of all these years I have convinced myself that if ever I found you again we would not waste time looking back, but only look forward. Life is too short, and we have lost too much time already, to be consumed with regrets. You do not have to explain yourself to me, but only tell me this: I have been waiting for you; will you return?"

I just sat there, too startled to say a word, so he said, "Take some time to think," as he pressed into my hand a slip of paper with instructions for contacting him written across it. "I will wait to hear from you," he said, and then he was gone.

I have thought of nothing else since then, and in my mind I have made and remade my decision too often to count. But finally, this morning, it came to me—the thought I had been fighting against has finally settled into me. Perhaps you see it already, and are surprised it took me so long to admit. He has not changed at all, not one bit, still the gracious, gentle man I loved. As for me, I have changed so much that aside from my face there is little left that he will recognize after more than a few moments in my company. I am the ripple in the river that ran so wide it disappeared, and can never be recaptured. What is left is only a memory of the person I meant to be, the person I could have been with him. How can I be now anything more than a disappointment to him? He may not harbor regrets, but my life is defined by them, and this is the one I cannot bear.

So I will walk to the post office this afternoon, and send the telegram I have composed. I have given it much thought, and decided to disguise it as a business message, for what would the postman think of me if I were more forthright? My reply should arrive by evening, under cover of nightfall. It will read:

"Thank you for your proposal. After serious consideration, I am not interested in pursuing it further. Please do not attempt to contact me again regarding this offer."

3. Elena's Story, Summer 1992

$\mathcal{T}$hree things soon conspired to change everything.

First, Calixta recovered from her scorpion sting. Four months later, apart from her size, one would never guess she had defied death so diligently. But she never grew again. Granted, she filled out, growing a paunch as she aged, but in dimensions of height and length she never managed to surge past the size of a six-month-old German shepherd. Since six-month-old shepherds tend to be large, this startling side effect did not diminish her much. Years later, when she and I returned to the States and shared a boxy apartment, the fact that she only achieved half of the one hundred twenty pounds she aspired to actually came in handy. My shepherd stood small, but what she lacked in size she made up for in sincerity, as if she pledged to spend the rest of her life repaying me for my refusal to dig her a shallow grave and replace her with Cali the Second. Though stunted in stature, her spirit emerged uncrippled.

Second, the schoolteacher who taught in the village high atop the mountain crest broke his leg. If I remember correctly, a soccer game did him in—one of those friendly Saturday afternoon pastimes from which everyone retires with bruised eyes, broken noses, and busted lips. When I imagine it happening, I envision the endless TV replay zoom ins on Joe Theisman of the Redskins and the two defenders—one pouncing from behind and tackling his thigh, the other aiming from the front and grabbing his foot—halving the bone in his shin as if it were a cracker. The teacher's injury must have happened the same way, for the bloody bone exited his leg with a jolt and protruded through his skin into the stagnant air. During the same game, another man got cleated in the balls and a creamy red mush oozed from his left testicle, but everyone agreed the teacher's injury looked worse. It was that bad. So bad, in fact, that the teacher's family decided to transport him to a hospital, where traditionally one only goes to die, and the school shut down due to his imminent demise. That he didn't die but instead recovered fully meant little at the time to the schoolchildren; whether he stayed dead or instead took six months to heal, either way he wouldn't be riding his motorcycle over the mountain pass for two seasons, so the repercussions in the village stayed the same. The school remained closed.

Third, the local minister of youth services—my Guatemalan counterpart—set his inebriated sights on me. He almost got me, too, the night the rains started. For three months every year, between June and September, between dinnertime and eight o'clock, it rains. Not drizzling dash-from-the-car-to-the-house-with-the-groceries, manage-to-get-in-before-you-get-too-wet rain. Nothing so simple, this waterfall of pent-up humidity, this downpour crashing to earth with a wail of thunder. Pity the unprepared ground it lands on. The first night this heaven-sent hailstorm hits the parched earth of the desert, it hunts for a place to pool. Imagine my shock when the water chose to course down the slight slope of my yard and collect inside my door.

All these years later, it is hard to recreate the fear I felt, knowing of course that it was merely a storm. But it surprised me so with its ferocity. The wind groaned and shook the tins on the roof, the day turned black as midnight, I felt the thunder rattle in my teeth, and bright flashes of lightening lit up the water pouring into the house with a short-lived electric energy. I clutched Cali to me and cowered in the farthest corner, where within fifteen minutes the water whorled around my calves. The wind whistled through every cursed crack in the roof, windows, and walls, little tornado tempests that sent all the baskets suspended from the ceiling rafters (to prevent rats in the food) spiraling like carnival tilt-a-whirls in manic circles above my head. Drenched Dorothy and Toto, we climbed up on the rickety table to await the passage of this strange twist in Oz, half expecting witch's feet might materialize beneath the door. Had the window not blown in and a stroke of lightening streaked the sky at that precise moment, I might not have seen the demon who arrived instead.

The youth minister lurked beyond the fissured glass. His face—too pinched, too pointy—bore a camel's shape, carried way out in front of him, always thirsty, perpetually stalking his next binge. Full up with liquor, he hunted a meal; his hungry eyes settled on me and envisioned a savage feast. No man ever before looked at me that way. His intention suffocated me and I struggled for breath, but my fear only stirred his fire, as if the scent of my anxiety triggered a taste long dormant. His tongue circled his lips which the sudden flash of light distorted to maniacal proportions. Thus prepared, he leapt at the hole in the wall, blessedly too small for him to either reach me or propel through, although his lunge set Cali to hysterical barking. Grabbing a butcher knife in one hand, I held her back with the other, afraid that when their standoff moved to either side of the metal door she might accidentally claw open the flimsy latch which prevented his entry. He screamed horrible threats, shook the door. I planned to kill him if he broke through.

Then quiet.

"¡Elena!"

I screamed, let loose of Cali, and dropped the knife into the murky lake that had been a floor. I had been so focused on murdering my assailant that the second voice, the second face in the window, startled me more than the first.

"¡Elena!" the gentle shopkeeper's son shouted again. "My father sent me to check on you. Are you okay?"

"Yes," I said, running to the window, touching his hand through the hole in the glass. The youth minister had disappeared, but the boy wore handprint bruises around his throat to prove the struggle.

"I am going after him," he said. "Stay here. Do not unlock the door. I will come back for you."

Huddled together on the table again, cold, wet, exhausted, Cali and I waited, the knife lost until daylight, a fork clutched in my striking hand instead. The boy came back later to help me clean up and report this: The minister reappeared only once more that night, mistaking my elderly neighbor's home for mine. He rode a stolen horse which he drove through her door, expecting to find me inside. Instead, he rode his steed right through—in one end of her house and out the other—as she pummeled him on the legs with a pot, assaulting him with a bevy of furious curses. His sure surprise still makes me smile.

Do you want to know how justice is served in Guatemala? No police, no arrest, no fine, no community outburst, no social condemnation, no professional ostracism. He is a drunk; drunks attack women. Unless I took responsibility for removing myself from the situation he would get me eventually, and then, since I had been warned, it would be my own fault. So this is how Cali's recovery, the teacher's accident, and the minister's assault played out: I needed to leave town, the faraway village needed an interim teacher, and Cali's life no longer depended on proximity to Lupe's chicken farm. Evacuation forced me into the mountains.

* * *

If I said I began packing immediately, it would hardly be the truth. I hardly had anything left to pack. With each turn of the calendar page more of my belongings had disappeared into the ethereal vacuum of space, into the hands of my friendly neighborhood burglar. One moment I possessed everything I arrived with, and in the next breath something else disappeared. A cookpot, a shirt, a shoe, a week later its mate, the hairbrush (tired of borrowing it while on the premises, the thief finally absconded with it altogether). Beleaguered by the depravity, I had taken to hiding those things I truly wanted in the rafters or in the crooked limbs of trees in the yard before I left the house, zealously debating the worth of my worldly goods, and occasionally leaving those items with the least practical or sentimental value in plain view in the hope they'd be chosen over something I didn't want to live without.

The dexterous thief and I played this game of wits until the day she got greedy and weighed herself down with something that prohibited grabbing and running. When I returned home unexpectedly mid-afternoon after the storm, I caught her dragging my mattress out the back door.

Dumbfounded, I gawked as the geriatric from next door struggled to get the Sealy off the porch. Talk about a wolf disguised in Granny's clothing! My presence hardly deterred her; she greeted me loudly and shamelessly: "Good! You are back. Get the other end—I am an old woman, for God's sake, and you are young. Carry this. I'm moving it into my house."

"What do you mean?" I asked, flabbergasted. Too stunned to move, I shouted at her from my defensive stance twenty feet away. "That is my bed."

"Not anymore. Now it is mine."

"How can it be yours—" I asked angrily, using the more familiar tense, *tuya* (taboo with the elderly), and dragging out my words to imply contempt "—if it came from my house?"

She maintained an air of practical formality. "It didn't come from your house. It came from my daughter's house."

Now thinking I've implicated her without cause (has she moved the bed from her daughter's home to my porch en route to her house?). I squeeze past her through my doorway to peer inside my room. Sure enough, it *is* my bed she is now dragging across the yard.

I sprint to catch up with her. "This is my house; the bed came from my house!"

She stops and stares at me, forcing air from her belly out of her mouth—"Phew"—with an intensity that causes her lips to shimmy like a whinnying horse. Then she spits and discards me with a backhanded slap to the air between us. "This is my daughter's house, she is only letting you stay in it. If it is my daughter's house, it is my house, and if it is my house, the things in it are mine. So now this is my bed, and I will sleep in it. Help me carry it."

So I'm renting the house from her daughter. This is how she slips in and out so easily: She has a key. And the upper hand.

"But I am paying money to live here," I whine, "and the bed is part of the deal."

She senses my resignation. "Phew," she spits again, and shoves the edge of the mattress into my hands. I am losing this battle; I am carrying my bed toward her house with her. Then I notice: She is wearing one of my shirts and her hair smells like my missing shampoo.

"The house has been empty a long time," I reason as we maneuver past the *pila* and toward her front door. "You never wanted the bed before."

"Correct."

We both commence huffing as we haul the coveted Sealy through the heat into her home.

"So why do you want the bed now?"

"Ah," she says, kicking aside piles and piles of pilfered items to clear a place for her newest prize. "I want it now because now it is special."

My toothbrush just got booted into the far left corner of the room (I recognized its ergonomically correct green gem handle as it flew through the air). It distracted me, but only for a moment. "What makes the bed so special now?" I want to know as the mattress falls to the floor.

"Because now," she says, smiling broadly and patting my hand, "it is yours. It is a gringa bed. Now it is special, and I will sleep in this special bed."

Who can argue with flattery of that sort? I turn to leave my bed, my shoes, my soap, my brush, my cookpot (her weapon against the drunk!), my shirt, my shampoo, and all my other superfluous belongings in her home—she is almost free of me—when I finally ask, "What will I sleep on now?"

"*Fíjese*, too bad for you," she mutters, shoving me through the door and slamming it behind me. "That is not my problem."

* * *

In spite of the minimal packing involved, the mountain move took preparation. First and foremost, I needed a horse. For the past few months I had trekked across the summit to the hideaway village twice a week, had helped the teacher and had run an after-school club. I observed that living there, I would need to pack in my own provisions, and I knew better than to think I could transport it all on my own back. Eighteen kilometers stretched over seven thousand vertical feet of a hard uphill climb between San Marquesa and Linda Vista. First, the hitchhiked ride to the town in the foothills, then the clamber over the steep abandoned creekbed littered with rocks like castoff shoes: children's moccasin pebbles to men's double-wide boulder boots. From there a steady uphill weave along the ridge edge, a fluctuating back-and-forth that made the ascension twice as long, but prevented the descentor from pitching headlong toward the bottom like a runaway downhill skier minus the skis. A reprieve at the first peak, a jaunt across three left-over lava fields from a more calamitous era, a riotous joke on the hiker, a hilarious sleight of nature's hand. The calm before the storm.

The first time I hiked up I sank discouraged to the ground, not understanding how I had reached the peak without reaching the *aldea*, "tiny town," recognizing too late that what appeared from the valley below to be a mountain was actually two—a mountain within a mountain—and that this halfway mark meant I still had just as far to go. I neglected to bring water, and leaving at 9 AM without eating, I now found myself parched, starved, and stranded under the sun of high noon. My legs throbbed, my stomach growled, my head pounded, and I sucked in air with the pathetic intensity of a drowning victim. Then diarrhea blew through me so urgently I hardly got my dress up and panties down before it poured onto the path. The personal debate that raged hinged on whether to wipe myself with my sock or my underwear. Witness the bizarre internal discourse:

"The sock is pretty disgusting, full of foot sweat; do I want it touching me *there*?"

"But what if I take off my underwear and someone can see through my dress?" (Can you see me, holding the edge of my dress to the sun, testing to see if I could make out the shape of my extended hand behind it?)

"Walking the rest of the way there and all the way back without a sock could be pretty painful. Are the blisters worth it?"

"Someone might find my discarded underwear and how gross is that?"

I finally used the underwear, already slightly soiled from the struggle to remove it in time, balled it up, and hid it behind a cactus. (Need I mention that I never went anywhere again without toilet paper folded into my sock, a backup stash padding my bra?)

I continued marching on over the green iron ore deposits breaking up from under the soil, past the slabs of white marble mogulled along the mountainside, beneath the hawk that circled me in the sky, along the path deeper into this Star Trek-ish terrain, oblivious to it all. My muscles no longer ached; they stung. I felt like a steak set to scorch on a red-hot grill, I burned so badly. With each step I motivated myself with this desperate bodybuilder's workout mantra: "I'll have a great butt, I'll have a great butt, I'll have a great butt. . . ."

If the beginning of the hike exhausted me that first day, the last little portion almost killed me. The *aldea*, visible now, loomed a half kilometer above on a precipice accessible only by a path so steeply graded that here it had been paved with a handmade mortar of sand, marble, and ore to forestall the landslide that so obviously wanted to happen. I leaned over and took it hand over foot. Like a weakened animal, I crawled rabidly toward the first home.

You can see why the crazy drunk wouldn't pursue me there.

Like I was saying, I needed a horse.

Easier said than done. In San Marq, few people own horses, and the ones who do don't want to part with them. Outside of San Marq, people own tired, starving, aged, worm-ravaged, beaten, bowlegged, depressed horses. Not the kind I wanted. Word finally came, as it does here, from mouth to ear, alerting me that a man on the other side of the river had a healthy horse to sell. Loaded with half a year's savings equally distributed between both socks, both bra cups, and both shoes (robbed, who would think to look in so many places?, I might still

57

survive with some money), Cali and I aimed for the river determined to buy a horse.

The river had risen with the rains. Brown rolling muck shot past, a chocolate milkshake of mud, water, sand, tires, trash, twigs, and one puny dead pig. To cross, a poorly designed rope footbridge stretched between two barely-anchored trees. Delightful. I relished crossing this suspended suicidal invention, especially dragging the dog with me. (Send her home!, I hear you urging me, but it wouldn't work. Ever since her illness, she shadowed me; every time I left her home she Houdini-maneuvered her way back to my side. Ten minutes, tops. Either I took her with me now, or locked her at home, crossed alone, and waited on the other side for her to miraculously catch up with me. Nothing but a big waste of time.)

Carrying her—out of the question. By now I had lost fifteen pounds and continued to dwindle, and our weight ratio of 60:110 prohibited throwing her over my shoulder. So I scooped her up by her front legs, stood her up in front of me, and walked her across. Dumb, dumb, dumb; what a horrifying maneuver! Rope burns seared my elbows and under-arms from desperate clinging; petrified clawing sliced bloody gashes into my forearms. Suffice to say, on the way back, the horse would swim, I would ride, and Cali would paddle along next to us while I held tightly to her collar.

Two hours later, we found the horse, a skinny little pony-donkey mix padlocked into the abandoned one-room adobe house next door to the farmer's home. People do not typically corral field animals in homes around here, and it worried me when they 1) refused to explain the purpose of locking it inside and 2) recoiled at my request to free it from the house for a better look. That the family all stood back a good five feet while I peered through the hole in the wall to see the animal dwarfed in darkness in the corner, that the wife—or daughter, or aunt, or whoever she was—let out a small, not-quite-stifled screech when I reached my arm inside to coax it nearer, frightened me. The farmer tried to negotiate with me, but I didn't want this scary not-quite-horse creature.

Just as my patience expired, the farmer's brother rounded the path, tugging a pretty red pony struggling under a massive load of firewood. No, not just massive. Inhumane. And there sparked the insane stimulus, motivated by equal parts impatience, exhaustion, and empathy, which propelled me to heedlessly purchase the pony. I never test-rode him, never inquired as to his health or history, never tried to bargain, but instead immediately disclosed how much money I carried, rooted it out from the concealed caves in my clothing, and paid all eight hundred *quetzales* for the sole purpose of immediately removing all the wood from the bay's back. Animal rights activists, applaud! Impulse shoppers take note: This is what is known as a VERY STUPID purchase.

Hopping onto his bare back, chugging away, I christened him Ebenezer, a biblical name meaning "Rock of Strength," although in truth my Eben deserved the somewhat more abbreviated moniker "Rock," defined as hefty, dense, and hard to move. I walked the path from the river to Eben's farm in two hours, I rode it back in two and a half. Head hung low, he appraised and assessed every step, contemplated the dusty path, concentrated on his own gait with a vigor suggesting that for him the process of walking came not subconsciously, but instead required intensely focused mental energy. Confronting the water on our return trip, calculating the process of passage, the horse—in consort with the dog—balked. Decided not to cross. But he set his wits against the wrong person, threw down the gauntlet at the wrong time, for if this was to be an argument, some strong-arm tactic, I would win.

I like a good fight.

This is both a boon and a burden. In a family where tempers flared with persistent frequency, I learned to manipulate words and wiles and wield them like a freshly sharpened scalpel; not my best trait. But the regular fracas steeled my guts and gave me the gumption to stand tall beneath the mantle of challenge. When Lupe and all the others questioned my relocation ("An *americana* cannot live in that village, in those conditions. . . . ") the opportunity to prove myself against some long-held misconception propelled my enthusiasm. Skepticism motivated me, a dare spurred me to excel.

My mettle proven in the sweet town of San Marq, the more primitive conditions of the *aldea*—no running water, no electricity, no bathrooms (no latrines, even!), no roads, no stores, no protection, no fallback options—lured me. In truth, this move to Linda Vista merely marked a subsequent roll of the dice, the next advance action in this board game of Life, played out not at the kitchen table with friends during summer break, but in a foreign country, alone, far from the safety of home. To confront the mountain and survive would be to scuffle with myself and come out clean, to scream my doubts up into the hills and have the echo return strong, secure, and steady.

Inured against failure, no animals stubbornly planted on a riverbank would stand in my way or delay my progress.

I coaxed. I cajoled. Finally, I stepped back and pinched them, causing them to leap from my ministrations straight into the river. Thus we started across like I planned: I rode Eben and held tightly to Cali's collar. You can imagine how long this lasted.

About ten feet out, sensing the lack of land beneath his front feet, the horse reared, plunging me into the murky sludge. Free of my grasp, the current carried Cali swiftly downriver. I trod water, the horse struggled, the dog got swept away. I manhandled Eben, who flailed furiously, buffeted by floating debris, while yelling encouragement to Cali, who turned and battled valiantly against the tide in our direction. Closer . . . closer . . . closer, until with a final mighty surge of energy, she burst from the water and leapt onto the horse's back where she clung like a withered saddle. Plan be damned, here's how we paraded back into town: I swam, the horse got pulled, the dog rode triumphantly home. For the crowd that quickly collected to watch this circus procession across the river, our antic likely defined for them the term *gringa loca*, "crazy American." As a harbinger of things to come, it heralded for me a surreal escalation of cultural inanity.

* * *

I want to say things came together easily after that. I want to skip over the next month of finding a house, borrowing a "moving" truck, breaking its axle and stranding it six thousand feet in the sky, coercing dozens of little kids to carry my stuff the last one thousand feet balanced on their heads. I want to shave off a few of the details, and beg indulgence if I do. I just want to get to Linda Vista quickly and fill you in on the first day.

Oh, the first day! It packed a year's worth of surprises into twenty-four hours and then threw a few more oddities into the mix for variety. The schoolchildren, bless their hearts, came to my aid at the outset; they formed a flustered line of industrious ants and shuttled my belongings between the hobbled truck and my new house. Viewed from the slope below, they morphed into a gyrating band of household products—a chair here, a box of books there—dwarfing the fascinated assistants beneath my privileged possessions. Everything had been pawed through mercilessly by the time Cali, Eben, and I caught up with the tail end of the motley contingent. How novel we were, what rapture we inspired! The day our threesome moved to town marked a turning point in history; prior to that year no white person had ever ventured into (let alone moved into!) Linda Vista.

I turned my willing *ayudantes*, "assistants," to task, placing my goods into whichever of the two buildings they belonged in. This new house consisted of two huts set near each other on a precipitous perch, a kitchen space and a sleeping space, both made of mud, both with roofs of thatch grass and floors of earth, one 8' x 10' with a raised adobe fire pit and open doorway, the other 10' x 12' with a rope frame bed and thin wooden door. Isolated atop the peak, my house sat highest of all, commanding a view that encompassed the village, the road, the valley, the river, the vista beyond. Had I not known better, I might easily have believed the sun rose in the morning and set at night using this spot as its landmark, its navigational point fixed in time. Timeless, these huts, which truth be told had been erected rather recently; the landowner built them on the uppermost edge of his cornfield as a wedding gift for his eldest heir, who defied tradition and moved away.

I cannot begrudge the son his action, nor question his motivation. To live in this remote location defied conventional reason. The farms and cornfields clung desperately to steep slopes, the elementary terraces comprised of soil that hardly hung onto the earth a full season before sliding away. My own home balanced on a perilous shelf backed by a few trees, surrounded by scrub, approachable only by scrambling over some rocks—hand over foot on the way up, feet before butt on the way down—onto a declivitous footpath that wove through the cornfield behind the school, the only public building in town. I had a reason to come here, a job to do, and a time limited one at that, which made all the difference. Had I faced a lifetime in these hills, maybe like the boy and his bride I would have run at the first chance. That so few did intrigued me, haunted me really, as if they lived addicted to home and hamlet, bound here by birth, magnetized to the ground on which they first walked. They made or grew everything they needed, or at least scraped together the minimal provisions required to subsist. Of the twelve families who lived in Linda Vista, the seventy citizens or so, I bet less than two full handfuls had ever ventured so far as San Marq.

Ostracized by the self-proclaimed gentry of the lower elevations, this close-knit tribe clustered on the peaks and circled tight their ranks bound by blood. I can only guess at the history which no one knows: the squabble, the feud perhaps, which drove one large family with its extended collection of siblings and uncles away from the valley town below up onto the bluff. By the time I arrived, every family there belonged to each other from ages long past, and grew evermore re-related through the entangled mix of marriage and breeding. With limited choices, a cousin will do. The children knew too little to hide the markings—the sixth toe, the extra finger, the telltale harelip—so they accepted me immediately. I imagine most of their parents at least appreciated my dedication, but of the adult households, I only ever came to know three. The rest didn't treat me badly, they just didn't treat me at all. Like ghosts, they inhabited shadows beyond my view. I might live there, but I would never be of there; I therefore did not merit acknowledgment.

That first afternoon, I fielded oh-so-many inquiries as the kids unpacked my boxes, rooted through my collected chattel, imagined outlandish uses for items they had never seen:

"What is this?"—bookmark, vitamins, sunscreen.

"What do you do with this thing?"—spatula, stamps, hanger.

"How does this work?"—lighter, thermometer, scissors.

"What is this for?"—nail file, athlete's foot cream, flea collar.

We launched into a civics lesson extraordinaire, detailing the use of each and every item, practicing its application on self and others. Their questions fascinated me; my answers fascinated them. Their utter unfamiliarity with my luxuries confronted me with my consummate privilege, so I framed truthful definitions of the objects' purpose in such a way as to downplay their utility. Better they think my things frivolous treasures than items not worth living without. Six months from now, when I depart, Linda Vista may be forced to wait through a half century or more of globalization and gentrification before her next rendezvous with a pair of tweezers.

Only one item stopped me short, assaulted me with a flustered rush of refined prudishness, and left me tripping over an easy explanation. Looking up from a detailed discourse on the many uses of dental floss, I saw two prepubescent girls had discovered a box of tampons. In a blazing display of industry and dexterity, they had already ripped the seal, torn the individual packaging, dispensed with the applicator, and now each spun a tampon like a propeller blade in the air, anchored to her pinky finger by the string. Charmed by the imbedded fragrance, one teenager, Alma, sniffed the Tampax and rubbed its soft matted cotton across the bridge of her nose while her brother shot a third feminine hygiene product into the ear of the boy beside him, using the disposable applicator as a bazooka launcher.

"*Qué bueno*, I like this," Alma muttered as she tucked her tampon behind her ear like a fresh flower. "Tell us what this is."

I possess no inherent affinity for discussing crude bodily processes. A product of parochial schooling, my sex education consisted of one half hour in sixth grade when they divided our two classrooms by gender. The nuns showed the girls a Modess maxipad, and the priests . . . well, I guess they told the boys what the nuns were showing to the girls. The taboo and indecent subject was never addressed again, not even on the playground, so stunned were we all by the abhorrent subject of human development. On the home front, in contrast, my parents spoke openly about sex: It is something married people do at night in bed, and it involves the husband lying next to his wife and putting his penis in her pee-she. That's how babies are made. End of story.

At about the same time the nuns waved the maudlin Modess disgustedly before us, I unearthed a *Playboy* magazine from beneath a friend's living room sofa during a sleepover, which explained things a bit more cleverly. However, my clandestine discovery also reinforced the perception that nakedness, fondling, and raucous fun are subjects which should deservedly remain hidden from virtuous eyes, stifled beneath large pieces of furniture in the dark. At age eleven, I knew well the implications and repercussions (could almost sense the depraved scene) if I did not covertly return the magazine to its hiding place after perusing the pages by moonlight.

Lest you think I didn't get the whole thing figured out in time, you'll be happy to know I eventually got the picture, had my share of fun-filled fumbles as every good and lucky teenager should. But I still didn't know the proper names for the things I did. I happily used the parts, I just refrained from labeling them. For God's sake, I thought I peed out of my clitoris (which of course I didn't know was called a clitoris) until well into my third decade of life! In fact, I still falter when forced to speak of my bottom area: vagina sounds so crass and clinical to my unaccustomed ears, and pee-she, the term of my youth, plain ridiculous. I guess I still try to skirt around the facts a bit, choking on the proper phrases annually at the gynecologist's.

So try explaining, in Spanish, the purpose of a tampon and—much worse!—where you put it, to a bunch of boys and girls in the Guatemalan outback.

I like to think I am honest with children, treat them like people, not possessions, address them with respect and age appropriate equity. But on this occasion decorum tempted me with the cheater's out, almost convinced me to play the part of the fair-skinned European plunderer with Victorian sentiments too cultivated for uncultured lands, urged me to demurely mutter, "It's a private thing," as I curtly collected the man-handled delicacies and crammed them back into the package. Instead I said, "It's a special thing for girls, and when you girls and I are alone, if you remind me, I'll tell you about it." Which they did, and I did, trying with grave sincerity to nonchalantly handle the terms I could hardly pronounce in my own native tongue. Not wanting to bias them, I feigned cool, pretend chic, laboring to mask my discomfiture. Nevertheless, their disgust poured forth, mirroring back to me the cloistered self I wish I hadn't felt the need to be at age eleven.

That discussion directly preceded the death of the snake.

Or, more precisely phrased, the filleting of the pit viper.

While I terrorized the girls with the tampon tale the boys machete-hacked two tree limbs and dragged them into the house, where I meant to suspend them from the crossbeams of the roof as a "closet" bar for my dresses. To reach the roof, I needed to hoist myself up onto the wooden corner post of the bed, the closest thing to a stool, so five of us grabbed hold of the side and yanked it from its corner exile, disturbing the lair of the heretofore dormant but now aggrieved reptile. The viper sprung to a coil and slung its head up and back, unfurling its body to loom over us, eyeing the strike zone of Alma's hand which still clutched the bed frame nearest its fangs in her paralyzed grip. A furious flinch. Then lunge.

The rest transpired so quickly that even in reflection I cannot slow the action down enough to identify the order of the events. What I do know is this: In my memory I skip from the vision of the ravenous snake set upon Alma's hand to the sound of the boys' voices, calling me from the door, alerting me to the fact that the serpent had expired. Their voices stopped me. Blood splattered my legs, a machete fell from my hand, scalish skin littered the ground. The children, strung out on adrenaline, drugged on the high of the kill, jockeyed for position as the lead storyteller, filled in my blank spaces with their lionized rehashing of the slaughter:

"First, you grabbed the machete . . . "

"It was *my* machete . . . "

"You pulled it right off his belt holster . . . "

"And then you leaned across the bed . . . "

"No, you jumped right *over* the bed . . . "

"In one bound! . . . "

"And you cut off its head . . . "

"Before it bit her . . . "

"And sliced it into little parts . . . "

"And killed it dead!"

The snake, head and body pretty much intact, but with some deep slices to rather vital parts, settled the subject of my reputation. Whereas ten minutes ago I had been a curio cutie, this unplanned, uncharacteristic, and unprecedented reaction launched me into the stratosphere of saint and savior combo. I suddenly morphed into a gringa of gargantuan proportions.

And this concluded only Act One of the evening's menagerie mania.

* * *

The landlord stopped by later that night as darkness descended, and brought me some light. He carried an old mayonnaise jar full of gasoline, with a saturated rag poking from a hole punched in the lid, which we hung from the rafters with a rusty piece of wire. The flame threw enough light for his purpose.

"Excuse me," he implored, hat in hand, head bowed, "but if you will allow me, with your permission, I would be pleased to show you which of the bugs on your walls will do nothing to you, and which ones will kill you for certain."

He stepped toward the wall next to the door. "If it is not too much trouble," he continued, not making eye contact, but staring at his feet, "may I please borrow an object for beating?"

I handed him a sneaker.

Following his raised gaze, I realized my walls crawled. Ants, beetles, spiders—Thwapp!—he plucked a splattered scorpion from the heel of the shoe and held it inches from my nose, looking at me for the first time.

"This is very bad," he muttered.

"Yes," I told him, "I know about those. Cali stepped on one."

"And she is alive!" he enthused. "She is a strong, special gringa dog!" He stared at me then, deeply, for a moment, wondering perhaps if I, too, possessed the power of protection from these creatures. Then he returned to task, scooped a furry spider the size of his palm from the mud wall, shook it onto my bare neck.

"That one won't do anything," he said.

"But this one," he continued, turning back to the wall and pointing at a smaller spider, leaving me to pluck the tarantula from my own neck and toss it out the door, "this little one is very dangerous. You must work hard to kill them all before you go to sleep, or in the morning you will wake up dead!"

We killed fourteen bugs that night, fairly evenly divided between the kill-you-for-certain spiders and the maybe-not-so-bad-for-gringas scorpions. Left the tarantulas, ants, beetles, worms, rats, and bats alone. As I sat wide-eyed and sleepless that night beneath my mosquito net, balanced on a cotton bolster padding the rope frame bed, I questioned my sanity, searched for some historical reference which might allow me to adjust to and endure the present circumstances.

I fell sadly short.

My family does not cope well with critters.

Once a bird flew down our chimney and scared us all to death. Once we saw a mouse in the kitchen and panicked. Once we stopped on a road trip to feed some geese and ran screaming and crying from the farm when they honked loudly and stampeded toward us. Once (when I was very little, but I remember this clearly) a feral cat sneaked into our house, ran wildly from room to room, and scratched at our dog's eyes, forcing Mom and us girls to squat for hours atop the fireplace mantel, the highest point, and await Dad's return from his weekly poker game so he could rid our home of the savage beast.

But the worst thing happened when I accidentally shot a Japanese beetle down my youngest sister's throat. We four females had been shopping, Mom and her teenaged daughters. Single filed, we bore our bundles toward the front door. Stepping across the threshold, I turned to say something to my mother behind me, saw a Japanese beetle crouched on her shoulder, flicked it off quickly so she wouldn't be scared. As fate would have it, I flicked it with miraculous precision timing just as Gabrielle, the last in line, her mouth even with Mom's shoulder, yawned. The beetle actually made an audible cracking noise as it whizzed past Gabi's teeth and crushed its armor-like hide on the back of her throat. Then it spread its flinty membrane wings and thwacked her tonsils before skimming across the roof of her mouth, wide open in horrified screams, the bug ricocheting ruthlessly off her gums, tongue, teeth. We watched the whole thing, transfixed in a dumb-founded stupor as Gabi shrieked and the beetle wings whirred and her mouth crackled with the sound of thwarted escape. It eventually flew out, but she never fully forgave me.

My Guatemala experience isn't a phoenix tale, no rise from the ashes, rags-to-riches story, but it still involved a bit of a leap. From this illustrious indoctrination, who would guess I would one day smear fourteen poisonous insects before going to bed, learn to sleep with rats nesting in my cotton mattress, their babies rustling beneath my skin, or dress in the morning and give three quick hops to release the hundreds of ants slithering inside my clothes? Asked one day to rank my life's accomplishments, I just might list this: I moved to the mountains, and I made it through the first night. In the face of fear, I persisted.

* * *

Twelve-year-old Alma attached herself to me, a symbiotic relationship I like to think bestowed on her some benefit but which, in hindsight, shone favor upon me. Yet in the beginning I thought her kissed by fate; pretty and lithe, articulate and funny. Thick, clean, shiny black hair, always combed, fanned behind her like a cape as she darted barefoot along the earthen footpath between her home and mine. Of all the children in the school she was clearly the smartest, the most engaging, the teacher's pet. She made it possible for me to teach.

While the children all knew me from my frequent visits to their school over the past few months, my move from the tourist's shotgun seat on the teacher's motorcycle to the throne oi authority at the desk in front of the classroom unsettled them. The first day, in response to my initial questions, the twenty or so five- to twelve-year-olds pulled their shirts over their heads and stared back at me through a sea of threadbare and malodorous fabric. Only Alma spared one eye, to wink at me conspiratorially before disguising her face, a sign I interpreted as meaning that while she supported the group display of shyness?, embarrass-ment?, terror?, she would ally herself with me in the end. So for half an hour I sang to soothe and coax them from their clothing. When that failed I opened the door to the schoolhouse and invited in the dog and the horse to riotous peels of laughter and astonished bare faced looks of impropriety. The spell broke. Thereafter, Eben lived out his days in the schoolyard, feasting on the spindly grass, lolling his head lazily through the window to alternately observe or snore through my lessons. Cali spent her mornings sprawled on the classroom floor, preventing the sobbing of one tiny tyke who wailed furiously and ceaselessly unless a canine body part snuggled against her ankle. And Alma cajoled the children uniformly beset by learning disabilities of genetic and malnutritious origin into participating in my dramatically unconventional scholastic endeavors.

We took nature walks as science lessons, and collected desert flora for artwork. We invented rhyming ditties to remember math concepts, and enacted historical events using my desk as a stage. We discussed biology while riding the horse, and nutrition while planting potatoes. Instead of traditional language arts, I taught the children to write their names, a monumental accomplishment in light of the fact that the lesson halted temporarily while one nine-year-old ran home to inquire as to what her name actually was.

Me: "Tell me your name and I'll write it for you the first time."

Her: "I don't know."

"Of course you know your name. Just tell me."

"I don't know."

"You mean you don't know how to spell your name?"

"No. I just don't know what my name is."

"How can you not know what your name is?"

"I don't know."

"Well, what does your mother call you when she wants you to come?"

"She says, '¡Ven aca necia!'" [Come here, you fool!]

"How do you know she's calling you and not your sister?"

"Because she points at me and has a special sound in her voice and I just know."

Me to the other children: "What do you all call her when you want her attention?"

Them: "We say, 'Hey you, come here.'"

Me to Her: "Okay. Run home and ask your mother to tell you your name."

Maybe names didn't matter to the previous teacher who, like so many, left his charges to copy letters, sentences, whatever, one hundred or two hundred times while he smoked on the breezeway and they "memorized their letters." I guess it escaped his notice that after all that training no one in this *aldea* had yet learned to read or write. Whether my few months interlude made any difference I will never know, but I like to think that for that brief time, for those few children, education suddenly became fun. My favorite tutorial: The afternoon I dragged over Eben's bucket of rain-collected drinking water and we all bathed faces, arms, and legs while exalting the benefits of proper hygiene. Afterward I pulled from my pack a gift, a rare treat I seized upon the night before while swinging in my hammock and reading an old copy of *Glamour* magazine sent by my mother and oddly undetected by the thieves who disguise themselves as customs officials and postal deliverymen. From this illicit bounty and a few other glossies I'd stowed away, I tore all the raunchy perfume strips from the heady pages. For the first time in periodical history they would be pressed into a use more illustrious than generating headaches and allergy attacks for the readers they assaulted. All the children lined up, wrists splayed with arteries exposed, as I swiped their skin with the odiferous strips. They thought they were beautiful. Every one stuck a hand beneath my nose so I could sniff him or her and remark how lovely each pupil smelled. In truth they exuded a disgusting odor: years of urine and dirt camouflaged by cheap perfume. But for one morning, they thought they were glamorous, so who was I to care?

Alma's little brother broke his stinky arm that afternoon during a midday game of tag. I rushed him to his parents, full of remedies and overflowing with good intentions. We could put into effect the emergency operating system designed to save my life were I bit by a rattler or beset by malaria: Send a Morse code message along the telegraph wire into the closest town, alert the mayor to meet me and the horse midway up the mountain with his truck, race us to a medicine man or (if we could spare the hours) to the hospital in the capital. I offered to accompany the boy, keep him safe, ensure his return to his parents. His fractured forearm, splinted, could be salvaged. A (my) perfect plan.

They listened politely, then shook their heads.

"It is very kind of you to offer," they said. "But it is not necessary. We would not want to trouble you."

"It is *not* troubling me, and it *is* necessary," I insisted. "I am not a doctor, but I do know that he probably won't ever be able to use his arm again if you don't get it fixed right away." I saw enough hobbled men begging on the streets to know well the repercussions of unfixed joints.

"If that is God's will . . . " the father demurred.

"If what is God's will?" I asked, suddenly angered, intuiting where his comment would lead us.

"If it is God's will that he be lame, then we cannot interfere."

"It is *not* God's will," I insisted, glaring at him, about to resume an ancient personal battle against my own mother and her newfangled Evangelical friends who believe that torpid contemplation manifests God's greater purpose for one's life. Divine inspiration through sedentary passivity. Poor God, I often lamented, even as a child. What a bum rap He inherits from people too preoccupied with their eternal salvation to take responsibility for their daily actions. Must God move this mountain—literally—to rouse and shake these dull parents to action?

I reiterated the bit about this not being God's will. "This is your will," I said. "Your choice. The fall was an accident. God does not want your child to be lame. You can fix this." Sensing money might be behind God's will, I offered to pay for the care. (Not that I had the money, either; I got paid subsistence wages.) Although my remarks must have enticed them, my words regretfully landed two degrees south of dead-on. If only I had the gumption to say it was God's will for me to pay for the treatment the boy might still be ambidextrous. Instead, my fainting fear of God maintained just enough of a stranglehold on me that I cowered at this critical moment and refrained from operating overt subterfuge in His name.

Instead I asked, "If God decided to send you some money, would you use it to fix your son's arm?"

"If that were God's will," they echoed.

I picked my next words carefully. "Since God knows you need money to fix your son's arm, if He sent you some money now, that would be a sign He wanted the arm fixed. Right?"

They nodded in prayerful consideration, a "perhaps" which I escalated to a "yes."

"If God decides this, then we will consider His wishes," the mother stated.

I decided to hurry God up a bit. I threw them what little money I had by hiring Alma to help me with my chores.

Yes, I actually thought five *quetzales* a week worth of good-hard-scrub on my dirty laundry could solve all their problems. At twenty-three I hadn't yet met problems much harder to solve, and I was still too

70

fresh, too new to her shores, for Guatemala to have yet stolen from me my naïve idealism. She would rob me soon; grab hold of me, give me a good flailing, wrench from my embrace the sense of personal omnipotence fueling the perception that a single person can make a difference. Oh, how I grew to hate Guatemala for that! (In all likelihood I would have lost that indefectibility on my own—as my father likes to say, all young Democrats eventually become old Republicans—but now I could always hold her responsible for having swindled it from me first. How convenient it is to throw the mantle of blame for our own evolving psyches onto someone else's shoulders.) It wouldn't be until much later, when I had put many years and more miles between us, that I could let time temper her lessons—teach me to conserve my energy and pick my fights—yet reclaim enough of my sense of self as separate from that place to rebuild my diminished faith in the power of the individual. After all, had I not believed I could make a difference, I wouldn't have gone to Guatemala in the first place.

Everyone thinks of joining the Peace Corps at one time or another. The Good Samaritan instinct coupled with the lure of intrigue wraps into a coaxing package for every post-JFK ask-not-what-your-country-can-do-for-you bonafide believer. Everyone bursts to share their inclination—

"You were in the Peace Corps? I thought of doing that, but then . . ."

"Wow, you joined the Peace Corps? I wanted to do that before . . ."

"Guatemala, really? With the Peace Corps? I planned on volunteering once . . ."

—so that sometimes, in a new crowd, I don't even mention anymore that I went, just to escape their stories of missed opportunity. The whole wide world wants a bit of the glory—for that is what it is, I swear!, I double in size in their eyes when I say I did it—but the stark truth is that of all the people who actually make the phone call, request the application, only about 2 percent serve a whole two-and-a-half-year tour and come home to tell about it. Come home to the other 98 percent and the rest of the population who anticipate stories of sweet children and native villages draped in fresh morning dew. The temptation exists to wrap a filmy gauze around my narratives; talk about the precious parts, weave wonderful party anecdotes that make everyone smile and say, "I really should have done it!" I wonder, I worry, what they would do with the truth.

The other problem, of course, with launching into the tale is that everyone craves a peek at my motivation, and they expect it to be lofty, indeed. But I maintain, in fact I insist, that the best of intentions can often hover behind the most mundane of impulses. First, I needed to get away from that college boyfriend. Four years together moves you into the decision-making territory of convenience-based options, where staying together seems the easiest, if not the right, choice. I sneaked a quick peek at his journal once (I scold myself, still), encountered this: "Everyone thinks Ellen and I should get married, but I just don't think that will ever happen. I don't think she's the one." It hurt, for a minute, until I realized with relief that I empathized with his sentiment. One of us needed to make a clean, final break, and I didn't think he had it in him. Also, I wanted to learn a foreign language. A gifted student, I actually failed Latin, got a D in Spanish, despaired of ever mastering another tongue without the prompting pure immersion provides. Finally, I dreamed of adventure, a tryst with the world, an escape from convention, a dare of dynamic proportions.

Then, as sometimes happens, when the timing is right and the self is ready, life drops into your hands a chance. Tilts it right up in front of your face.

Fate beckoned to me from within a *Cosmo* cover. I'm not kidding. A poorly written but nonetheless captivating article about a Peace Corps Volunteer who fell in love with her African colleague, an article which aspired to romance, but mostly wound up being a diatribe on the plague of AIDS and male disloyalty, piqued my interest; not in the girl, but in the concept. I mentioned it to my parents, they objected. . . . You know the rest already.

It sounds superficial, but sometimes the simplest of motives directs us toward the most complex of destinies. I'd have to go back twenty-three years, stir up a lifetime of rooting for the underdog, weeping for the hurt, sympathizing with the beleaguered, to construct for you my soul's trestle across which the superficial swifted me to Central America. Because really, do you actually think I could have done it, could have succeeded, if I hadn't been primarily yet subconsciously steered by the desire to make a difference in a life other than my own?

Of all of them, Alma needed me more than I knew.

* * *

72

She started, like I said, by helping with my laundry, a two-person job if ever there was one. Linda Vista boasted one spigot, an ancient rusty contraption midway between the school and my house that diverted a trickle of secluded creek water toward better use. On days when rain refused to materialize, and my fifteen-gallon bucket sat outside the door gathering only dust and cicadas, it took two to balance the bulging basin on the back-and-forth journey to water. We usually made our return only to the boulders beneath my home, as there was no feasible way to drag the sloshing liquid up and over, so I'd shinny up the rest of the way alone and toss my dirty things to her below. With little plastic bowls, then, we dipped water from the tub, dampened the clothes, spritzed our sweating selves, and laughed. We worked well together. Laundry took forever for me, less time for her, more accustomed as she was to the motions: a speedy swipe with the fat orange ball of soap, a rigorous rub on the rocks, a final dousing of clean water, and a quick wring. While the predilection to treat my clothing as delicacies consumed me and I dawdled over my private underthings, she beat upon all the other articles with abandon and finished in half the time. We talked ceaselessly, giggling often as we lazed among the drying outfits arrayed along the hillside like overturned crucifixes beneath a dominant sun. My inept perseverance tickled and endeared me to her.

With the water left over from our conservative efforts, we gave each other a frugal weekly hairwashing. It made sense, wet as we were, and already covered with the sticky slime of substandard soap. (The smell of that soap haunts and taunts me even today. It overwhelmed the Guatemalan market and grocery odors of curdling cheese and plastic-wrapped spices, dominated only occasionally by the rancid scent of dead-too-long meat, and it wafts after me still, oozing its pervasive baity perfume from the Hispanic *bodega* in my current hometown, a lurid siren call. I can't help visiting there every once in a while, just to smell the soap.)

If the acrid fragrance enticed me, that bouquet most closely approximating Jean Naté and toilet cleanser, its pungent temptation intoxicated the mosquitoes. They feasted on my skin slathered with soapy residue, and dined to the point of explosion, full up with blood. While Alma largely escaped their assault, they flocked to me with the fervor of a crowd to a curiosity, a rampant mob assailing my foreign body. Arthropodal racial profiling. Which is not to say the bugs bit only when lured by soap; they bit always, only more fervently when sudsy. They chowed through Skin-So-Soft and Bull Frog. The only workable solution for my chickenpox-like hide came via a bottle of military-issue bug repellant with the lamentable side effect of peeling all my skin off in flaky layers. It also served as a photo transfer medium. One day, having just applied the potion, I reclined into a hammock with an oft read but still rereadable copy of *Glamour* magazine propped in my lap, and stood up an hour later to find the supermodel cover image transferred in full color to my thigh. For the week it took her to peel off, the tattooed visage of Cindy Crawford smiled up at me from my leg.

"You do not look so well, Miss Elena," Alma said, eyeing the swollen bite marks, the scaling skin, the upside-down woman plastered above my knee. In an effort to make me feel better, my bruised vanity as plainly obvious as my swollen skin, she offered to restyle my hair, my best and only unblemished feature. Which is how we came to wash each other's hair after dispensing with the laundry.

We hung our heads, in turn, into the wash basin, then scrubbed them with the laundry soap. Her scalp was more tender than mine, and wore bruises she attributed to falls. So I touched her softly and pampered her, attention she melted into. She smiled wide at me before switching sides. She loved to play with my hair and I loved to let her. I shared my new brush with her and was not afraid. We gathered the laundry and let our hair dry. With each day, she lingered longer.

For all the time we spent together, I knew so little of this young girl. She spoke when addressed and then of my dog, my horse, my house, my life in America. The weather. The school day. A month after our arrangement began, I knew only what I saw: she liked to color while sitting at my table beneath the fading light of the setting sun; she hated tamales but loved tortillas and could whip them together with a soft artist's touch; she bruised and cut easily, and picked at her wounds when sitting quietly. But I did not know her parents' names, the vast number of her siblings, what she ate for breakfast. These things I could not see directly, and she shielded them from view. The most I ever truly learned of her came in a fast and furious whirlwind borne on the smoke of my attempt to kill us both.

Not that I meant any harm.

Alma sat on the ground inside the kitchen hut, petting Cali, my little battery-powered tape recorder pressed against one ear, the volume full tilt. Packed with electric cells long overdue for replacement, their energy drained, REM sang in a slow and distorted manner so that the words

74

became less a dancing ditty than a drawn out prophesy: "Itttt's theeeee ennnnnd ooof thee wooooorllld aaas weeeeee knooowww ittt. . . ." She sandwiched her head between the dog's belly and the recorder, stared into the coming night, and bit her lip. I tried to cook.

All the food in the kitchen I carried into these hills or the villagers gifted to me. I made flapjacks often, flour, eggs, and water being easy to mix, and out of desperation and hunger continued to do so even when ants invaded the flour and speckled my cakes with their charred bodies. I boiled stale pasta and ate it sprinkled with a touch of salt. I survived on the oranges, eggs, and tortillas in the hands of the children who waited in a bountiful line outside my bedroom door each morning to share with me their family's food. Last night, on his way to check on the two pigs corralled beside my home, the landlord's son brought me a crab.

"How sweet," I said, startled. "You have brought me another pet."

Quizzically, he looked at me. "I have brought you dinner," he said.

I meant now to cook the almost dead crab, for whom I had tried to salvage a life in a pot of shaded water, but who clearly intended to die. Since he was about dead anyway, Alma, Cali, and I would split him for supper. Sadly, the gas *tambo* to fuel the cookstove had run out of juice, impossible, of course, to refill here, so I built a fire.

I don't have good luck with fire, afraid as I am of the matches with their incendiary little tips, and I always seem to generate more exhaust than flames, this day serving as a prime example. It started well enough, my Girl Scout—inspired teepee of wood, and I threw the match into the pile without burning my fingertips. I blew softly to inspire combustion. Smiled at the smoky wisps of success. But instead of the grand conflagration I expected, a pyrotechnic display of skill over which I could boil my deceasing dinner, a portentous puff of gray haze grew. A storm cloud ascending. The eruption engulfed us—not the flames, they didn't exist!—but the thick noxious smog that burst from the woodpile, slipped its heft into our choking airways, and plugged up our eyes with a filmy dark screen.

I dropped to my knees and reached toward Alma and Cali, coughing in a soot-stained ball on the floor, when a scorpion the size of my palm landed on the back of my hand. Another one hit my head and bounced off. In a cruel reversal of fortune scorpions shot from the sky like hexed heaven's manna, dozens and dozens of them crashing upon us. With a mighty surge, I shoved our three bodies out the open doorway. If the toxic cloud wore a silver lining, here it is: We escaped unstung.

I stared back, mouth agape, into the room consumed by the twisted locust curse, watching the torrent of scorpions pour out the door, and contemplated the magical jinx of my misfortune. It was as if I had opened a miraculous universal portal, through which the molecules of smoke took shape as stinging beasts.

"You smoked them out," Alma stated as if in response to my bemused imaginings.

"Hmm?"

"You smoked . . ." a hacking cough interrupted her. I rapped her on the back; she shrunk from my swing. "You smoked them out," she repeated, pointing to the thatch roof where—of course!—the scorpions lived and from where they fell, stunned, when I depleted their environs of oxygen.

Alma's teeth sported a smoky film. We would breathe black boogers for two days.

"I was scared," Alma stated, quietly.

"Wow, so was I!" I said.

She looked at me incredulously. "No you weren't," she said. "You're never scared."

"Yes I am," I said, and chuckled a bit. "A lot of things scare me."

"But you saved me. You saved me today, and you saved me from the snake."

"That doesn't mean I wasn't afraid. Sometimes one must behave bravely even when scared."

"I used to be brave, too" she said, and turned her body to face mine. She cupped her hands around my cheeks and stared at me deeply with her dilated eyes, as if to confront me with the message she couldn't state. "Now I am scared all the time."

Her gaze spooked me; it said things I didn't want to hear. We sat face to face for a moment, silent, until I coughed up a gob of pitch phlegm, and the noise of my sputtering broke the trance. I moved to ask her what frightened her, but she was already up, back to business.

"You don't want to do that again," she reprimanded, speaking of the smoke-out. "You need some *ocote* to start the fire, and it will work," she continued, referring to the resin-soaked pine nubs I had never heard of but which, apparently, everyone else used to spark their flames. She dragged the bucket of rainwater over and we began to wash our hands. "You know," she said, an idea kindling, "it might be better for you if I were around more to help you do things." She spoke quickly now, a rush of hope. "I wouldn't be in the way, I could sleep in the hammock, and I won't eat much, and I'll help you all the time so that you are safe. . . ." Her voice trailed off, expectant, a one-time proposition to which I need only capitulate. Clearly she had thought up this plan and waited for the right moment to hatch it. Her false-front offer concealed a gamut of veiled need.

"But Alma," I stammered stupidly, "your family would miss you . . . and I'm doing okay, I'm figuring things out . . . and besides, I'm not going to be here that much longer; the teacher will be back soon. . . ."

She waved her hand at me and smiled wanly. "It's okay," she said, and that was the beginning of the end for us. I saved her one time too few. She stopped coming around so much after that, her visits tapering off until I saw her only at school, where her answers drifted and her affect dulled daily.

Sometime later, in graduate school, I would learn to name all the symptoms I spied—the bruises, the flinching, the self-mutilation, the depression—and sort them into a diagnosable category. It would make me feel better to think I didn't understand it then, but I have to admit I was beginning already to ignore what I couldn't alter. Brave as I tried to be, I still sometimes turned my eyes from what I feared. I saw Alma blossoming into a woman, and I knew—oh yes, I knew!—that in a Guatemalan household of older macho men a woman is not a safe thing to become. I will always wonder if hers was not the life in which I actually could have made a real difference . . . and failed to do so.

The only memento of our friendship, a pile of *ocote* pine piled daily, surreptitiously, on my hearth. For my safety.

4. ALMA'S STORY

*I*n the beginning of things, right when I first knew Elena a little but not too much, I thought three thoughts and here they are:

1) Strange
2) But pretty
3) And maybe a little bit out of her mind

The first time she ever came up here to our *aldea* she walked up and we all saw her coming and stood on the road to watch her. Even though we thought that she was going to probably die before she got here and that would be a shame, it was a little bit funny too because of how red she was (I never saw a red person before!) and also the way she wobbled with dizziness was a little funny to see. When Rosa gave her lemonade she got better with rapidness, and then after that she sometimes rode on the back of the teacher's motorcycle and it was probably better for her health and helped her not be so red all the time, but you have never seen anyone look so weird on a motorcycle as the *seño* did.

Sometimes the teacher he gives rides to the men like Hernando if they have to go down the mountain to a political meeting or sometimes if someone needs medicine he rides down on the back of the teacher's motorcycle to get the injections from the pharmacist. But a woman doesn't ride on a motorcycle! It's a little indecent! Of all the females only the *seño* rode the motorcycle, but my mother said not to worry because the *seño* did that because she is not really a woman, just a foreigner. Still, I think it's strange. And I don't know how she stayed on the motorcycle. All the men, when they ride on it behind the teacher, they wrap their arms and legs all around him to hold on very tight because the teacher goes downward very fast on the hill and sometimes the rocks on the road grab the motorcycle and throw it up into the air for a moment like they're mad at it. Then it is a good thing to be hanging on tight. But the *seño* she kept all of her arms and her legs just to herself and only put her hands on the little bar on the back of the seat. So even though her walk was kind of wobbly when she came up here I have to say it is true she rode the motorcycle really good and never fell off even though she is a woman foreigner.

That isn't the only thing that is strange, but that is the very first thing.

Fortunately, she is very pretty to look at, so even though her comportment was often very odd we wanted to be near her most of the time. My grandmother always said: "Life is hard. We are born to suffering. So in order to revive your *espíritu*, focus on something beautiful in your resting time." When Elena got here, I mostly focused on her for my spirit's sake. Some of the older women worried at first about how she'd use her power due to her hair like fire and her eyes like the blue sky, which they said gave her too much control over the elements, but the elements were very favorable during her time here and that made everyone happier with her. In addition to bringing us good weather she also had other powers like she could talk to many of the animals such as her horse and her dog, and even the snakes seemed to find her favorable. I once observed to her that the mosquitoes very much liked her big white legs and why did she not just talk to them and ask them to stop biting her like she could talk to the dog and make it do things? She said she would consider that, but mostly was just happy someone finally appreciated her thighs. I don't really understand that reason, but that is because they have different reasons for things if you are a gringa.

So like I said I thought these three thoughts at the beginning:

1) Strange

2) But pretty

3) And maybe a little bit out of her mind because the day she moved here she told us a very crazy story about bleeding and babies that in addition to being crazy was also very disgusting. Elena said that women bleed out of a hole near their urinating place every month which means you are old enough to have a baby. She said *americanas* but not Guatemalan women stick some string and good-smelling cotton up inside (INSIDE!!) their urinating place hole to catch the blood. She also said that if you have sexual relations with a man in a bed and he puts his urinating instrument inside (INSIDE!!) your urinating place hole that maybe you will get pregnant and then you won't need the stringy cotton for a long time.

At first, when I heard it, I thought there were a lot of problems with her crazy idea. For one, urinating doesn't have anything to do with babies. Everyone knows that babies are angels that come to earth, sent by God. If the angels are happy here because you treat them with kindness and they like you they stay and turn into children. But if you let a dog in heat or a *bolo* drunk man give it the evil eye, or scare it with a loud noise, or if the mother goes outside and turns her breast milk cold, or if you do anything else that is bad or evil or think of a bad or evil thing, then you make the baby unhappy and it might choose to go back to God as an angel. Just think how unhappy a baby would be to get urinated on, so that part of her idea has to be wrong.

Another thing is that I asked her what happens when she gets all full up of the cotton?, and she said that you don't get filled up, you take out one bloody cotton after a few hours and you put in a new cotton. That sounded okay except she said you don't wash the first one, you throw it out, and I asked her where?, with some nervousness, because everyone also knows that if you step over a bloody bandage lying on the ground you will get skin eruptions. She pointed to a tree up high on the hill behind her house and said she would probably bury them there, and that is good because I never go near there anyway so I should be okay.

Finally, after thinking about all this that she said, I decided that in addition to being a woman foreigner she is not a Catholic. Jesus Cristo and the Virgen would never let such awful things like bleeding and pokes in the urinating place happen to a Catholic person. And so for a while her being a gringa and a pagan explained her weird ideas. But like I said, these are the thoughts I thought at the beginning. Later on, I found out that Elena was more right than I realized at first.

* * *

Our teacher broke his leg and went to the hospital so he is probably dying and that is why Elena moved here so that she can be our teacher in the school. This is somewhat unfortunate because without a teacher we would not have to go to school. My mother says school is mostly a waste of time because all you learn at school is to read and to write and who ever needs to do that? Instead you could be at home learning the important things. But sometimes the priest comes to visit us up here and in addition to the mass and the confession of sins he says the children should go to school for a year or a few years and that this is the rule. My parents say we should not sin by breaking rules so that is why we go to school.

I don't know if anybody told Elena that school is just a rule for a few years before we can spend our time at home again learning the important things, because she is very earnest about her teaching of all these unimportant things. Her earnestness is fun though because in Elena's version of the school we get to play and sing and the animals come inside the schoolhouse and she gives us rides on the horse. This is our town's only horse and we all admire him very much because he is FAT! This is one very strong, fat, healthy horse! My aunt Rosa's husband Hernando loves this horse so much that he took down some of the barbed wire from his pig corral (which makes the pigs happier because everyone knows that pigs prefer to walk free) and finished fencing the schoolyard so the horse can live there. The yard has the greenest grass to keep the horse fat and the barbed wire makes a superior fence because barbed wire is not made here, it is from another country and speaks another language, so the coyotes are unable to talk with it and strike an agreement to pass through which keeps the horse safe inside the corral.

In addition to the horse rides we play tag with the dog during our breaks and make pots out of clay and plant a garden. I like the garden work a lot and am always very eager for my time to dig. By looking at Elena's watch we know that if the fast-moving line goes around five times that is five minutes and it means the next person gets to use the hoe. We have planted squash and zucchini and some flowers, which Elena says are not for eating but just for bringing joy, and also we planted potatoes. The *seño* taught us a good trick for figuring that if every potato grows ten eyes and you have ten potatoes to start with, that makes one hundred eyes and plenty of new potatoes!

These potatoes are a new food, which the *seño* says she will cook for us so we can taste them. Rosa's husband Hernando grows new food too, in the shape of unusual trees with different types of colorful oranges on them. My mother says that it is unnecessary to try these new foods because what is wrong with the food we have?, and that if you try too many new things you might forget who you are, and the spirits do not bring good fortune to those who try to be better than what they were born to. So we eat beans and tortillas at home, but I am thinking maybe I might just have one small taste of Elena's new gringa potato someday to see how it is without eating so much that I turn into someone different and bring evilness into my family.

I can make very good tortillas! By the time I was four or five my mother says I could make tortillas almost as good as she could, although of a smaller size because with short baby fingers it is not possible to tap out a very sizeable tortilla. Making the tortillas is always my favorite part of the day. Early in the morning with my mother we soak the maize in the limewater before even the sun rises. When other things start to come awake like the birds and the men we are already grinding the kernels into *masa* on our *metates* which we got as our birth presents on the day we were born. I am lucky I was born a girl so I got a stone *metate* which is to me a very valuable thing—the very best thing I have!—so I could grow up knowing that my task would be to make food for a family. If I had been born a boy I would only have gotten a birth present of rope for leading around animals which is the little boy's job, and everyone knows rope is not as good a thing as stone. Rope wears out, but a *metate* lives forever. By the time I was four or five me and my *metate* already could do really good at our adult responsibility.

I don't know what my mother did without me before I got born. She had a lot of work, that is one sure thing! I am not the oldest, but just the oldest girl who's alive and so no one worked with her in the house before I came because boys cannot make tortillas or fetch water or clean clothes or light the fires. Only I can do that with my mother and she says she is very lucky I came along after the dead baby girl because with my two older brothers growing strong they had enough field help already and I keep her from being lonely.

(Except I must interrupt to say that now that the one brother has a crooked useless arm my father is again eager for the younger ones with two healthy arms for working to grow up fast!)

The mornings are the very best time of the whole day. I learn from my mother who talks to me while she works and tells me the words of the Bible and the catechism she memorized from the priest—memorized it after just one time of hearing it! She is so smart! I say back to her the words and the rules about the sins and she smiles and tells me something that is our private secret, something I cannot tell the boys because of their being boys it would make them jealous, she tells me that of all her children I am the most special one of all. Because of this she lets me do some of the adult things like when we got a new pot for the black beans I got to be the one to tell it its job and hit it five times with the stick (instead of my mother!, the mother always does the pot training in the other houses!) so the pot would understand its place and its use and do its job well throughout its life.

I feel that my father also appreciates my special capacity because in the morning after he eats his tortilla and drinks his café he always every day stops next to me and puts his hand on my head and says, *"¡Qué bueno!"* with a very big smile and gives me a pat which is just for me. I never heard anybody else get the same special *¡Qué bueno!* because even when the boys get a *qué bueno* which they don't very often get, it is only a little *qué bueno* like nice work but not a big *¡Qué bueno!* with the special pat every single day. My mother always smiles at me especially big after that, after my father leaves, like in spite of all the hard work she does every day the thing that makes her the most proud is turning me into someone my father admires. This is our special ritual that has happened forever and it is what makes the mornings the best time of all.

A little while ago my oldest brother who is a few years ahead of me, maybe he is sixteen or seventeen or some age that makes him not really a boy brother anymore but a man brother, he began to pay special attention to my good work also—finally he noticed! While I cooked the tortillas and he ate them hot he began to stare at me working like he is full of admiration for me. Then I started getting a *¡Qué bueno!* from him also with his hand on my hair. I can tell he likes my hair. Everyone likes my hair. It is very long and I sit with the comb and the little mirror every day when I wake and make it smooth without knots. It is one of the things that makes me happy and is different about me than about the other women with their hair that is kind of ugly and not nice to touch. I can tell my hair makes my brother happy also because with his *¡Qué bueno!* instead of a pat he puts his fingers in my hair and rubs it a little between his fingers for the soft smooth feeling and has a look in his eyes like he is looking at a piece of chicken on his plate which we hardly ever get, so the look is of a very special something that you can't wait to swallow. He must have great admiration for me to give me such a look, but you should see my mother's face when it happens! She looks as if that piece of chicken fell off the plate into the dirt and got stepped on, a look like sad and mad and scared all together.

The bad part of this is that my mother's new look gets aimed at me because my brother he just stares back at her like, so what? Like he doesn't care what she thinks, which is true because now that he's a man it makes him the boss of her. But I don't want this new look of my mother's aimed at me because it makes me nervous like I have done something wrong and I don't understand. I wonder what happened to her big smile? Where is her old look that says, You are my proudest thing!

Instead what happens is that one day after my father's *¡Qué bueno!* but before my brother's, my mother gets a new idea all of a sudden and says to me to quick take some of our hot tortillas to Elena's house so that she will have some breakfast, she needs breakfast, she is much too skinny, she is a gringa who can't cook, she probably doesn't have any food. I do not understand my mother's urgency to make me leave the house during my favorite morning time when I am made to feel most special, and I am saddened but only until Elena awakens and opens her door to the surprise of me and yells, *"¡QUÉ BUENO!"*

Now this is my new routine to leave before my father and my brother finish eating, before anyone can touch me and say kind things to me, so I have to get all my loving morning attention from Elena, but she gives me so much that it is enough.

* * *

I have a big honor now which will bring great pride to my family, thank you very much to the *seño* and her really good ways of explaining things.

At first though things started out in a not so good way when Elena said to our class that when we grow up Guatemala will probably be run by cooperatives and to get into practice we should set up a cooperative in our school. She said that what a cooperative does is gather together a group of people to elect a few leaders like a president and a president's assistant and a person to guard money and then they make the choices of what the group gets to do like build a latrine or a dam. When Elena said that one of the boys stood up and said, "I'm not being in a dam cooperative!"

So Elena said, "We're not forming a dam cooperative, that's just one example that I gave."

So he said, "Well good because that's the kind I'm not being in because I'm too young to die!"

Suddenly, Elena's cooperative idea started to sound rather dangerous and I made the sign of the cross for the Trinity protection and so did the girls near me. The boys started out trying to be brave but then began to shift and make moves with their feet as if they might suddenly run out of the room.

Elena asked everyone to please stay calm. She said: "Nothing bad is happening except that we have a misunderstanding. Perhaps I have chosen the wrong words to use that have led to your confusion so I will try to state more clearly. Dam cooperatives do not kill people."

It sounded to me like the same words she used the first time and the same boy said: "No! You are wrong! My mother's sister's cousin's husband who lives in Quiché said the white missionaries made a cooperative to build a dam there and the town elder he told them to leave a hole in the top for the water's spirit to escape through at night, but they told him there is no water spirit and that is not how dams are made and then guess what happened? They built it their way and angered the water and the very first day after the dam got finished all the men in the cooperative got found dead with their chopped-off heads sitting on top of the dam!"

When he said that the littlest girl in our class started to scream and scream until the *seño* ran and snatched her up. *Seño* yelled, "Stop! Calm down! We have discovered our misunderstanding. You probably didn't know this, but in the region of Quiché of which we're speaking there is a war between the guerrillas and the government which is very sad. One of the terrible things about this war is that many Indians there are being murdered by the army by having their heads chopped off. That is what happened in the story told by your sister's friend's cousin's . . . person in Quiché."

We all thought about this for a moment and then the boy said, "But you probably didn't know that an angry water spirit is helping the Quiché army by chopping off all the Indian heads in the dam cooperative!"

Then Elena said, "Ay, Jesus!"

So I said, "We may be poor and we may not have much water, but at least we're not Indians!"

And Elena said, "AY, JESUS!" even louder and sat down with a thump on her desk. We all waited to hear what she would say next about the fate of our heads.

Finally she said we would take a vote. She said anyone who did not want to have their head chopped off and anyone who did not want to start a dam cooperative should raise their hands. I raised my hand very fast and so did everyone else! "Good," she said, "this is democracy. The whole class has decided together not to do this, so now we will no longer talk about dead bodies, beheaded people, or water projects."

Instead we talked about clubs, which is where a group of people gathers together to elect a few leaders like a president and a president's assistant and a person to guard money and then they make the choices of what the group gets to do like build a latrine or something else that isn't a dam. In our club, the leaders would get to collect ideas from the rest of the class and help the *seño* decide on the lessons we learn. When she asked, three boys stood up and said they would volunteer to be class leaders and the *seño* said, "Thank you, this is good, but we need some girls too."

One of the standing-up boys said: "What do we need girls for? They are not smart enough to be in charge!"

After that my friend yelled, "We might not be smart, but at least we're not Indians!"

Then *seño* yelled, "¡AY, JESUS! We are not talking about Indians anymore either! But just so you know Indians are smart, girls are smart, and anyone who is smart and has wholesome desire can be a good leader."

But my friend said: "I don't think you are right, *seño*, because men are always in charge so they must be smarter and know how to do many more important things than women—except for you *seño* because you are not really a woman, you are a gringa." Oh, that gave the *seño* a wild-eyed look! She grabbed some charcoal, drew a line on the wall with the word "Men" on one side and "Women" on the other and said that we would conduct a test. She said, "Tell me who is capable of building a terrace so your maize does not slide off this mountain?"

"The men!" we shouted.

"Tell me who knows what to do for a crying feverish baby so it does not die?"

"The women!" we shouted.

Each time, she put a check in the column for men if we said men and for women if we said women. She asked many questions like who is capable of getting milk from an ornery goat?—check for the women. Who can defend the house from a rabid dog?—men check. Who can dig a well? Who can mend a machete-slashed arm? She asked so many questions and at the end she helped us do a count and do you know what? There were just as many checks for women as for men! *Seño* said: "Twenty-two check marks for things Guatemalan men are better at and twenty-two check marks for things Guatemalan women are better at means equal smartness and equal importance."

I thought this was a very interesting new idea until one of the boys said, "Not equal—because the man's work is harder!" I started to lose my faith in the *seño's* idea because I think the boy is right.

But then Elena said: "No! Man's work is not harder, man's work is just different. Look at our list. Man's work is more physical, but woman's work is tiring too. Man's work is strong in muscle, but woman's work is strong in spirit. Both demonstrate equal strength, equal smartness, at doing different things."

One of the standing-up boys, the one who wanted to be president of our club, said, "Without the man the family would not be able to live though, for who would grow the food?"

He is proud, yes for sure he is! He spoiled the *seño's* idea with that thought of his, and we all said, "Yes, he is right!"

But Elena only smiled and said: "Without women, the man would not be here to grow the food because without a strong woman to give birth to him—something no man wants to have to do!—then that man would not be here in the first place to grow food for his family. And in the second place, without the woman to make the edible meals out of the materials the man grows, we would all be eating hard unshelled beans which would either get stuck in our throats and make us choke to death or get stuck in our insides and make our butts ache." Oh, we laughed and laughed when she said that, for like I told you she is a little bit indecent!, and the standing-up boy ran totally out of contradictory thoughts. But I think she did not want his feelings to be hurt and she said: "We are both right, you and I. Without the man's work we would not have food and without the woman's work we could not eat it. Which means one person is not more important than the other. They are of equal importance, equal strength, equal smartness. And in this classroom, they will be equal leaders."

We voted and now I am the co-president. Me and the boy whose butt would ache without his mother and her edible beans.

For her help in securing for me this great honor that will bring good favor upon my family, I thanked Elena very much after we got back to her house after school. I know this will make my parents very proud of me, their only child who is the co-president, and I tell the *seño* that to show my thanks I will do some extra work like whatever she needs done at her house like fetch the wood or cut back the bushes or remove the dead insects from the floor, but she says that no, we should celebrate. Only I am not familiar with celebrate. Elena says that celebrate is time to rest and play and be happy about something good like being the co-president. Even though I think we should get some work accomplished she says no, no, and here is what we do:

Elena tells me to lie in the hammock and Calixta the dog gets in too. Calixta licks all the dirt off of my feet, licking one toe, then the next, with her tongue tickling all between my toe spaces. Elena sits on the ground and pushes us with one hand like we are a leaf on a big tall tree and when we swing near her she shakes a paper in the other hand so that a big cool burst of air lands on my face. My favorite music from her magic music box is singing its song and I think, celebrate must be the thing they do in heaven, and this is my thought right before I start to fall asleep but then I realize suddenly—I am almost asleep! I jump up to wake myself, flip the hammock, hurt the dog, and bang my knee, because the sleep will ruin my celebrate. The bad things happen in the sleeping space.

* * *

I know it is true that your *espíritu* can wander during sleep and your soul can leave your body for hours or days while you dream, especially if you have done a bad thing or have an enemy trying to bewitch you. So I know that these things that are occurring are my own fault and that if only I can change something about myself I will be protected, but I do not know what it is I need to do to make it stop. I have thought and thought about anything I maybe have done. Was I not a good daughter? I have been a good daughter! I do all my work and I do not complain. Have I had envy? I have not! I am pleased with my station and do not wish for things I cannot have. I do not fight and I only do things to others that I want them to do to me. I hold in my mind good thoughts and still these things are occurring, so what am I doing wrong? What have I done to make this happen?

Until I discover what to do to make it stop all I can think is not to go to sleep so that the dream will not come, so that the evilness will not haunt me when I close my eyes. In our room together it always felt safe before with my mother and my father in the bed where from my space on the sacks on the floor I can see their bodies through the crisscrossed ropes hanging down. I hear my brothers breathe together near me in the same in-out-in-out when they lie down with their chests against each other. Always the night started cold but grew warm inside, and if I woke up I could smell the safe smell of my family until the dreams started and then even the smells changed. I think it is an animal—someone's spirit animal sent to punish me that grabs my face with its big paw and presses me into the pile of sacks, pulling on my dress, sticking me with its claw, and hurting me down there. I lie still like dead, like the possum, until it goes away. I think then, I cannot sleep! I cannot let this dream come back.

But even that I am not good at anymore. I try to keep my eyes open after my brothers go to sleep, but the night is very long. I try to listen for sounds, like a sqwack or a thromp or a shh-shh-shh and then try to think of where the sounds came from to give myself something to do, but it is so quiet in the night that my eyes start to close. If I realize quickly enough that sleep is coming I can jump up or pinch myself until I see the next morning I have made myself bruised and sometimes it works, but sometimes it does not because the dream comes anyway. It gets me and sometimes afterward when I am trying to stay awake to not let it come again I hear my mother crying. I see her body shake through the crisscrossed ropes and I wonder if it is coming to her dreams too? But I do not cry or do anything else except stay still like I am dead and fight not to sleep.

Because Elena is the one who knows about blood in the urinating place hole I decide after much thinking that she is the one I should talk to one morning when I see the claw scratches on my legs and blood nearby my urinating place. Normally, I walk to her house through the *milpa* where I can collect the squash from beneath the corn plants to give her this extra food, and even though this is the long way she is still not awakened when I get to her house. But today I saw her already up, with the horse out of his corral, walking down the rocky path behind the school together with the dog so I ran straight up the hill to meet her. I was almost out of breath when I caught her and asked, "Where are you going so early?" She said she had a meeting in San Marquesa and then needed to bring back some supplies. So we could not have our morning time today because of her hurry. She put her bag on the horse, jumped up behind it, and kicked him to go fast away, but I said, "Please with your permission may I ask one question about the cottons you have for blood?"

She stopped the horse who threw his head back with anger and bit the dog and she said with some exasperation, "What Alma? I am in a hurry!"

I told her I thought I maybe needed a cotton for my urinating place.

"Did you get your menstruation?" she asked.

And I asked, "What is menstruation?"

"Menstruation is what I told you about, how the blood comes every month because you are old enough to have babies."

I said, "I think it is blood because of getting clawed."

She had a look of very much confusion with wrinkles on her forehead and said, "Is blood coming from your urinating place?" I nodded yes and she said, "And do you have aching pain down there or in your belly?"

I nodded yes and said, "Especially at night!"

Elena said, "Then that is your menstruation which is perfectly normal and nothing to worry about." I told her it doesn't feel good and I'd prefer it not to happen to me because I cannot sleep but she said that is normal too and that it should stop in a week or so and that I should talk to my mother about it because she is in a hurry and has to go. Then Elena is gone so I do what she said. I tell my mother that something hurt me and there is blood on my urinating place.

This is not a good thing Elena told me to do. My mother with her back to me, her hands in the *masa*, started to shake and shake and suddenly made a noise like a bird with its wing in the cat's mouth, a scary screaming groan and with her doughy hand out she spun and hit me so hard on the face that I fell right into the dirt with blood coming from behind my teeth, my mother who never hit me before did this!, my mother who loves me!, how could she do this? "Shut up!" she screamed. "Shut up!" She wore some other mother's mean scary face, and her shaking hands spit the uncooked *masa* down on me from her fists until she cried. Then she bent her face down beside me in the dirt and moaned, "You were so special." But her hands scared me and I scooted away when she reached for me causing her to cry louder and run out the door.

I should not have followed her because that is not my place, I should have stayed away, I should not have listened to Elena because this was an idea that was not good, but instead I ran after my mother who ran through the *milpa* and from far away I could hear her and my father yelling. I do not know all the things they said. I just heard some parts like my mother screaming, "You have to send him away!"

Then my father yelled, "He is a good worker!" I couldn't hear the rest then until my father said how if I have a baby it will prove I'm fertile and could help me get a husband, so Elena must be right. This must be menstruation. I must be ready to get myself a baby.

All the yelling scared me and I decided to turn around and go back to the house, to fix this mistake I made of telling my mother. I ran home but my oldest brother, he is there. He knocks me down and pulls me by my hair, not gentle touching but hurting touching, into the corner of the cornfield. It hurts my hands and my face drags on the rocks and the sticks stick me and I say: "Ouch! What? Stop!" But he grabs my face and crushes my mouth closed with his hand like the claw in my dream and calls me fucking bitch and his other hand rips my dress and he jumps on top of me, and bangs me hard giving me the menstruation pain! He pokes me, just like Elena said could happen! This is not my brother!, not my brother who rubs my hair and says *¡Qué bueno!*, not the one who looks at me like a special thing! This is the bad dream! I must be sleeping; I will play dead, I will be the possum and this will end.

When he is off me he says to say nothing to anyone or I will get hurt, but he does not have to tell me to say nothing because this was only a dream; it is not real so I will not tell anyone. Just look at these terrible things I make happen when I tell people about my hurts and about my dreams.

* * *

When Elena first moved here I felt sad for her being all alone with only a dog and a horse and no family to love her and live with her. I thought that she must have great loneliness and be distressed by the aloneness with no one to give her comfort. So even though she has many more things than me like three dresses instead of one dress and her own machete and a magic music box I thought in the beginning when I first met her that God gave me more of the blessing on account of putting me in my family and not kicking me out of my own country to live alone somewhere else. Many things changed though when the dreams started happening and sometimes now I feel the most alone of everyone even the *seño*. Of all the things that changed here are the things that changed the most:
1) My father
2) My mother
3) Me

My father drinks the *guaro* now and spends all the time in the field or somewhere else even when he's not working so I do not see him often, not even in the morning. He does not talk much to me or to my mother with never a *qué bueno*, not even a small one. My mother does not make the tortillas with me anymore because I am too tired and also she does not say the catechism and her eyes are droopy and baggy and black like she cannot sleep either. For me, there are only small changes, not the ones I wished for. The biggest change is that I am not anybody's most special thing anymore.

Elena said the menstruation would be over in a week, but it did not end, the dreams still come, even though the blood stopped and it does not hurt so much. It even feels like a feather tickling me sometimes since I got used to it but I mostly have learned not to feel it. When the menstruation happens, I put my thoughts on other places. When the evil animal spirit gets in my brother I think good thoughts to try and make the menstruation end. I think of good animals like the Calixta and the way she jumps on the horse kindly and stays just a little bit ahead of me all the time during tag. If I close my eyes tight with my hand smooshed down on my face I can even think I am the Calixta, I am the one who can run fast and far from anything bad, I am the one who sleeps in a warm bed with Elena and shares her food, I am in a field with the horse and warm sun and good grass and then when I come back the menstruation is over.

So even though the menstruation is not as bad, these other changes in my family make me sad, especially my father's and my mother's changes. What has happened makes me miss them, even though they are still here. So like I said, I am the most lonely one, even more lonely than the *seño* who does not want me around either, and I have felt much confusion.

When after many months of thinking I could still not think for myself of what I did to make all of this happen, I asked my mother one day: "What has happened? What have I done wrong to make everything change?"

Even though my mother is different in many ways she is probably still the same smart, and my mother said, "We have all sinned. Pride goes before the fall happens."

So see, she is still smart and that is a true thing. I don't know about the falling part, but I remember having some of that pride. Even though I didn't eat Elena's potatoes I was the co-president. No one else in my family ever tried to be co-president before, which is maybe what my mother meant when she said the spirits do not bring good fortune to those who try to be better than what they were born to.

So finally I buried my mirror and do not think anymore of looking at myself as someone special. I will be like the other women, like my mother, like the Virgen, and I will put my mind on taking care of the men and the family without thinking about myself or any of my pride. I strain hard to do my tasks well with extra suffering like putting too much heavy water in the buckets so the metal handle cuts my hand as I walk the long way from the spigot across the rocky path without sandals. This is my confession for having my sins. This is my way of telling God I am sorry for my pride so that maybe the punishment of evil can stop. I do not even let Elena wash my hair anymore. I let it be dirty and if I ever think of my father's hand on it patting or my brother's hand in it rubbing it special I pull some of it out to remind myself that special is a sinful thing.

I can tell you that this penance is working, now that I act more like a normal woman of sacrifice and am becoming fatter too like the women get, because the dreams they do not happen to me as much. My mother says my baby should be here soon and that must mean my sins are almost forgiven, if God is sending me an angel to have for my own. Sometimes during the day, during my chores of collecting the squash or washing the clothes, when I take a little break due to my tiredness and hide behind a tree in the woods where the dreams cannot find me resting, I think about the baby that God will send me. I think that if it is a girl I will name her Elena so that right from the beginning she is born to good things, and will not be afraid of turning herself into someone different and making evil come to her family. A baby named Elena can be happy and plant flowers for joy and kill snakes if she wants and have long beautiful hair.

My baby named Elena will never have to be afraid like me.

5. ELENA'S STORY, AUTUMN 1992

It would be simple for me to allow this tale to digress and then degrade into a scathing denouncement belittling and chastising the Hispanic male. I admit my bias plainly, and if you have not noticed yet you will see soon, again and again, the tortured roots from which my proclivity springs. It is my hope that in being forthright my prejudiced statements may be judged on a balanced scale that takes into account the troubled experiences that birthed them.

My father-in-law once remarked to me, in reference to his tour in Vietnam, that when he first returned he couldn't speak of it at all. Then he could speak with nothing but anger. These many years later, he says, finally, he has acquired the right perspective. I fought no war per se, but I empathize with his statement. When I left Guatemala I swore I would never return—the plane couldn't leave the tarmac fast enough!—and I stubbornly refused to look out the window, hoping only to banish the sight of her from my eyes and mind. I would have woven for you a furious yarn had I dared, at that time, to put pen to paper. But the years pass. I would like to go back now. Tell the land I forgive her, and thank her, too.

Would you believe that on a recent Sunday morning, over a cup of juice, wiping the sleep from my eyes, I found the name of one of the towns where I lived next to the AP byline in the weekend edition? How I gobbled up the words! It was a silly story about some circus dolphins stranded in a tiny pool in a highland town when the man who stole them from the sea ran off and left them behind. "Oh, I know how you feel," I thought, touching the page of printed words, "you fish out of water, you victims of some villainous man." But while my heart bled for them, I also had to laugh a bit; only in the Guatemalan mountains do dolphins swim in the village reservoir.

94

And then it struck me: I have gotten to that place where, looking back on my own experiences, I mostly just want to laugh, too. I can picture it easily: The bad man having run off, a gentle one remaining behind, not knowing any better, slipping a tamale to the marooned mammals. Giggling with glee when they splash him. Running home to his family, throwing back the front door, yelling with delight, "I have caught for us the biggest fish!"

What I am trying to say is that there were a few good men.

A number of them lived in Linda Vista, and here is how I know.

Midway through my mountain sojourn I hiked down to San Marq to replenish my supplies. Toilet paper, peanut butter . . . these things ebb more quickly than you might think. In the tradition of all good alpine travelers, I waved goodbye to everyone along the path out of Linda Vista, shared with them the purpose of my trip, told them I would be back before sundown. Eben shuffled downhill, the empty duffels tied to him with chaffing ropes, prepared to haul back my own goods and the perish-ables for which every family had pressed into my palm one *quetzal*, fifty *centavos*—"A bag of *azúcar*, 'sugar,' Miss, if it is not too much trouble? With the humblest gratitude might I request a small bit of rice?"—hat in hand, twisting skirt edge between gnarled fingers, passing to me their last few pennies. Eben would return loaded down.

I made good time and visited friends in San Marq, purchased supplies, packed the horse to overflowing. I started back toward the mountain at 2 PM. Barely moved one hundred feet.

"Elena!" a small child screamed, rushing up to me. "Come now, come now! There has occurred a horrible accident! We need you, come!" she sobbed, tugging my dress. Cali ran ahead of us, Eben moored to a tree. The far-off screams crescendoed in piercing decibels as we thundered over the cobblestones back toward San Marq. I galloped to keep pace with the panicked child, who steered me across the back porch of my old house and into the yard of the elderly neighborhood thief. The one who had requisitioned my bed. The old woman lay on the ground next to a roaring fire, wailing an agonal moan. An immense iron cauldron canted, disconnected, from the brace that supported it over the flame. Tipped on its side, the massive pot leaked the last few spoonfuls of boiling corn mush, the rest having coated the woman's bare legs from groin to toes in a hissing, bubbling, cooking mire.

Four other women arrived just as I did, beckoned by the cries.

95

"Water!" I screamed, and pointed to the *pila* uphill in my former yard. I reached to scoop the steaming soup from the old woman's thighs, but it sent searing pain roaring through my hand, and I reflexively retreated. Yanking the little girl's shirt over her head, I used the material to swipe off the top layer of ooze. The four women raced back from the *pila*, a tiny half-full plastic bowl of water in their collective eight hands.

I glared at them furiously—this itsy token to vanquish the flood-burst of fire?

"*No hay nada,*" they said simultaneously, meekly, "there is nothing else to bring you water in."

"Help me," I said, and we grabbed her upper body, dragging her roasting legs over the dirt, stones, sticks, broken glass, to the *pila* where we used our hands and skirts to splash the water onto her burns.

The woman's whole body quivered, her head lolled, and every few moments through her clenched teeth an anguished groan seeped out.

"Is there a doctor?" I asked one of the four female assistants.

"No, there is you," she replied.

Stupefied, I bent to examine the injured legs, ballooning with blisters, bleeding a clear viscous cream. "What am I supposed to do?" I asked, peering back up at her.

"You are supposed to fix this," the first lady said.

"What makes you think I can do that?" I asked, incredulous.

I am a hypochondriac. I had spent my whole life to this point fretting over each earache, searching out and measuring moles. I counted sneezes. Last time I gave blood, before leaving the States, I had to recline, with cold compresses, so as not to faint. My fair skin, blue eyes, red hair, and freckles predispose me to illness; I know this for a fact. I have been told over and over. "You must take care of yourself," my mother reiterated throughout my youth. "Your body is more delicate than most. You are not like other people." I embraced the role of the ill, basked in the special status my dainty nature afforded me. In a corner of my heart, I learned to put faith in this weakness, for behind the façade of suburban paradise, attention was meted out less for merit than for shortcomings, as the latter were more rare. I got the most care when I contrived an affliction.

In spite of my hypochondriacal neurosis, I pled ignorance in the face of actual malady.

"What makes you think I can fix her?" I repeated.

"Because you are Elena," said the second woman.

96

"Because you are the gringa, *la americana*," said the third.

"Are you sure there is no doctor?" I asked again.

"Ay, well, there is," said the fourth. "But *fijese*, I just passed him. He is asleep in the ditch, drunk. I tried to wake him and he spit on me and I could not make him move."

So here now is the truth. They needed me to fix her because there was no one else who could. They trusted me to help. They put faith in my education, believed in my skills, and required my strength.

"Bring me a bed sheet—a clean one," I said, standing.

We fashioned a rickshaw of the sheet and transported her to the Sealy. I rummaged for clean cloth and we wet these shirts, some slacks, and a towel, and draped them over her toasted limbs. I told the women to give her lots of water to drink, showed them how to pat her legs with cool, soapy water three times a day, made them promise to keep her shaded and off her feet. I found the Tylenol she stole from me months ago, and measured the pills into little pain relief piles, instructing the helpers to administer a dose at the sun's rise, apex, and demise, and then again at the moon's crest, peak, and disappearance. Explaining the old woman could not be left alone, I cautioned them to check her forehead regularly for fever. When someone manifested a needle, I made them promise not to lance the blisters.

"Show me your feet," I said to one of the neighbors. "See these blisters?" I asked, pointing to the road-weary boils we all grew on the bottoms of our soles. "It is good and fine to poke holes in these shoe sores. Walking blisters can be burst. But her burn blisters," I said, releasing the Samaritan's foot and returning my gaze to the patient, "are not like blisters from walking; the swells she has now are not the popping kind," I explained. "Her blisters will prevent infection. If you open them, like a door, in will walk the germs."

Having done all I could, I turned to leave, but not before pulling aside the caregivers.

"When the doctor awakens," I insisted, "feed him much coffee, and tell him the gringa said to bring to this woman some antibiotics."

That is how it is I came to leave San Marq so late, and walk home in the dark.

Don't think I didn't know better than to get caught out alone by the night, but that streak of stubbornness propelled me toward home. I did not want to have to unload the supplies and find a place to bed down with horse and dog. I figured, hell, I'd walk fast, we'd make good time. I figured wrong, and dusk descended.

Rumor has it these hills are rampant with haunt, the ephemeral vestiges of spirits wronged and wandering, lost. I heard them in the creak and groan of the saddle sacks; their undead fingers grazed my skin every time Calixta's fur brushed against my shin. A ghostly presence inhabited every shadow just beyond the path, and breathed steely breath down upon me from the gathering clouds. Eben neighed a deep throaty rustling, again and again, tossing his mane beneath the swarthy starlight. We three converged, a huddled silhouette against the encroaching night.

The ghouls of my nightmares threatened us least. With the declining temperature a bevy of wilds materialized from their lairs. I anticipated rattlers, glared into the underbrush without seeing, strained to discern their ominous vibration from that of the wind, of our feet, of my blood bolting rampantly through me. My animals listened, too, their furry ears twitching, their heads spinning to-and-fro in furious apprehension. So fixated on what might sneak upon us, we neglected to notice the pack of vultures until they loomed straight ahead.

They fought us for the road, for the fox dead in the center of their grim circle. Writhing, they threw back their bulbous heads and screeched a horrified death song, these minions of the underworld. Shook at us scabrous talons. Rippled with resentment. The leader, threatened, lurched toward us, unfurling his monstrous wings in a corybantic flailing. I held back the rearing horse, quieted the growling dog, fell back a few paces, and conceded defeat. Our party stepped slowly, deliberately, around the deathly scene.

Of all the menace we tiptoed past this unlucky night, however, it was an encounter with man I feared the most.

Too many female Peace Corps Volunteers get raped—four during the time I lived there. One on a rowboat idle along the Caribbean coast. Two, at gunpoint, while browsing in a crowded town square at midday. Both virgins. Another, in her second assault, was plucked off a public road by a man in a pickup who laughed at her tears and mocked, "What? Did you not like it?" I loved Cali for who she was, but I acquired her for what she could do for me. I liked that men cowered from her. I counted on her to save my life and she did not disappoint me. There is a reason I took her with me, always.

On this walk, thankfully, her services remained unenlisted as we crept stealthily upon the sleeping village.

I could just barely see my house now, far away on the crest, ringed in fire.

From the path through the *aldea*, my house, visible only by virtue of its incandescence, seemed elevated halfway to heaven, as if the stars lingered there to rest, waving, shivering, against the coal black hue of the surrounding countryside. I counted six . . . seven . . . eight flaming weevils licking the sky with their red-orange tongues. Perhaps this kindling meant to beckon me, a lighthouse savior guiding home our lost, tossed, wayward crew. Or perhaps, instead, my house was burning down.

If so, the pungent aroma of splintering wood and incendiary thatch hitchhiked on the back of an easterly wind and skirted away before we caught up with the breeze, for the night smelled only of the dirt we kicked up beneath our feet, of horse sweat and animal droppings and ripening corn. We meandered along, no purpose in rushing to watch a blaze that cannot be contained. My hand already stung with blistered welts from my attempts to squelch the combustion of the woman's legs earlier in the afternoon. Enough fire for one day. I was tired. Let it burn.

The closer we came, the clearer my vision. The house was not alight—instead, eight burning bushes morphed into eight gigantic glowing candles which finally became eight torches ablaze in the hands of eight waiting men. Eight men circled my home holding fire in the middle of the night.

I am of the opinion that if practiced, one can learn to sense intent, to interpret an energy, either malicious or otherwise, and with honed skill react in foreknowledge of what is to occur. Guatemala started to teach me this. Not that I ever became fully skilled in the use of the power, for my ability to prevent an action based on my sense of it beforehand always lagged. When real evil approached it pressed on me—that is the only way I can describe it. I presaged its advance with the rapid constriction of my pores and a strangling in my chest. I knew enough to be scared, but not always in time to avert assault. Like the time, wandering lost in the capital, when I knew, moments ahead of time, that I would be attacked from behind, and then felt the groping hands; on the bus, when I actually lunged from my seat to shout a warning, but not in time to avoid the turn and the guerillas waiting in the trees; and worst, the night I slept through the approach of my stalker, only to come awake in time to hear his last few footfalls echo against the patio outside my door before he lunged against it. In matters of true presentiment, I deferred to the dog, who had been waiting in quiet anticipation to lunge into battle with that stalking intruder while I still snored softly in my bed. As a judge of character, I trusted Cali implicitly and acted on her whim, my Geiger counter of safety or threat. She knew the nature of every heart.

So on this night, approaching eight men in waiting at the top of a remote mountain, miles and miles from refuge, too far for a scream to matter, I doubted my own calm until Calixta rushed forward and licked the proffered hand of the man at the head of the group.

"*Buenas noches*, Elena, good evening," Hernando said, removing his worn brown hat and bowing slightly, a fleeting nod of respect. The torches danced, throwing gargantuan shadows onto the walls, and in their reflected glow I recognized this man. In his house I initially sought refuge the first day I hiked, parched and sick, into these hills. His wife, Rosa, squeezed me a fresh glass of lemonade, then another, then another, and watched me, smiling, tender, while I drank the full weekly ration of her family's sugar. Hernando's brothers stood with him now, and his brothers-in-law, my landlord, their older sons, and one adolescent boy trying without success to be manly who sat propped against the side of my house, asleep, a thin trail of drool leading from his mouth to his shoulder. He must have been there for hours.

"We hope we have not alarmed you," Hernando continued, "and we do not want to further trouble you, as you must be tired from your long journey. However, earlier in the day, a child noticed a family of five rattlesnakes crawling up your wall and slipping into your house."

The landlord, shuffling up behind Hernando, cleared his throat to beg indulgence. "Please pardon me," he said, his hat clutched in his aged hands like a prayer cloth, his head toward the ground, "but if you will allow me to humbly point out that it was *my* son who noticed this." With that, he ceremoniously swept his left arm through the air, moving with deft showmanship and fine style, holding his hand suspended in the space beside him, above the sleeping boy, as if to call attention to his most astounding of prizes. "This son, of mine," he said, glancing at me, a smile tugging the corner of his lip.

I knew the boy from school, from his crab-for-dinner gift, from his tending of the two pigs near my house. "A fine boy, he is," I said, and the landlord smiled at me fully.

"You said you would return tonight," Hernando continued, "and we worried that if you entered without being aware, you might be hurt. So if you will allow us to enter first, we will make sure it is safe, and then we will leave you."

I removed the padlock and the eight men, with torches and machetes bared, crammed into the little room. They searched, respectfully, and exited. "It is safe," Hernando said, "the snakes must have crawled back out. We wish you a good night."

So the eight men with torches returned home, to sleep a precious few hours before rising for their fields, their harvests, their families, their animals, their awesome responsibilities including, of all things, me.

* * *

I once played the guitar. I once played many instruments and I play them no more, which is to say that I played until I conquered and then I ceased. It was the challenge, more than the music, that excited me. I learned and learned until I got good, and then I played and played until I got bored. An all-or-nothing mentality which I think engrained in me early and which I can most precisely correlate to breakfast foods. As a youngster I vexed the world, and particularly my mother, with absurdly persnickety eating habits, so that when she hit on something I tolerated she fed it to me so often that it made me sick. I never ate a bowl of cereal, a fried egg, oatmeal, waffles, or any of the standard morning fare that makes life simple. So when I suddenly announced a craving for pancakes, pancakes appeared on my plate every day until the taste would never leave my mouth and the heretofore delicious pancakes acquired the savory tang of moldy dough. This precipitated a switch to little pizzas individually and laboriously created with handcrafted sauce on toasted English muffins; I ingested so many so frequently that to this day I cannot eat toasted bread. Even milkshakes full of rich ice cream (and, unbeknownst to me, a raw egg) pleasured me only until such time that their regular appearance at the breakfast table became a drain on my appetite.

And so it was with musical instruments, as with so many other things. I played until I felt accomplished and then I stopped and forgot all my skills. This is my manner: I skip from one challenge to the next with a vengeant focus on mastery and a hyper energy which takes such momentum to maintain that it simply cannot be sustained over a long-ish period of time. My hobbies evolve on a constantly rotating basis so that six months from now I will be enjoying the delight of some new-found diversion which in a year will no longer hold my interest.

Careers dull for me after a while. (My mother, who has always wished me to be a writer, gushed with joy when she heard I started this book and envisions a life for me of creative literary pursuit. "Mom," I keep telling her, already feeling the pull of some other undiscovered accomplishment, "let's just see if I can finish *this* one.") I am the consummate jack-of-all-trades.

There was a period, directly coinciding with the start of my life in Guatemala, when I feared this predilection marked me as the bearer of some sort of latent personality flaw. "I am too fickle," I thought. "Something is wrong with my attention span. I am unable to focus." But as I aged, not in years necessarily but in experience, and perhaps through a dawning independence sparked in the Guatemalan mountains, I decided—slowly at first, and then more deliberately—to disallow myself, primarily, and then others by proxy, to label my nature as labile. Whose business is it if I do not persevere endlessly; have not the fates always smiled on the creators? Instead of assuming the title of flighty or changeable which the world might have tagged on me, I decided to reframe my tendencies in the most positive light. My capricious craving of change is an enviable character strength. Who cares how well I play the guitar?

Who, indeed.

"Can you play the guitar?" the Catholic priest asked me. We stood beneath the overhang of the schoolhouse, where the entire community of Linda Vista assembled for mass on this most rare and revolutionary of days when the priest visited. A middle-aged man with a gentle face and a tolerant temperament, he journeyed up to the parishioners on the mount twice yearly or so, a sojourn that few other priests had the constitution or musculature to make. He brought with him his holy implements in a cracked leather case, and a guitar strung on a woven strap across his back.

I opened my mouth to answer him yes, then closed it again, thinking no. Finally, with a coy smile, I replied, "Not really . . ."

"No one here knows how to play," he said. "But I have faith that someday someone will learn. Show me what you know," he said, pushing the instrument into my hands. The rest of the townsfolk milled around, closing in and watching carefully. I played a few chords, showed off some fancy finger work. "My prayers have been answered!" he shouted. "I have an accompanist."

He intended for me to provide the musical portion of the mass!

"Father," I stammered, "it has been a very long time since I played." The irony here is, I last played at a Catholic mass. I learned at age seven, so as to participate with my mother in the radical new Sunday service officiated not by organ, but by strings. An activist guitar group of eight adults and one seven-year-old child. I played until we were not Catholic anymore.

"However," I conceded now, inspired to greatness by the priest's look of glee, "if you give me the sheet music, I'm sure I can fumble through."

"There are no sheets of music," he said. "You must play from your heart."

"I don't know any songs by heart," I insisted. This wasn't precisely true because I knew three, but they were all inspired by seven-year-old sentiments and entirely inappropriate for church.

"Let the spirit guide you," he stated calmly, anointing my head with his hand.

The assembled participants all took their seats, in the grass, on the concrete breezeway, squeezed into child-sized desks. The priest arranged his vestments, and cued me to initiate the processional. The entire gathering took a collective deep breath, prepared to explode in pent-up song. For this reason, of my three memorized choices, I dispensed with the idea of playing "Yankee Doodle." No one but I knew the words. And so, limited in scope to two options, and determined to save the holier "Silent Night" for the recessional (to carry us through the upcoming six month spiritual drought), the priest strode into the schoolhouse grounds to the harmonic cross-cultural strains of "Happy Birthday."

"Happy birthday to you, happy birthday to you, happy birthday dear—" Here everyone paused a moment before chiming in with a discordant mélange of names: "God, Jesus, Father." One sweet spirit even sang out, "Elena," which I thought was a kind tribute to my ceremonial contribution. "—garble garble garble, happy birthday to you."

The priest proceeded nonplussed, as though birthday celebrations regularly coincide with the start of mass.

He wasn't too far along, though, before he began to lambaste the Evangelicals and lost my good favor. Here is the thing, which I must be honest and disclose: I am not much of an Evangelical fan myself. So that you will appreciate this, I will share some history. As I hinted earlier, I grew up Catholic, but my family (or I should say, my mother, and then—begrudgingly at first but wholeheartedly in the final tally—my father, too) left the Catholic Church to become born-again amid great commotion and ruffling of family allegiances which would remain disturbed for many years. That my sisters, and I in particular, never fully embraced but instead rebelled impulsively against this paradigm shift caused prolonged agitation in our household. Frankly, I suspect we would have revolted against Catholic dogma too as we aged, believing as we do that spirituality is an inclusive and individual process, but it is easier to oppose the religion which expects one to raise her hands, speak in tongues, and be slain in the spirit before a possessed crowd during the most insecure and troubling of teenage years. The fervor of the Evangelicals has always made me nervous.

But the fervor of American Evangelicals pales profoundly in comparison to the enraged spiritualism of their Guatemalan counterparts. Spurred on by missionaries who, I know, originate most frequently from my own country, these modern-day Christians are intent on saving souls through a warlike fixation on the acquisition of spirits. This attempted conversion is perpetrated most commonly through nighttime religious services broadcast publicly to the interested and disinterested alike through a complex system of strategically placed loudspeakers. Linda Vista, thank God, lacked electricity, and we were all therefore spared these attempts at our loyalties. But elsewhere, in every town cursed with electric power, the setting of the sun commenced a litany of prayers, pleas, and threats which crackled over the rooftop sound system with a virtually indecipherable roar. For at least three hours every night, and sometimes, not infrequently, during all-night vigils, the Evangelical congregations screamed upon their neighbors a woeful stream of vituperations. They wailed in sorrowful lamentation. Screeched with unbridled joy. Shouted the love of God across unstable microphone wires that vacillated with their own shrill feedback. Pled for the sinners' hearts with a high-pitched, ear splitting shriek.

One night, suffering from flu and fever, besieged already by a headache, I retired early to bed. Suddenly, through my window—I swear!, right through my very own window!—the nightly Evangelical ministry started in. (Clearly, this incident occurred after I moved from Linda Vista, but I jump ahead to make my point.) I leapt from my bed alarmed, accosted by the proximity of the ruckus and decibel of the noise which caused my head to throb in time with the attendant trumpet accompaniment. Someone had installed a speaker on my roof. Without thinking, I charged out of the house in my pajamas, my hair a Medusa-like tangle, and rushed around the corner to the church. I cannot over-dramatize the impression I must have made, flinging open the big wooden doors with a crash, barreling down the center aisle with red swollen eyes, insane hair, in my bedclothes, trailed by my stomping and growling dog.

To say you could hear a pin drop would be to imply that things had not quieted down sufficiently. The trumpeter froze wide-eyed, his lips a perfect circle around the mouthpiece, and the singer's tongue protruded from her mouth in an unfinished C minor. The audience arrested their enthusiastic swaying with arms still in the air, on a collective inhale, and forgot to breathe back out. But for my furious footfalls and the click of Cali's toenails on the floor, the room stood shocked by its own silence.

I stormed the pulpit and thrust my arm forward to point in the face of the preacher.

"I am going out of my mind!" I shouted. "I am very sick, and you are making me crazy!" (In hindsight, I know they all misunderstood and took me, literally, to be sick in the mind and going nuts.) "If I cannot get a decent night's sleep, I will die!" I screamed, exaggerating for effect, "and if I die, I will come back and haunt all of you!" With this I swung my arm around and pointed at the assembled believers, who gasped in even more air so that they all looked ready to hyperventilate. They may be God's soldiers now, but they are Guatemalans first, and superstition therefore courses through their hearts in more plentiful measure than blood and plasma. "I just want some sleep," I muttered over and over as I retreated for home.

While not my most culturally sensitive moment, my lunacy did result in the desired outcome and the entire town slept peacefully for one night. Of course, the feud reinitiated the following evening (although the speaker had by then disappeared from my roof), this ongoing polemic between Catholics and Evangelicals.

I think the most distasteful thing about the Christian religions is the utter disdain they display toward one another. This is not by virtue of their beliefs, which are, by circumstantial necessity, of a shockingly similar variation. It seems at times to be motivated by little more than body count, with the greatest prestige, tithes, and heavenly position going to the organization that fills the most pews. Yet in tiny towns like Linda Vista, I hardly understood the need for infighting, and the Catholic priest shocked me when he used his whole homily as an invective to criticize the Evangelical movement.

I leaned toward Rosa, Hernando's wife, who sat beside me (the woman of the delicious and lifesaving lemonade), and whispered my surprise.

"Ah yes," she whispered back. "Catholics hate Evangelicals."

"How do *you* feel about Evangelicals?" I asked.

"I am an Evangelical," she replied quietly.

"I thought you were a Catholic—you are about to take Catholic communion," I stammered.

"I am a Catholic."

"But you just said you were an Evangelical," I murmured.

"I am an Evangelical."

"This is not making any sense to me," I said in hushed tones, one eyebrow raised.

"Well yes, I can see that," she said. "I am a Catholic *and* an Evangelical."

"That's not possible," I insisted.

"Anything is possible," she demurred. "I am a Catholic when the Catholics are in town, and I am an Evangelical when the Evangelicals are in town. The way I figure it, the difference isn't with God, it's with the people here on Earth who practice the religions. And so since there's only one God, the same God for both Catholics and Evangelicals, I don't think it matters whom I go to church with, just so long as I go."

Nothing nearly so sensible got said the whole rest of the day.

* * *

Rosa enjoyed my company and I hers, and though our lives veered in diametrically different directions, there are things we have in common. We stand at the same height, although she more plump and I more gaunt, and our hair, though of different colors, hangs to the same length. Our complexions are both smooth. We bite our nails. Born in the same month, we share an astrological sign, which she knows nothing of and I do not believe in. Rosa is only a year older than I.

She has six children.

Her house resembles mine, a kitchen hut and a sleeping hut, but hers is smaller and also has a porch. From the end of this porch she watches for me, for she can see my door if she tiptoes and leans slightly forward, and every morning without fail when I awaken and step into the day, the first thing I hear carried on the newborn breeze over the *aldea*, the schoolhouse, the cornfield, the path, the rocks, is her joyous voice greeting me: "*Buenos días* Elena, good morning!" Always she has prepared for me the Guatemalan breakfast staple which I gladly accept and look forward to: scrambled eggs, black beans, tortilla. What I do not finish for breakfast she rewarms and serves me for lunch, so that in this way she ensures my return to her home after school, which starts around nine and ends around noon.

I like to look upon her as I stroll toward her home, for I feel we share a sensibility. She is always sweeping the tamped earth that makes her floor, her porch, her patio; or she is potting a discovered flowering plant in a chipped cup or concave rock; or she is watering the natural greenery that flourishes around her house so that it stays green and lush and nice to look upon; or she is straightening the sticks and rag dolls with which her children play, sorting them into a pile on the end of the porch, so her yard is smooth and bare and free of debris. Rosa and I appreciate beauty. Even in the most difficult of circumstances, we take what little there is and arrange it in the most flattering of manners.

Not everyone is so inclined, and this more than anything made my adaptation to Guatemala difficult. Of all the adjustments, both mental and physical, which must be made daily if one is to acclimate to a foreign land and culture, I believe I coped with the most profound conformations the easiest. I muddled through the language, and adopted the customs of respect and decorum which facilitate immersion. I made friends. In my mind I held fast to a quote from Elizabeth King: "I find that it is not the circumstances in which we are placed, but the spirit in which we meet them which constitutes our comfort," and I refrained from focusing on the privations which no native noticed. Few immigrants fared better.

But I could never reconcile myself to the minimal level of cleanliness and the absolute indifference countless Guatemalans demonstrate toward their surroundings. Many live in what can only be described as rank squalor, and try as I might not to judge, I remain baffled by these conditions. While I do not pretend to know what it is to be raised in an atmosphere of deprivation and hardship, I do not accept the liberals' excuse of imprinted indigence. There are people who have so little yet keep everything neat, organized, and cleansed, while others more materially blessed live in filth, worse than pigs (an animal which makes efforts, after all, to be clean). I have visited whole villages where the residents dump trash into ditches along the roads, allowing it to overtake the pathways, an invitation to animals to root and fight viciously over the scraps alongside children who play covered in muck, while everyone behave as if oblivious to the stench and disorder. I have visited other towns where the populous burns their garbage, sweeps their walks, and grows red, purple, magenta bougainvillea over their walls in a profusion of pink-hued perfume. More often, however, the two opposites bump up right next to each other, the cared-for home flanked by the distressed, so that group mentality cannot be said to account for the difference, proving in my mind that cleanliness is an attitude, not an economic or social condition. There are people with simple dirty faces, a hygienic shortcoming that cannot be avoided when one's floors, walls, and roads are built from the earth; than there are people additionally smeared with meal residue and snot who attract flies and are covered in lice. Once, at my wit's end, I picked maggots with my stubby fingernails from a little boy's nose where they feasted on a crust of many days' mucus.

This child, a student of mine, was related, I believe, to the three teens who gave me the most trouble. They lived downtown, which is to say in the five or six houses which occupied the lower elevation of Linda Vista, separated along a boundary invisible to me but distinctly clear to the residents of uptown, including Rosa, who could point to a space in the air there and say, "Here is where everything changes." And she was right, for while all the cornfields intermixed out there in the hills and the men labored side by side, their children attending the same school, social visits never broached this line, for downtown was dirty and the reputation bad. The proverbial train tracks threw down their signal flags even here, and warned, "Do Not Cross."

I had no reason to know these boys, too old for school and living on the opposite side of the *aldea* from me, but they came and found me. I saw them lingering sometimes on the path below my house, and when I waved hello they simply stared back at me with sullen, silent faces. The sense they gave me always made me call for the dog and they would walk on. Sometimes I felt watched, which I attributed only to my own paranoia, until I found them one day with their eyes on me when they should not have been.

I did not have a latrine or a place to bathe. The landlord kept promising to dig me a pit, but it never happened, so I dug a hole for my own feces, shoveled it in, buried it beneath a tree. I urinated in a designated spot set back from my home and bathed fast with a sponge and a bucket of accumulated rainwater behind the back wall. All timed carefully so no one would see. Until the day they did.

I squatted, Cali beside me, for she relieved herself alongside me as she did everything else, when with much commotion and a bone-jarring bounce a boy fell from his camouflage in a tree twenty feet above and behind me. His brothers leapt from the limbs and dragged him away, so that by the time I turned a startled pirouette I saw only the back of their heads and shoulders bounding over the bluff, but I recognized them by the crud in their hair, their soiled shirts, and the fact that the three always moved together. How often did they hide there and watch? How much did their voyeuring eyes see and what might they return for and when?

I began to worry, and then Rosa came to call.

This is unusual because for all of our visits, she never came to me, I went to her. Something was up.

"I do not want to alarm you," she said, "but I think you should know that we heard a rumor—" which must have been more than just a rumor, for she would not have come based only on conjecture "—that those three nasty boys from the awful family downtown had plans to break into your house. They boasted that on the night of the new moon they would climb over your wall and slip beneath the roof to rape you."

This did not surprise me, and I slept prepared for such an attack with a butcher knife beneath my pillow, a machete below my bed and Cali locked inside with me, but to hear that the plans had actually been laid sent a shiver along my skin.

"But do not worry," Rosa continued. "I think we have fixed this problem. I spoke to my two sisters first, and then we three talked to our husbands and sent them to talk to the boys and their parents, which is where they are right now. They are telling them this: My sisters and I consider you now to be a sister, so that we are not three but four. And if you are a sister to us, then you are family to our husbands, as if you were one of their own wives. Our men will say, 'Since the gringa is our family, like a wife, anything done to her will be avenged by us. So if you go through with your disgusting plan, know this—we will kill you.' So I think you will now be safe, but I wanted to tell you so that if there is any more problem you will report it to me, and I will tell my husband. I will lend him to you to protect you, since you have no man of your own to guard you."

To thank them, for she was right, the boys never bothered me again nor appeared anywhere near my home as far as I knew, I took the remaining film in my camera and photographed the three sisters and their families. While the indigenous do not like to have their pictures made, thinking that in so doing you steal their souls, the Ladinos love the attention. On my next excursion out of town I developed the film, enlarged the prints, fashioned frames from twigs which I lashed together. Rosa called my attention to the picture on each of my visits, saying proudly, "Look, look at my lovely family!" and she hung it from a nail on the porch wall during the day and transferred it inside with them at night.

So it is that the image moved in and out with her baby, her youngest, a one-year-old, who passed his days suspended naked in a hammock. During the day he swayed on the porch and at night hung in their sleeping room.

I have heard it said that many Guatemalan youngsters learn to walk later than their U.S. and European counterparts because of the delayed balance effected by this pendant first year. Equilibrium distorts after a year of suspension. However, these dangling bottoms allow excrement to seep out of baby bodies and drip through the hammock's rope to land upon the ground, obliterating the need for impractical diapers. Once toddlers learn to walk, but before they learn to control their bowels, they totter naked around the premises so their waste fertilizes the ground instead of soiling clothing. So Rosa had two perpetually naked children and while she scooped up what she could of their poop she obviously had no control over retrieval of urine. A dark patch of well-watered earth hovered below the infant's hammock and also littered the property, so that the mother always knew where her two-year-old played by the puddle in the yard.

Rosa's three other children, a three-, four-, and five-year-old, darted always underfoot when I visited, so curious and excited by my presence, while her sixth child threatened to burst momentarily from Rosa's expansive belly. One or two always hung from her swollen breasts, while a third often waited in line for milk. Despite our age equity, I thought, the gulf that divides us could not be more vast:

I wore braces when she married.

She still struggled to write her name when I graduated from college.

I pledged a sorority while she birthed her first child.

She learned to till fields while I prepped for graduate school boards.

I studied investment strategies as she struggled to feed eight with food enough for four.

She settled down forever as I took off to travel far, far away.

Nevertheless, our lives crossed, and against formidable odds a friendship forged.

* * *

Rosa shocked me one day with a cavalier comment: "*Fíjese*, my sister's baby died this morning."

Fíjese, as you may have already conjectured, is the chosen vernacular for bearing bad news. As I understood it, keeping in mind that I lacked a lifetime's understanding of its subtle nuances, *fíjese* combined calamity with an aspect of fate so as to abdicate the speaker from all responsibility for righting the wrong. Its definition stretched from sorrow to slander, with a gamut of meanings:

"I am so profoundly sorry . . ."

"Ha, ha, ha hahaha . . ."

"Too bad for you . . ."

"Now's my chance to stick it to you, gringa . . ."

"Prepare yourself for the most horrible news you have ever heard . . ."

"Prepare yourself for a line of absolute bullshit . . ."

Just prepare yourself. Anticipate a letdown. Grab onto something strong to hold you up, steel your nerves, call on a saint. *Fíjese* is the Guatemalan's way of asking, "Are you sitting down?" and can appropriately preface any of these comments:

"What a shame you walked twelve hours to get here. Even though the sign says 'Open' we closed early for a party and cannot help you until tomorrow."

"You know the money you loaned me, which I was going to pay back this week? Well, I don't have it and probably never will."

"I don't know where you will sleep now that I have stolen your bed." (Remember that one?)

As much as I loathed and feared the sound of the word, I did with time become fluent in its use. Said with a fawning smile and a tilt of the head, it equaled a flirtatious beseeching of forgiveness, as in: "*Fíjese*, remember the truck you lent me to move my belongings to Linda Vista? Well, the axle broke and it's stranded at the top of the mountain." Said with a droop-eyed look of mirth, it excused etiquette breaches as an act of goodwill: "*Fíjese*, I have developed a terrible allergy to cows and if I eat these brains—which appear to be deliciously prepared!—I will get itchy bumps all over my body that are contagious and since I would hate to infect you I must sadly abstain from partaking of your meal." You can see where the catch phrase could be used to my advantage, too, as the recipient's only response is a slow, obliging, understanding nod. So sad for you.

Much as the word wore many hats and proved utile in a profuse number of instances, it seemed a bit supercilious to describe the death of an actual person with such nonchalance.

"Oh my God," I replied to the news of the baby's death. "How horrible!"

"Yes, it is," Rosa said, sighing, and I saw real sadness in her eyes for her sister and her niece, and she looked for a moment about to cry. But then the mood passed and she shrugged. "It is also good."

Rosa's sister's twelve-week-old baby, her eleventh, never flourished. While no one fully expected the baby to live, we all hoped for the best. Or so I thought.

"It is good that the baby won't suffer anymore," I agreed.

"Hmm?" she asked.

"You just said it was good that the baby died," I said, "and I finished your sentence: so that it would not suffer anymore."

"That's not what I meant," she said.

"Then what did you mean?" I asked.

"I meant that it is a good thing this one died. They already have ten children and she's getting too old to have any more, and if it hadn't died they might not have had an angel."

"What are we talking about?" I asked her, something I found myself asking frequently.

"They almost didn't have an angel!" she said.

"Rosa, explain this to me more clearly, please. I have no idea what you're talking about."

So she explained: Every family needs an angel to intervene for them with God. Without an angel there is no one to pray to, no one to ensure the rains fall and land on your crops, no one to hear your confession of sins or grant you God's forgiveness.

Dead babies become angels.

In a country where infant mortality is exceeded only by illiteracy, where malnutrition dries a mother's milk and dysentery sucks at the guts, babies die like leaves drop in autumn. Transient gifts. Ephemeral beings. To forestall sorrow and prepare for the worst, these little ones are treated as evanescents—no names, no dreams, no attachment. They will be fed and bathed and clothed and treated with the general kindness afforded a visiting seraph until their robust growth indicates they have chosen to stay of this world. Only the ones older than three months can be loved and christened, or the parents might die over and over from grief for their departing newborns. So the myth of the angels must have begun to ease the repeated sorrow of death. But at some point the coping method became less a defense mechanism and more of a goal. When I asked, Rosa admitted ruefully that her family did not yet have its own angel. "But don't worry," she assured me. "We have plenty of time yet. I am still young; we will have more babies."

I accompanied Rosa to the child's funeral, a small affair. Hernando did not go; he had to tend his own field and that of his brother-in-law, so that the other family could take the free time to bury their baby. I stood back a little way from the mourners as they dropped the infant into a hole halfway between the house and the edge of their field. A rough-hewn handmade coffin enclosed the limpid body, so little wood, which if I overheard correctly used to be a slat supporting the parents' bed and blankets. With only a table, some chairs, a bed or two in everyone's home, spare wood is hard to come by. I wonder: Now every night, when they sleep, and the cotton bolster dips into the divot where the coffin wood used to lend its support, how will they keep from thinking of the baby decaying in the yard?

No one cried but it is not to say they did not grieve. Angel or no, whose heart is so hard that it does not crack when, shovel in hand, the dirt hits the box of hopes and dreams and covers it over until its very existence is in doubt? The mother, she is the one, when the men go back to their work and routines, and the siblings run off to play, who will carry with her the child who died. Some say it is in gray hairs, wrinkles, or an affect of depressed perseverance. But I see it in Rosa's sister, in a deft movement few could have noticed, a slight of hand as she turned from the grave. She grazed her belly with her fingertips, as if to wonder, was it here?, and if her womb answered back, which I hope it did, with a twitch or a spasm, then I believe she will always touch herself there and in doing so she will not think, "I have ten children and an angel," but say to herself, "I had eleven babies."

No one cried, which is only to say they bore their loss privately.

No one cried because this moment came years overdue.

No one cried because, to fight off the tears, they repeated again and again that ten healthy children is a miracle. Really, we are blessed.

* * *

I wedged myself into a slatted chair in the corner of Rosa's kitchen. I curled my feet onto the seat beneath me and tried to balance on the unforgiving wood, sandwiched between two children fighting for my lap and a chicken pecking for crumbs beneath the table. (Give me a rat to dangle my toes in front of, send a bat to swoop upon me, I will not care. But good God, these chickens with their violent beaks and gouging toenails, banish them all!) "Maybe you should put the chicken outside," I whispered to the son, and he thought about it, but then shook his head, no. So instead I positioned him in front of me, and he thought he sat on my lap for favor which made him happy, but actually he functioned as a barrier between me and the bird. We three, the boy on my lap and the boy beside me, shared a cold tortilla, but the crisp blackened edges had begun to peel and the corn flavor ceded to the scent of mold. I kept an eye on the fresh tortillas roasting on the *comal* in the opposite corner.

Two mangy hounds, one missing a large portion of a floppy ear and the other with no tail, fought over a bone in the middle of the room, too close, I thought, to the toddler crawling naked across the floor, but Rosa watched unperturbed. She also let her children play with sticks and never thought to fear for their eyes. I, in contrast, learned a lifestyle pre-occupied with precaution, carrying the scissors pointy end down, shielding my eyes from errant BBs, and walking slowly around the rims of pools. Once when I saw her son running with a knife and I yelled for her to grab it quick, before he fell and gored himself, she laughed at my concern and said, "Don't worry, he'll be fine." She allowed her kids to eat food that fell on the ground, and they lived.

There is a saying: With absolute poverty comes absolute freedom. At its most elemental, perhaps this statement begs the question: Have you ever actually seen someone eviscerated by scissors? Shoot out his eye? Can convention and decorum and fear of death prevent the child who runs near water from drowning? Rosa did not waste her time on this and other stupid stuff; her full, hard life denied her the opportunity to worry over outlandish possibilities, and her children were no worse for the cuts, bumps, or scratches that life dishes out. She did not turn the handles to the back of the stove; the fading singe on her five-year-old's hand would remind him sufficiently not to touch the hot *comal*. The boy on my lap wore a gash above his eye that would heal.

The brawling dogs ignored the little girl.

With one hand Rosa washed her new infant in a plastic bucket on the edge of the raised *adobe* hearth, while with her other hand she flipped our tortillas. I removed the plate that covered the bowl of yesterday's beans. With one hand I flicked away the flies over the food, while with the other I peeled three oranges. The earthen walls that rose from the ground surrounded us on all sides and blocked the sun. We lunched together in the unnatural dusk of noon.

"Have you thought of a name for the baby?" I asked.

Rosa turned and smiled a full broad smile, her eyes alight with rebellion. She did not heed advice. She named all her babies too early and enjoyed doing so. "I have named him Fernando," she said, and hugged him to her breast.

Sitting, she chose the fattest tortilla and set it aside on a plate with the largest portion of beans for her husband who walked through the door. Sweat drizzled from his hairline in rivulets over his cheeks. With a shrug of his shoulder and a swipe of his forearm he erased the perspiration from his face before bending to kiss Rosa on the top of her head. "*Gracias, buen provecho*," he said, wishing us all good digestion as manners dictate, but speaking in essence only to his wife. His workman's hands grazed her face as they embraced, and his fingers, dark from the fields and smeared with soil, softly stroked the edge of her ear. A tender, private caress. I lowered my eyes.

Of all the Guatemalan couples I ever met, Rosa and Hernando are the only ones I understood to be lovers. Not that the rest didn't have sex, for the astounding number of children attested to this fact. But husbands do not generally nuzzle wives. No one threads their fingers around another's palm on the streets or in the houses. The man does his job and the wife hers, and if they exchange a glance between them it more frequently looks like a glaring indictment of, "You're not planning on bringing that bloody carcass into my kitchen, are you?" or "Is there nothing you can do to keep that baby from screaming in my ear?" than a weighted, longing, lustful stare.

Guatemalans are a stoic people; not overly demonstrative with their affections, and rock solid in their delineation of roles. I bucked many, many standards. I rode a horse. I lived alone. It confused and perhaps disturbed them that at twenty-three I had no husband, wanted no children. When I decided to move to Linda Vista to temporarily assume his role, the male teacher scoffed at the suggestion. "This is a stupid idea you have," he said. "You will never be able to do it. No woman can live in those mountains," as if dozens of women didn't already live there, but what he meant was what all Guatemalans, male and female alike, meant, for I heard this sentiment often: that none of those women could have done it either without their husbands to care for them, which, having lived there, I do not believe is true. But what everyone begrudgingly excused in me with a roll of the eyes and a flip of the hand, as if to say, "These *americanas* are impossible to understand," they disavowed in their own women.

Women knew their place. Men worked very hard, either toiling in a field, a shop, or other business endeavors, and they earned the right to play as hard and drink and eat and relax. Women worked just as hard in other ways, cooking, cleaning, and caring for children, an Ozzie and Harriet lifestyle, you may think, of traditional standards and role assumption. But whether it was the nature of the work, so taxing and exhausting—I know I hardly felt amorous at the end of my own day— or whether these separate tasks kept them so focused in opposite directions, I hardly ever saw couples converge. The shopkeeper and his wife worked alongside each other behind a small counter, he doing the selling and she the cooking and serving, but they never bumped into each other, not once in the course of the day, in such a tiny space. The mayor and his wife dined together every night, at opposite ends of the table, and if they passed a plate between them he held one end and she grabbed the other side, so that in the course of the evening they never touched. In over two years, never did I see anyone but Rosa and Hernando embrace.

While I cannot know the libidinous leanings of a country, the salacious undertakings which, in spite of outward appearances, may unfold behind closed doors, it is not difficult for me to imagine these sexual unions resulting in nothing more than perfunctory couplings for obligatory purposes of breeding. But Rosa and Hernando at least are partners in more than propagation. He lingered over her hair as he finished his kiss. She turned imperceptibly and grazed his chest with her cheek. They danced a slow love song of subtle practiced motions. The children chuckled, I blushed. He pulled up a chair, and sat so close his knees must have touched hers secretly beneath the table.

"Congratulations. I hear you have named the baby," I said.

"Yes," Hernando answered, stealing a few quick bites of food before heading again for the fields. "We have named him for his strong and very handsome father," he said laughing, with a puffed-out chest, amused at his jest. "We have christened him Hernando."

Rosa stroked her husband's hand, grinning at his humor.

I sipped my lemonade, confused for a minute, until I realized I must have misheard Rosa earlier. "I misunderstood you before," I said to her, spooning more beans onto a son's plate. "Here I've been thinking you said the baby's name was Fernando."

"I did," she replied. "His name is Fernando."

"But . . . what . . . ." I stammered, "Hernando, didn't you just say you named him after yourself?"

"Yes, I did. His name is Hernando," Hernando reiterated and spit a hard piece of bean onto the ground. A little boy belched.

"Fernando," Rosa said again, emphatically, with a wide toothy grin and a kiss to the babe's head.

They continued to cuddle and I stopped asking. Full, I threw the remains of my second tortilla beneath the table, where the chicken fought valiantly for a moment before losing it to a dog. Finally Hernando said by way of explanation: "Rosa doesn't like the name I gave the baby, so she named it something else." Although he tried to be serious, to feign a sarcastic admonition of her insurrection, he couldn't help but smile. He moved too slowly to hide it behind his hand, and she caught sight of it, giggled, and boxed him softly upside the head.

They stood and performed the woman's work of clearing the table together. He does not care about the baby's name or his right, as a man, to make that decision. He married a woman he loves and always will. He cares only for his wife's amusement.

This is their joke on the rest of the world.

Fernando it is.

6. Rosa's Story

My life is a life that is full of good luck. When I said this to Elena, she agreed about this idea with me. My life is simple but not hard, as it could be, and has had many happy moments in it with more to come, I am sure. I have a very special husband. I have healthy children. I have an *americana* for a best friend. I have many blessings that others do not.

I will always remember as extra special the year Elena came to live with us. It was the same year my middle child, Fernando, my sixth, was born. My two birth sisters were well fed and without illness and, if you count Elena as one of us, like I did, then we were four sisters living happily together that year here in Linda Vista. After a too wet winter with much chill, Elena's arrival was a good omen. The time she spent with us was a good time, with a fine harvest and pleasant weather and much to do and talk about together. The year of Elena was a fine year.

I most enjoy the years, or the days in the years, when something different than what is ordinary happens. So you can imagine how fun and unusual it was to find a gringa walking toward my house that first day. It was clear from all of her huffing and sucking for air that she was not accustomed to walks into the mountains, nor did she look at first to have the constitution for the effort, as small and as fragile as she appears. On her first visit I invited her in and made her a glass of lemonade. I kept refilling her glass with the juice from the lemons my husband Hernando grows in the grove beside the house. I have a memory of going out for more lemons at least five times—or maybe six times—before Elena stopped drinking. I knew right from the beginning that she would be a good friend to me because she let my children climb on her lap and we smiled in a sweet way back-and-forth at each other while she drank and drank. Always she said in a kind way, when she finished one glass, that she was very sorry for the imposition but please could she have some more. When I said after the sixth glass that there were plenty of lemons but no more sugar she drank that last glass slowly. I liked her right then because I know what the lemonade without the sugar tastes like, but she did not reveal the horrible sourness. She only said in a most polite manner, "Thank you very much, my thirst is now gone and I do not need any more lemonade."

Lemonade is a simple thing to make. I do not know what I do that makes it so, but everyone says that my lemonade is the best. It is how I first won the affection of Elena and also, before her's, of my husband.

Hernando and I grew up together and spent three or four years studying every day in the same schoolhouse as children. But children do not generally notice each other and I can remember nothing remarkable about him from all those years. Then there was some time after that when I was in my home helping my mother and he was in the field assisting his father. We did not see each other hardly at all in those years. It was not until I became a young woman, and began to have eyes that noticed boys, that I really saw him again for the first time. It was in the year and at the time that my parents died of the cough.

Because I was the youngest I was still living in my parents' home and the task of tending to them fell to me. They had been sick for some time, with my sisters' husbands doing the work in the field that my father could not accomplish. I kept the house and did what I could to make my parents comfortable, but the cough is too much for one young woman to prevent. Finally, seeing that their health only continued to worsen, my eldest sister took the coins she had saved for the year and gave them to her husband to buy some beef fat with. It is said that beef fat and sugar water can cure the cough, but we had no beef to make fat with in our village, so my brother-in-law went off our mountain with his youngest brother, Hernando, to find the cure for my parents' cough.

If it had not been that the bandits got Hernando and his brother in the hills below our village, and beat them black and purple and took my sister's money, then maybe my parents would not have died. But instead the bandits got them, and they lay there in the road for a day until they could walk. Then they walked to town slowly and had to spend too much time begging until someone gave them what they needed for free. So by the time they climbed back up the mountain to our village in their painful manner, my parents had already died and we had their bodies prepared for the burial.

So it could have been a very sad occasion when Hernando and I met again for the first time. He was very bruised and in much pain, and my parents were dead and I was an orphan. But because I was already moving my belongings to my sister's house I was there when he arrived with his brother, who is my sister's husband, and I assisted in the care of these two men who arrived too late to be of use. I do so like to take care of people with what have been called my gentle hands, and I helped to wet the rags and remove the blood stains and tend their wounds. I also was instructed to make some lemonade to soothe their parched throats. Later when we were married I said to my husband that when I first put my hand on his beaten arm that day I knew he would be my husband. And he replied to me that he knew this same thing after I pressed that first delicious glass of lemonade to his lips. So even though it was a time of sadness at the loss of my parents, I had much new feeling and excitement in tending to the body of Hernando.

I said to Elena that only God knows why it is I have been so much more lucky to have found such a good husband when she is so very unlucky and is still all alone. I pray every night to God that He will shine a blessing on her as He has on me, and end this great burden of aloneness that has been laid upon her. Even at the difficult times in my life God has been good to me and answered my prayers. You see how He sent me Hernando to turn my attention from the death of my parents. It was an odd blessing the way the circumstance occurred for me, but it made it easier for us to make our decision to wed.

When my sisters met the men who would be their husbands there was a long period of getting to know each other. Also, they had to wait to see if all the parents approved. First, my parents and the parents of the boy had to meet and discuss at great length all the good qualities of their children. Then it took some time to accumulate the means to offer the gifts from the boy's family to my family. During all this time my sisters had to wait, not seeing the men who would be their husbands unless the boys came to visit our father to bring a tool or a chicken or something to demonstrate their abilities and their good nature. Only when our father agreed to the marriages could they stand in each other's company on the porch or walk in the road, and then finally they were allowed to come together.

For me and Hernando, though, it was different. We were in each other's company much during the time of his recuperation as I was the only one in the family without children and therefore had the time to attend to the men's wounds. Also, with my parents dead so suddenly and everyone's minds on other things we were often left alone and became sure of our intentions quickly. One day, after spending much time telling me about his experiments with oranges and lemons—cutting the branches from one type of tree and securing them to the trunk of another, so that the many different varieties grew from the same tree!— he also began to brag of his ability with animals and his idea to raise some goats for milk. When he began to tell me of his smart plan for building terraces with stones for structure I told him he could stop crowing about himself like a wild rooster. I said, "You do not need to convince me for I have already decided to become your wife." This made him smile, and that is all we ever needed to say of that.

It worked well for us that my sister was already married to Hernando's brother and the families therefore were already known well to each other. Also, with my parents dead it fell to my eldest sister and her husband to approve of Hernando, and of course my brother-in-law approved of his own brother so that went simply. Finally, my parents' house was empty and already prepared for us to start a family in so we did not need to wait for Hernando to build us a house. Looking back, I think it only took a week or so for everything to get approved instead of many months, and that is how it came to pass that we married even before his skin returned to its normal unbruised color.

My sister spoke a blessing over us on the porch of my parents' house, under the post where they wed themselves some years before. My mother-in-law wished us fertility and long life, and my father-in-law counseled Hernando to behave as Joseph, the carpenter, who gave his wife and child a good life through the efforts of his own hands. Then we ate the tortillas that my sisters and I cooked and when everyone left I lay with my husband in the room where I was born.

I told Elena that when she finds a husband not to fear the wedding night because the loving is a good part that no one talks about. Until then, I told her, I would share with her my husband in all ways but that one—and she laughed when I said this and said, "Thank you very much, but I am happy to leave the loving to you!"

This is how it must be when a woman has a sister without a husband and without any parents to guard her. The married sister instructs her husband to offer his protection to the unmarried one, so that she will be safe and cared for. My husband did this job well. He built a fence for Elena's horse and allowed me the extra allowance for more food so that

Elena could take her meals with us. Also, he let it be known that he was responsible for her honor and in this way we assured her safety. It made me very happy to lend her the assistance of my husband, because this is how sisters take care of each other. This is how families measure their love. Mine for Elena is deep.

* * *

I have a photograph of my whole family. It is the most special thing I own. Elena took for us this photograph one day with her small black box called a camera. It is a large-sized photograph with wood all around the edges to keep it safe and I don't know how it came from inside the small black camera box, but Elena says that in truth it did. I keep this photograph hanging always where I can see it, outside when I am outside and inside when I am inside. Even on those days when my children cry too much or roll in the dirt or pick things out from inside their noses, I can look at the picture and it reminds me how lovely they are and how much I do love them.

Not always is it easy to keep the good loving thoughts all throughout every day. I try the best that I can to keep our house and our yard in order so that everything will have a place and be neat and as clean as I can keep it. But oh, six, seven, eight little children all running everywhere at one time can make an orderly house a difficult thing to have! I know that my many children are a blessing and that it is God's rule to have the most that are possible, but sometimes I have to ask the Virgin and the Holy Spirit to remind me how to see the blessing when they have all sat down in mud. Or when they all start to sneeze and cough and make vomit at the same time. Or when there are four that want the milk—who cry loudly for the milk!—and I have only two breasts to give it from at the same time. On those days I have to try very hard to be the good mother I should be.

What I do not have to try hard to do is make the babies. There are some very unfortunate women who do not make very many babies, but Hernando and I make a baby all the time. One baby every year. One baby comes out, another goes in! I am very grateful for this blessing of many babies from God, although I notice that with the more I have the more tired it makes me. That is why, sometimes, there are days when I think I do not have the energy to be a good mother. On those days I stand in front of my photograph and I pray. I keep praying until I can look at my photograph and think, "Look at my lovely family!" Then when I can do that I know that I will be okay for that day.

Because Elena does not have any children she has more energy sometimes than I do and she is a willing helper so I let her assist me. She can chase after the children and catch them and bring them to me so that all I have to do is bathe one while she runs after the others and for that I am grateful. Sometimes though it confuses me the way Elena behaves with my babies. For one thing, she likes to take the tortilla and break it into small pieces and feed it to the children one tiny piece at a time. A meal with Elena can take a long time to finish! I think that when she has many babies of her own, all hungry, she will see it is easier to give them one large tortilla each to suck on and crawl off with. Also she tries to have her eyes all the time on every child, so sitting with her in peace while they play is not an easy thing. She will jump up and run quickly to bring it back if one steps onto the road or over a hill. Don't you agree it must be that Elena got lost often as a child, and was not returned quickly to her family? For it is as if she does not understand that any-where the children go someone will recognize them and bring them back to our house after a short while. The one other thing I notice that is very unusual is that Elena always questions me in a nervous way when the boys play with their machetes. She thinks I should take them away, but in what way then would the boys learn what their adult roles will be? I have to say that it makes me sad to realize that poor little Elena must not have had many good things to play with in her childhood, but it also makes me happy that my children have such fortunate lives.

Even though her behavior can sometimes be amusing or odd, Elena is a very kind aunt to my children. She has had good practice. Elena is the oldest of the three children in her own family and it is always the oldest daughter who is the best at taking care of children because of all the care she gives to her younger siblings. After all the siblings grow up, it then becomes the task of the youngest daughter to take care of their parents when they turn old. So that leaves only the middle daughters with the life of ease, but neither Elena nor I would know about that, being the oldest and the youngest like we are. We two understand what it is to work hard for your family.

Because she is a hard worker for family—even for my family which is not her own first family that she was born to—it is difficult to know how it is she could have left her family behind and come to us all on her own. I have asked her about this question and she has said that in *los*

Estados Unidos it is normal for the children to grow up and go far away from their families, but I do not understand how this can be so. I have considered all the problems that would come from going too far away, alone, and there are more problems than I have fingers to count all the problems on.

Hand on the right side:

Thumb: Who will keep you warm on the cold nights, without the whole family to share the bed together? Who will say the prayers for you when you get the cough or the lung rattle from all this cold aloneness?

First finger: Who will collect herbs and boil them and pour the healing juice down your throat while you lie flat in the house, unmoving, with fever? Who will remember that the spicy herb most often used for the lung rattle gives you red itchy bumps and know instead that it is better for you just to have the prayers and the heat cure?

Tallest finger: Who will know that you are cranky when you are sick, and also cranky in the morning during the first hour after waking, and be sure to talk to you only quietly in a small voice during those times?

Next to the last finger: Who will know that chamomile tea is your favorite and have it ready in the cup for you to sip while you awaken? Who will be the one to recall that the cup with the blue trim and no cracks on the rim is your favorite and save it for your use, just as a kindness?

Smallest finger: Who will be aware by the way you push aside your tea—without you ever even having to say a word—that your heart is hurting? Who will set aside their chores and sit with you without needing to talk or question you, just so that you will not be alone in your sadness?

Hand on the left side:

Thumb: Who will rejoice with you when your sadness is relieved? Who will bring you a flower from the field or a lovely found feather to hasten your joy?

First finger: Who will know the stories of your youth, the ones you most love to hear, and tell them again and again in the moments when you most need to laugh? Who will laugh as you do—with a "snort, snort" like a rutting pig—so that your laugh does not sound strange or awkward but only normal?

Tallest finger: Who will think that you are the smartest or the bravest or the best at some simple task? Who will know that you can make a clover with your tongue, and believe that this is an amazing thing?

Next to the last finger: Who will take your side in a dispute with a neighbor or a shopkeeper, and defend your name against cruel remarks in the street—even, indeed, while arguing privately over some silly concern?

Smallest finger: Who will love your children and give them the breast and raise them to remember you if you die while they are young? Who will be there to say your name fondly when you are gone, if not your family?

* * *

Fernando's was an easy birth, as the sixth birth should be, as all other things were easy in the year of Elena. It was not at all like my first baby's birth—now that is the one that was scary and hard! Hernando and I had been married almost a year and though we lived the life of two adults, keeping the house and planting the fields like a man and a woman do, my body was yet that of a girl. It had not before been stretched and bent to the task of mothering, and that made the first the most difficult birth.

My sisters said they would see me through it, and that I should come find them when either thing happened: either the water ran down between my legs, or I got the cramps like from eating a diseased piece of chicken, only without having eaten any chicken at all. I expected that only one or the other of those things would happen, because they said *either* thing, so I got my first shock when the pain started shooting from my front to my back, from my top to my bottom, at the same time that the water dripped out of me. I thought the pain had made me urinate with my clothes on and I felt so embarrassed I went to change, but the stain was not yellow and it did not smell like urine smells and it kept oozing little by little all down my legs. It took me some time to put on new clothes and find my sisters who were together in a field collecting beans. By then I was in much pain and also very angry.

125

I fell on the ground when I saw them and I yelled, "You did not tell me it would feel like this, and with the pain and dripping water *both*!"

In a too calm voice, my oldest sister replied, "There are some things that are better left unsaid."

To her I said back: "And there are some things you say that are not true at all! This is not the pain of eating a diseased chicken part! This is the pain of a diseased chicken dying over and over again inside my belly, with its bony claws and sharp beak STABBING at my insides!" (I still remember how the word STABBING got accompanied by a sharp pain, like a real chicken was in there and poked at me to make my words true, and the word STABBING got shouted so loud it rang out many times in the mountain's echo.)

For that they made me walk home without any help while they carried their beans. (Beans! What is so important about beans?!) And my oldest sister said as we walked along: "Shh, you must be quiet so you do not scare the young girls! There is nothing wrong with you! Walk normal! This is all normal!"

"Not normal for me!" I shouted, too loud, to make sure they knew how very angry I was with them for what was happening and for them not being more concerned for me than for their beans.

Finally, after a full day of this, back in the house on my bed, they got more concerned. Of course, I am here telling this to you now, so you know I am healthy and also I have forgotten the most terrible part of the pain. For that reason it will probably not sound as scary to you as it was to me then. But in the dark night of the second day, with the candle throwing its shadows around the room and the blood on everything, I was very much frightened. And so were my sisters. Their looks changed by the second night, when they did not turn their eyes to my eyes, which said to me, when I could still focus my attention on such things, that they were more frightened than I. Oh, how I wanted my mother! In the beginning I cried out for her again and again. My one sister sat behind me with her arms wrapped all around me for comfort, while the other waited between my legs, but sisters are not mothers—it is different. My mother was dead and could not help me anymore. But as the second night grew darker and the shadows got bigger and the blood kept leaving me, I know for sure that my mother came to me. It is as if the pain got lifted and my mother's cool hands stroked my face and brought me rest. My sisters say it is at that time, after too much pushing and with glassy half-dead eyes closing, that I began to whisper over and over, "Let me die" (for it must be that I wanted so much to go away with my mother).

The rest is just a good story now, for I am well and no one died. Also, there are many years now that have passed since that night. Many moons have set and risen again since I moaned, "Let me die," and my eldest sister—who could see from her position between my legs that the baby had decided never to come—took up the knife. When she walked into the room carrying it they say I sat right up and yelled angrily with new energy, "Don't kill me yet!" That is how they knew I would not die, they say now with voices full of laughter. I say now, when teasing, that they should have taken their chance when they had it! But of course all my sister did was to cut open a bigger hole in me, big enough to reach her arm up in and pull the baby out, so that we both could live.

But the sixth birth was not at all like the first, thank you to God and sign of the cross. It was not as bloody. (No need to cut open the mattress afterward and wash the cotton and restuff it with new hay.) Nor was it as painful. (All I needed the knife for this time was to chop off the baby's cord, and because the knife was already right there on the kitchen table next to me where I'd been cutting the avocado I only needed to wipe off the green flesh on my shirt before making the slice.) And it was fast!

I was in the kitchen preparing the lunch, waiting for Hernando to come in from the field and Elena to return from the school with my eldest son. With each child the pains had come faster, but never before and never again did they come in such a hurry. There I was just chopping the avocado for the guacamole like any other day when the water swept out, and when I reached down to check myself I touched the beginnings of a head! I was suddenly afraid that if I went out for help he would get born on the road, in front of my children and the neighbors, so I stayed there in the kitchen by myself. With one hand I pressed to keep his head in, and with the other I moved the avocado onto the ground and climbed up on the table while the labor came. With my skirt still on I gave only maybe ten or twenty hard pushes, without crying out at all, so my babies playing in the yard would not hear and come in and be frightened. It was hard and fast pain and in trying to be quiet I bit my tongue so my mouth bled, but not my female parts too much. When I knew he was ready to come out I leaned up on one elbow and with my other hand I tried to catch him so he would not slip off the table and smack his head on the ground, and I was very fortunate—he stayed on the table with me. It is also fortunate he came as fast as he did, for I had time to put the baby's sac in a bowl outside, finish mixing the guacamole, wipe the waters off the table, and set out the plates before my family arrived for lunch. It is my luck that I was smiling and washing a new baby when they all came in to eat, for only a short time before I was bleeding from my mouth and bursting from my bottom on the table where they gathered to take their meal.

It had been decided before by Hernando and me, if she would accept, that Elena should be the godmother of our sixth baby. My other two sisters were already godmothers two times each, and one three times!, but this baby would have his own special new godmother Elena. I assured her he would be a good baby to be the godmother of—a healthy baby—for I had done all the things right, like always. I carried keys in my pocket every day and did not eat any citrus or mango throughout the whole many months, even when I wanted lemonade badly, so he did not slobber excessively or come out with a twisted mouth. We burned the sac right away, and buried it the day he was born right after lunch, so he would grow up to have a normal and not crazy mind. And when the baby's cord fell off we wrapped it around the handle of an ax and put it in a tree, to give him strength. Because I could promise Elena a good godchild, she said, "Yes, thank you for asking me." (But she did not say this before inquiring about the responsibilities because, she said, "Rosa, you know I will not be here forever.") I think about her saying that, sometimes now, and I know she was trying to get me ready. But it was too happy a time to think of something so sad, so I ignored that last part she said and filled up my mind just with the joy of the thing she did for us.

Elena made us a fiesta. I told her there is nothing to do to be the godmother except say yes, but she said that in the United States there is always a fiesta for the baby when the godparents are picked and soon after she left on foot and said, "I will be gone two days—be ready for fun when I get back!" Two days we waited and waited, all the time wondering, What will happen when Elena returns? Something special maybe, something rare and unusual!

My sisters, too, became excited, and their husbands also. We watched from our porches and sent our children in turns to wait at the curve at the steep end of the road on the edge of Linda Vista, and when they returned to change the shift we would rush out and ask, "Have you seen her yet?"

All the other families noticed our excitement so that soon the whole village was anticipating her return. But always the children said no, she had not yet been sighted on the road, every time we asked, until the end of the second day. The sun was already going down that night when my sister's second boy ran screaming up the road: "She's coming! Elena's coming! With a *truck*!"

You may not believe this, but not only did she return in a truck, but in the truck belonging to our very own mayor of the *municipio*! Elena made the introductions for the very first time ever between our politician the mayor and us his people. We had by then gathered around the truck with many of the men and boys jumping into the back of it when it stopped in the schoolyard. This is not all that she brought us, not just the mayor, but also what she called *un cine*. It showed pictures of people, moving pictures!, of people with strange eyes and very straight hair doing crazy fighting called kung fu with their hands and their legs. It is very hard to explain how the *cine* worked, but I will try to explain it so you can understand. How it worked is that in the back of the truck Elena had brought a machine that made a very loud brrzzz and it made the other machine with two big wheels that she put on the roof of the truck move the *cine* onto the wall of the schoolhouse. We were at first so surprised at the noise and the light and the movement but then we sat on the ground and laughed as a whole village together at the crazy moving people doing flips and cracking wood on their heads and jumping up high in the air. While we watched the *cine* making light on the wall in the dark night, Elena opened a big box and gave to us, every one!, what she called little ices. "Suck on it!" she said—and at first I was nervous and the others were too because it made a stinging cold feeling on my tongue and gave my teeth a shock. But Elena did it first so I did it also. Soon it made cool sweet water in my mouth that was the best thing I have ever tasted!

We sat up so late that night that we saw stars, and Elena and I talked on the porch until two whole candles burned away and no one else remained awake.

"Where did the *cine* come from?" I asked her after the mayor had driven the machines away and all the people had gone to bed.

She said, "I got it from the Chinese embassy in the capital."

"What is a Chinese embassy?" I asked her.

She said: "Every country has embassies—they're large buildings that one country owns in another country—where they give help to travelers.

Like if you came to visit me in the United States, and you lost your papers, you could go to the Guatemalan embassy and they would give you new ones."

"So the building where you can go to get help is the Chinese embassy?" I asked.

She said: "Oh, no, here in Guatemala there is a U.S. embassy for helping Americans—for an example, I went there once to find a doctor for Calixta. And oh, you will think this is interesting—they had the biggest dogs there that you have ever seen! Two big guard dogs, called Rottweilers, the same color as Calixta but much larger, guard the gate and are ready to attack anyone who tries to enter with bad intentions!"

"So what is a Chinese embassy for?" I asked her.

She said, "The Chinese embassy is for helping people who come from China—although they are kind enough to also help out other people of the world by lending *cines* about kung fu fighting."

"Where is this country of China?" I asked her.

She said, "It is far away, on the other side of the world, in a place called the Orient."

"This is called *el oriente* right here," I said.

She said: "Oh, no, this is only Guatemala's *oriente*—the east side of Guatemala. China is on the world's east side."

I learned many things of much interest to me that night of my baby's fiesta, by staying up late and talking to Elena. She knows so many things of importance that I will try hard to remember in case anyone ever asks me about these things again: The *cine* comes from a loud brrzzzing box; China is where they distribute kung fu; the mayor drives a blue truck and has a mustache; the Guatemalan embassy is where they collect and redistribute lost papers; little ices are better-tasting things even than lemonade; and the U.S. embassy is a good place to observe large dogs. But most of all I will remember that this was the greatest night that has ever happened here in Linda Vista, the night we talked and laughed until almost morning. It was that kind of a night where you think that all of the rest of your life will never be anything but more happiness without the pleasure ever coming to an end.

* * *

Elena has gone. She left when school ended, before *navidad* and the Day of the Magi, because she said the teacher would be back when the

130

school started again so she would not be needed anymore. I said, "To me, you are needed." But my need was not enough need to make Elena want to stay. I think this is the very worst thing that has happened to me for a long time that I can remember.

I let her be in my family! There is me and my husband and my children and my sisters and my Elena and her Calixta—our family! A good person does not leave her family! I know that she left her own first family, but I kept thinking it must have been because of them letting her get lost often as a child and because she did not have many good things to play with—but that we would give her our love and take care of her and share with her our food and never lose her and that would make everything be different. I trusted in her that because of all this we did, she would never want to go away from us ever.

But then she left and I thought: "I should not have trusted! I should not have given love! If I did not trust and if I did not love, it would not matter that she went away."

But even though I did not want it to matter, because if it didn't matter it wouldn't hurt so badly, it did for true matter so much that I could not think of anything else. How could Elena whom I loved hurt me so badly? How could she not know what it would be like for me to have no more special friend of my own, no more *americana* all for myself? I wonder, "Does she ever think of me all the time like I think of her, and does it make her sad to know that no one anymore is left here to tell me stories of exciting faraway places while I cook, and no one plays with my children while I do the wash?" Or does she only miss me sometimes, and even then not very much, like a fast thought when she is thirsty and the lemonade is not mine?—or maybe she does not even care like it seemed she did!, maybe she will drink whatever she is given and already forgets the taste of mine!

Everything has been craziness because of Elena going. The girls hang on my skirt all through the day and when my oldest son fell and cut his knee I went to pick him up but he said: "No! I want Elena!"

I said to him, "Elena is not here, so get up off the ground and stop crying!"

But he just sat on the ground not moving and cried louder so I smacked the angry look on his face and then not only did that not stop his crying but the girls started crying too and pulled harder on my clothes.

"Everyone stop crying and go play!" I yelled.

But they kept crying and said, "There is no one to play with!"

So I yelled, "Then play with yourselves!" and I shook them all off my skirt and turned to run inside to get away from all the noise, and what did I do? I stepped on the tail of the dog who was hiding behind the screaming children and he started to howl and it made everyone cry more!

All I wanted then was one glass of lemonade, one glass of lemonade with a great deal of sugar to keep away the headache that was coming. So I sat down alone in the kitchen with a glass and a lemon and the knife, trying to be calm despite the crying and the howling in the yard, and I cut the lemon in half and inside—worms! I took that sour lemon and with one big holler threw it right out the door, right out there toward those nonstop crying children, and SMACK it had the bad fortune to hit Hernando right in the face when he turned to come through the doorway for lunch.

"What is happening here?" he asked (in a rather calm voice for someone who got hit with a worm-full lemon).

"Nothing is happening!" I said, crossing my arms.

Hernando stared back at me for a minute and said, "*What* is wrong?"

I said: "Nothing is wrong! The only thing that would be wrong is if I had thrown the knife instead of the lemon at you!" (I got a bit of satisfaction from imagining the knife sticking out of his head.) Then I banged my face down flat on the table—the banging aided the headache some—and said: "Okay?! So nothing is wrong! Nothing is the matter! So why don't you leave me alone?"

I put my arms over my head to make it quiet, then, thank you to God, Hernando left and shushed the children.

But did he leave me alone? No! He came back and said, "This has gone on long enough; I can't believe you're still angry with Elena for leaving."

Ugh! (I couldn't believe he said that!) Ugh!, he made me gasp right out loud, that was such a stupid thought, and I said: "I'm not mad at Elena! What makes you think I'm mad?! Why should I care what Elena wants to do, or where she goes? If she doesn't like it here enough to stay then why should I care?"

With my face down on the table I could say all those things and act like they were true, but when I looked up to yell at him directly and he only looked back at me in a loving way, not a fighting way, I couldn't yell anymore and started to cry instead, and when I could finally talk again through the gasping I said to him, "Hernando, how could she have left us?"

And he said back to me something that started to change everything. He said, "Rosa, she was never ours to keep."

We talked then for a long time, without eating, remembering all the family we have lost. I cried again for my parents and I cried for the first time for my sister's baby, the one who died that autumn, the angel that we were all pretending not to miss. Sometime during our talking Hernando went and got from our bedroom the only photograph we have of Elena. When she took the photograph of our family that time long ago she called over our neighbor and gave to him the black camera box and showed him where to push a button, then stood with us so we could have a photo of all of us together. It is the only picture we have of her but it is a strange picture. She is standing there with us, but she is too tall, and it is only her body, without its head, that shows up in the photograph. All we have of her is her dress and her shoulders and a little stub of neck and that is all. It is as if she is there and not there at the same time, as if even then she was already starting—as she always said she would—to go away. Looking at the picture together, I said to Hernando, "Do not be mad at me for this, but sometimes I wish I could have gone with her, just for a little while."

He said: "But that would not have worked. You would not have been happy. You and Elena are too different. What is good about Elena is the excitement she brings, the new ideas, the things she will try without regard for what is traditional. What is good about you is the pleasure you bring to what is normal—the way you rock the children and make them laugh, the way you give me something to look forward to every morning. Your gifts are good ones to keep at home, and Elena's are good ones to take away and share."

I said, "She was always going to have to leave, no matter what I did, wasn't she?"

He said back to me, "It is as natural for her to leave as it is for birds to fly, so why be angry with either for soaring away?"

My husband, Hernando, is a good man. I am the luckiest woman I know.

So finally, I only missed Elena greatly. She has become part of the history and remembrances of my family. Whenever anyone asks now about the stain on the lemon tree by the kitchen door, we smile and tell them the story of the day Elena tripped into the trunk and scared us all, with the thorn deep in her scalp and the blood running all down her face, calming everyone else while we screamed even though she was the one who was hurt! It has become our tradition to soothe pains by saying, "Be brave like Elena!" and soon the tears stop.

The sound of her name makes glad not only us, but the horse too, for when Eben walks too slowly while working—more slowly than normal—Hernando clucks at him and says, "Let's go Eben, let's go see if we can find Elena!" and he insists it excites the animal and quickens his step. When I am alone I take pleasure in humming the tune she would whistle when she worked, and when the new milk goat had kids their names came to the children easily. The red one is Elena; the black one, Calixta.

So in some ways, though I believe we will never see her again, she is not all the way gone. She just waits for us to remember her so she can return and visit us in our thoughts for a while. It took me some time, but finally I realized there can be love even without togetherness, and that is how I have gotten settled with Elena's departure. For it is true, what Hernando said to me. She could never have stayed forever, just as I could never go.

7. Elena's Story, Winter 1992-1993

*D*uring the days and nights of change and heat a year slipped past me. A year ago I arrived here.

My parents escorted me to the airport, where we huddled together in an awkward collective, trying not to cry and not knowing what to say in expectation of many years' estrangement. Then my mother blurted out (in the way she is apt to do) a statement which, separated from all the reasoning preceding it, sounds nonsensical to anyone but me. I have learned over the years to interpret her backward and upside-down sentiments. I know without needing further clarification that when she says she has been to see the films *I Want to Tell You Something* and *The Three Faces of Eve*, she actually saw and appreciated the Julia Roberts movie *Something To Talk About* and the Barbra Streisand flick *The Mirror Has Two Faces*. So when she turned to me in the airport, leaned across the hard plastic chairs that hook together as if the seating itself could keep us from leaving each other, and said—

"Do you want to be notified if I die while you're gone?"

—I knew she had been thinking, "With all the elderly relatives in the family, someone is bound to die while you're away, and it is silly really to come home for a funeral; funerals are for the people who are living, not the people who die. I don't want you to think you need to come home to support us if someone dies, because I would rather that you had your adventure and did not feel pulled away from your new life, which I think will be an amazing thing, in order to fulfill some responsibility toward us. In fact, I would not want you to have to give up even one moment's experience for me, and I would die happy to think that even my own funeral would not rob you of the joys you are sure to encounter," but it came out as:

"Do you want to be notified if I die while you're gone?"

135

(Six months later I got a telegram from the embassy, which took many days to reach me, and said: "Mother gravely ill. Contact home." I thought, "Here it is—she has died!, and in an effort not to alarm me her dying wish was to send me a telegram informing me not of her death, but of her illness, so my father can break the news to me in person." Two days' travel to a phone, three days' dialing before someone answered on the other end. In those five days, in my mind, I missed the funeral and everything else, so that our airport conversation became an absurd reality. But then I got through, and they had been on an excursion, nothing more, and my mother heard of my distress and said, "Oh, that's so horrible what you've been through, I'm so sorry, and don't worry about me, it's only breast cancer." Somehow she managed to convince me, and still these years later I do not know how, that breast cancer posed her no risk and therefore not to fret, so I didn't and neither did I return home.)

As we tentatively agreed, in the crowded airport lounge, that they would send word of family deaths to me, and not hold it against me if I chose not to return, I noticed Zac. He sat alone, having connected from New York, thumbing to a fray the corner of the Peace Corps folder with the list of the clothes and other essentials to bring; I noticed his nerves before I noticed the blue folder with the flag and the stars on front and knew we were two of a kind. We called him over and he came eagerly. I cannot remember what got said, and it doesn't matter, for in just being there he became the most important person in my world. He made it okay to leave my family, because he adopted their role; he walked into the future beside me, and sat with me as I flew away.

Here it is that my memory dulls. Or perhaps in truth the memory never existed, but constructed itself only around fleeting observations. I have only snippets of recollection and they all center around sensation. The press of the glass on my forehead as we brisked away, for I pinned my eyes to the land of my home for as long as it remained visible. The THWAMP of the luggage hurled to the ground when we disembarked—mountains of suitcases, bags and boxes. Dragging my duffels, too heavy to carry, across the tile floor thinking, "Thank God for my father and for his duct tape holding us together." Guns everywhere, on everyone. Brown children surrounding me, swarming, begging for money, pulling my hair, touching my skin. A rose pressed into my hand, with a thorn still attached, so I bled my first blood on Guatemala as soon as my feet landed on her floor. Darkness. The night smelled differently.

136

I can only recapture that sense of place when it rains in the Oregon autumn, and someone lights a fire at dusk after a warm day that the night has cooled. I go outside then, breathe, close my eyes, and there I am again!, for the smoke, humidity, and smell of green things growing sends me back, and I can be for a moment—until reality sets in—alone in a crowd of people outside the Guatemalan airport. Eager, horrified, and excited, but mostly awed waiting for a midnight bus to carry me deep into Central America.

The Peace Corps scooped us all up, seventy or more Volunteers who landed together, and the anticipation alone likely drove the bus, but all is fog for me save the smell and the darkness and the churning of my stomach. In the morning we dispersed to local homes and families who sheltered us for three months of training, and here again I begin to remember.

Of the three-month training I will say little; what a bore it was to me, how I longed to be free! But thank God for it. Not the classes, but the camaraderie. Adrift alone in an unknown sea is never a good place to be, and these other Volunteers are the people who fashioned for me a raft and a life vest and with their coaxing voices called me into port when I drifted too far and almost got lost. One day, two months into it, the Peace Corps assembled a group of Guatemalan dignitaries to introduce to their trainees, and we each stood respectfully and in fledgling Spanish told our names, our hobbies, and our backgrounds. One elderly woman, hoping to impart her love of weaving, confused the word weaver, *tejedor*, with the similar *tenedor*, so that when she rose and addressed these illustrious guests she did not say, "I am a weaver," but instead proudly announced, "I am a fork."

I made myself tiny, hid in my chair, turned slightly to Zac, who sat beside me with his masterful Spanish, and raised one Scarlet O'Hara brow to ask, "Did she really? . . ."

He spied me from the side, avoided looking, restrained a belly laugh that disclosed, "Yes, she really did."

This became the battle cry, the secret code, the siren call. When training ended, and the Peace Corps gave us a bankbook, the name of a town, and let us go to it on our own, these other Volunteers lingered out there, just a bus ride away. All it took to summon one was a telegram saying, "I am a fork," and the recipient knew you had been too long alone, dropped everything, and came to be with you. Someone once stopped unexpectedly while traveling at the home of a fellow Volunteer, and found him stark naked, listening to loud music and in time with each bass note beating himself on the head with a lacrosse stick he oddly had brought from home, while pinning hundreds of cockroaches to the wall with little pushpins. He should have called out, many months prior, "I am a fork," and help could have come more quickly, but fortunately it did not arrive too late, and he is a successful lawyer now with an Ivy League degree.

Of training nothing more needs to be said, for here is the most essential point, which I cannot emphasize enough: Of the Volunteers I befriended right there at the beginning, these have stuck with me and will always be my heart's closest friends. Which is not to say that now, scattered throughout the world as we are, I see them or even stay in close touch. But if I were to walk down a strange street and encounter them, even from behind and at great distance I would recognize them, and with unbounded joy I would rush to them and without skipping a beat we would take up the conversation that interrupted in midstream when last we separated. Though many years stand between us, I would know of what they spoke and they I, for this is what it is to truly love and these are my forever friends.

I may never see Zac again, but to me he will always remain one of the dearest people the world ever guided to my side.

Nothing more does a traveler need than this, and in those years I tried to open my home to all, even the unknowns, who came from afar and were not as lucky as I to have arrived with a built-in group of comrades. An Australian man and an Israeli woman once knocked on my door. "G'day," he said, "we're looking for Ellen," and I knew immediately to let them in because only fellow Volunteers called me Ellen, to everyone else I am Elena, and so a true and trusted friend had sent them.

They carried directions to my house mapped on the edge of a napkin with an X-marks-the-spot over a smear of road food. These two stay glued in my mind, the Israeli and the Australian, of all the dozens and dozens who overheard my name on a bus, or shared a drink with an expatriate, or in some other way managed to bump into an American who said, "If you get tired, or run out of money, and need a place to stay for awhile, stop and visit my friend Ellen. She's a good cook and she's got plenty of room. Here, give me your napkin, I'll draw you a map. . . ."

I remember the Israeli because, years into my stay, dressed as I was in filthy patched clothes, she astounded me with the laundry lines of black silk lingerie she hung to dry in my yard. I thought, "This is why she's traveling with the Australian," or more appropriately, "this is why he's traveling with her." They met on a bus and, I think, stuck together only for the few randy nights at my house.

The Australian I remember because he said he'd been traveling for eight years, and I impetuously asked if I could look in his bag, for he carried only one small duffel which left me awed and full of respect. He kept two full changes of clothes, an extra pair of shoes, a journal with pen, three books (which I traded him for three of my own that he hadn't yet read, a barter he practiced at every stop), and a frying pan. "'Tis impossible to find a good frying pan in countries like this," he insisted, and I knew what he meant. In that moment he reminded me of my last night in America when I left my mother's frying pan abandoned on the bedroom floor, and I liked him immensely for it. We sat up all night sharing stories until I got tired and he went to lie down with the Israeli woman.

This became the tenor of my home when I moved from Linda Vista to Zataquepeque. It rang out with strange voices, a symphony of dialects, and crescendoed into the dark hours with the voices of people forging a temporary solace in an outsider's home. My house bubbled over with visitors, strangers and friends alike, so that I spent little time alone again.

Inasmuch as I provided a temporary safe house for the wandering sons and daughters of foreign lands, I kept close tally of those native homes to which I could also return in time of need. So it is that I found myself back in the house where I lived for the three months of training, back in Juanita's house, precisely one year after she first welcomed me the day I arrived in Guatemala. I traveled to her home again now, because when school let out at autumn's end for the winter holiday, Linda Vista no longer needed me. The recovered teacher would return with the new year. My bags packed, I therefore headed west, and stopped to visit and spend the night with Juanita and her family near the capital, where Cali and I were rewelcomed and entertained as long lost relatives are again embraced after too much time apart. "We will celebrate your return!" Juanita said when I straggled through the door, the prodigal stepdaughter passing back through town, and to do so she cut open the one-pound bag of M&Ms I gifted her a year ago and which she saved for months on end, for the most precious of occasions.

In retrospect, perhaps it is a blessing I stopped there so that she could save my life in the morning. But it can also be said that the detour itself drove me straight to the edge of my grave and forced me to peer straight down to the bottom, a scenic route I would have enjoyed missing. For I know with the conviction of the nearly dead and the clairvoyance of the resurrected that it was the M&Ms that poisoned me. You are thinking, I know, that the Mars Corporation will not appreciate this libel, and I am crazy to blame a candy for the disaster that followed. But I am guessing you have never been full up with worms, infested with amoebas, eaten by giardia, felled by cholera and poisoned—and here I mean *actually* poisoned—by your own food. Neither had I to that point, or I should say, neither had I yet become aware of my affliction, for had I known then as I now know and will never forget, sugar (chocolate in particular) stirs and aggrieves these intestinal fiends. They had been eating me for months, chewing my food before my stomach set to work, picking at muscle when food ran out, hungrily eyeing my liver. I had become skinny through more than exercise alone. Tonight the invaders would feast. A pound of M&Ms excited my interloping enemy and cost me dearly.

* * *

With the internal compass that guides us toward home and safe places locked on her unforgettable coordinates, I scurried along the unmarked road to Juanita's house. Cali bounded ahead of me, barking like a homing beacon, and tracked the irrigation ditch to her front door. The ditch, dug long ago, strove to encourage better drainage, but in a year the project progressed not at all so that I still had to squeeze myself between the malarial pools and the walls of the houses, turning sideways and skipping a bit in a forward shimmy. Instead of promoting progress, the unfinished ditch hindered all traffic, and stranded Juanita and her neighbors at the edge of an impassable pass.

I expected her not to be there.

Juanita is the only Guatemalan woman I know intimately who works outside of her home. Her grown daughter works alongside her, and together they slip out early in the morning in skirts and high heels to catch their bus. At night they sleep together in one room and lease the other to two male boarders, which worried me when I first moved in, but then the boys turned out to be kind and trustworthy. Of the husband I know nothing, except that he didn't exist. Juanita shared no personal secrets, but she made good marmalade and introduced me to chamomile tea; she brewed it for me every morning for three months and I have never again sipped a cup without envisioning her watching me silently from across the table. She sat solid in her chair, with a flat, blank, but not unkind face. In another life she would have made a good therapist, for her features gave away no clues as to her thoughts.

I found the spare key, in the same place it hid last year, so that I felt in all this time not one thing had changed. As if, perhaps, they expected me, and with much hope and anticipation continued to put out the key in case one day I decided to return home and could, in that jubilant moment, find my way back inside.

Inside is peculiar. Juanita owns a large home, with fewer possessions than even the most destitute. Aside from the requisite beds, in the five-room home there exist only three items of furnished décor: a battered dining table with mismatched chairs, an old oven, and an incongruously new and rather fancy dresser in my bedroom. No photos, no mementos, no gadgets. Where she stores her plates I can't imagine. But oddest of all is the treatment Juanita forced upon her walls. She painted her home as if in a compensatory manner so that the interior space might counterbalance the scale of destiny when one day her life weighs heavily upon it. In stark contrast to the monotonous routine of her days (rise, leave, return, sleep, rise, leave, return, sleep), the empty rooms resound with a cacophony of color and shout the submerged glory and joy within her upon the adobe walls. In a land of baby-angels, of earthquake-crumbled churches, of pit vipers beneath beds and sewage pools outside the door, so much enthusiasm in one place overwhelmed and unhinged my equilibrium so that I stood and swayed beneath this assault of good intentions. The garish and frightening palatial combination of Pepto Bismol pink, maternity ward green, and bile yellow converged in cataclysmic conjunction, a medical experiment gone wildly wrong, exploding its smeared residue across the entire expanse of the living room. Even a year of dust-filled winds and smoky fires did not dim the boisterous hues. Looking at the walls, for nothing else exists on which to gaze, I could see straight through to Juanita's soul; I knew too much.

"Ay, you are back!" Juanita shouted, surprising me with her early entrance before my eyes had finished their blinking adjustment to the strange space. Her full figure squeezed into a purple dress lent the room a circus flair. "We will celebrate your return!" she said, and out of nowhere the M&Ms materialized.

I am an unabashed sugar fiend in a land with no good candy. Guatemala's *dulces* pack no punch; the cane sugar, too pure from the field, does not incite that bloody rush and giddy buzz of processed and refined sweets. The chocolate—what a waste to even discuss it!—comes in crystallized clumps, and writing this, even now, I notice my tongue is involuntarily sticking from my mouth, where I am scraping off the lingering taste with the edge of my teeth, hoping to spit the memory out forever. Through her most concerted, focused efforts, Guatemala can offer up nothing so delightful as the M&M.

Of all the vices available to me as a young person—drugs, drink, tobacco—I chose the path of least distress and cultivated a sugar addiction. My grandparents fostered this natural inclination early so that as a wee little thing, a diminutive queen in a kingdom of doting affection, they catered to my affinities and served to me a soup tureen of vanilla fudge ice cream every morning upon waking whenever I spent the night. I ate half of a half gallon with a big-person spoon. When they died, their sons, my uncles, full of compassion and compelled by grief, continued the habit, and when I visited their homes I ran first to the freezer where sat this cool confection. I grew up believing ice cream for breakfast to be a venerated family tradition, and honor it still on special occasions. Nothing in the world tastes so good except, perhaps, the M&M.

My father is worse than I, his pockets a virtual candy smorgasbord, full up with good stuff. He dispensed M&Ms like allowance, which accounts for my valuation of chocolate above money. After his first mid-forties heart attack, when the doctor insisted he lose some weight and fortify his diet, when Mom started violating our orange juice with wheat germ, the M&Ms disappeared from view. But as I performed my weekly chores, and emptied the lint catcher after laundering Dad's pants, I sometimes pieced together the washed, dried, mummified paper remnants into the bottom leg of an M or the gentle curve of an ampersand and knew that even in failing health a person cannot live without sweets.

When Juanita placed the bowl of candy before me I ate every blessed M&M, a parched and empty camel slurping at festered water. Ignorantly gratified, I slept half a night.

I woke in time to hobble, doubled over, clutching my gut, to the latrine. My bowels exploded as gravity reached up, wrenching out my inside parts. My whole body shook in spasms. The diarrhea would not stop; it oozed a lava trail, and then my belly erupted in a watery chocolate gush that spouted from my mouth. I bent in half trying to aim all my waste down the same pit and instead washed my legs in vomit. Nothing ceased and it all hurt—shit from one end and puke from the other. My eyes watered, my nose ran, and save for my ears all the orifices of my body purged a watery goo. Had a fire sprung up around me I could not have moved to save my burning skin, so firmly did this agony clutch at me. I knew that if I ever gave birth someday the baby would surely slip from my body in a more graceful and forgiving manner.

At least two hours seeped away, and the cock began to crow at daybreak. A clear liquid continued to leak from me everywhere; my fluids brewed and percolated out with no remorse. This is what it is to die of dehydration. I began to separate from myself then, to leave my body which ached so badly and had betrayed me. In my mind I wandered away. But before I disappeared entirely, before the final curtain dropped on this perilous night, I collapsed to the ground and began to crawl, soiling myself all the way. Nonetheless, I moved toward salvation, toward water. Unable to stand, unable to drink, I dunked my arm into a puddle beneath the *pila* and sucked the sludge from my shirtsleeve.

This, then, is how Juanita discovered me in the morning: sweating out the rest of my life in a ceaseless, unconscious trickle, curled in a fetal position in the yard, the edge of my shirt wedged in my mouth. My lips still sucked autonomically, my instinct to survive off the water in the cloth alive and well.

* * *

I entered a long, dark tunnel with a holy light at the end, to voices calling me, "Come, come to us," a classic near-death experience birthed in the muddle of my myopic mind. For a moment I thought I'd reached heaven, but I resuscitated for real in cramped quarters beneath the burning glare of a lone lamp, where the nurses hollered into the hall, "Come, come to us, we need more help!"

The doctor's head, disembodied in the sea of white coats, white walls, white lights, cursed as he dropped my arm and the IV tube snaked away. "¡Ay, chinga'o! ¡No se puede!" [Fuck me!] I can't get it!" Just then the blood from my hand sprayed a long tall beautiful captivating arc and with its fountainous red rush rendered all that white a speckled print.

I disappeared again.

The rocking roll of the gurney with the sticky wheel woke me next, jolting over every broken floor tile in our rush to the next stage. "*No se preocupe*," whispered the pretty nurse at the head of the moving table, bending to console me as we hurried along. "Do not worry, Evelyn, you will be fine soon, go back to sleep." I almost did, too, allowing her soft hand to caress me into a drowsy dope, but some small cognizant notion suddenly gripped me and yanked me back through the misty fog.

I opened my eyes and said clearly, "I am not Evelyn."

"Shush," she said, "this will all be over soon."

I came back. Lucid. Full of fearful fury.

So it must be for drunks, teeming with liquor and out of their minds, who suddenly face a situation so dire that sobriety overtakes them and the effects of the drink disappear without warning. I have never been so conscious. I swung my legs over the side of the gurney, intending to stand and stop the extradition, but my bones were jelly and like a rag doll dropped from a window ledge I plunged straight to the floor, the tubes all pulled and stretched taut, but my mind stayed stone solid. "I am not Evelyn," I screamed, "I am Ellen! Not Evelyn! Not Evelyn! Not Evelyn! I'm Ellen!"

Everything and everyone stopped, my voice echoing endlessly throughout the acoustical hallways so that even when I shut up I continued to shout. "Check the chart," I begged over the sound of my own dimming cries. "You will see I am not who you think I am."

The pretty nurse, ugly now with irritation, grabbed the chart and shoved it in my face, pressed her finger to the name with a proctor's point, and said laconically, "Evelyn Umberto."

"Those are my initials," I said, "but that is not my name. I am Ellen Urbani, an American."

In that moment they noticed me for the first time, these harried hospital people, and in the slack drop of their cheeks and jaws they finally saw their obvious mistake. "Give me the chart," said a man in our group, opening it and muttering under his breath, "Jesus Cristo! Who is she?" Ignoring me, they slung around the accusations: "It is not my fault . . . You said to . . . He gave me . . . I didn't notice . . ." which ended with, "Where is Evelyn Umberto?" and they all looked around as if she hid somewhere close and in doing so saw me again sputtering beneath them. Wordlessly, they lifted me back up and returned me to the ER from where I originated.

I have always wondered to what fate they would have delivered me, had I not awakened and jumped overboard.

I struggled to stay awake thereafter.

There are only two hospitals in Guatemala where the U.S. government allows its Volunteers to be treated, and in proof of God's existence, I always fell ill within busing or driving distance of one or the other on the four occasions I merited hospitalization. Each time I moved I had to draw a map and turn it in, plotting the most effective landing zone for a helicopter in case a medical or other type of disaster forced the Marines to evacuate me. I still shudder to think of having to wait all that time for a rescue team to whisk me to safety, for you can see that under the conditions of rapid dehydration I might not have lasted long enough to benefit from the asylum. When struck, I deteriorated rapidly. Recognizing this, in all future circumstances I set forth for help at the immediate inception of the earliest warning sign. Since my awareness usually dimmed quickly, I once pinned to my chest a note written in thick red marker, "Sick—must get to Herrera Llerrandi Hospital," before boarding a bus, enabling the angelic passengers to slap me into consciousness and drop me out the door at the correct stop. From there I straggled the two blocks to the hospital of my own accord before collapsing in the lobby. On another instance, I hitchhiked atop a corn harvest, and rode the whole way staring into the sky with the husks at my back while a grizzled old man sang spiritual hymns and spoke in a hushed voice of the power of God, so that my illnesses all seem colored by religious experience.

Only foreign travelers and Guatemala's 1 percent rich frequent the private hospitals to which I rushed. These cost money, far more than the other 99 percent of the citizenry might come by in a lifetime. So, as I mentioned before, the poor only enter public healthcare facilities under significant duress and at their wits' virtual end, preferring generally to die of the simple illnesses at home without subjecting themselves to the horrors of hospitalization. I empathize with this, having seen firsthand the ghoulish conditions. When Doctors Without Borders passed through, I took a little boy so they could repair his harelip. His parents had begged and pleaded with me for some time to fix his mouth, so I leapt at the chance for the free surgery, and they did too, until they learned it would take place in a hospital and that almost erased all hope of cure.

"Ay, *Dios mio*," the parents said, "my God, there must be another way," but I assured them there wasn't. Surgeries cannot take place on

145

the kitchen table. In the end, they allowed me to take their son to the hospital, but only after extracting from me a promise never to leave his side and to be with him at every moment with my hand upon his body, for they assumed, I think, that I had just enough of a touch of the mystical, with my bewitching red hair, to see us both through the nightmare. What good reason they had to fear! Because only the most dire and those without hope wind up in these purgatorial deathtraps, every person is a worst case of burned off faces or leprous slough. The ones who get carried through the door all trail blood and lack a limb or have something jutting from them that doesn't belong there. Patients loll on the entrance ground begging for help and attention; the effluvium of their wet rot coats every Lysoled surface. Days later, eating dinner, picking flowers, you still smell the faint whiff of ether.

The crazies are locked up with the sickies, too, so that walking behind the physician, heading to the harelip surgery, I saw a bony hand grab at his coattails from behind a chained door and heard a voice implore, "Doctor, doctor, why do you always fill me with the desire to eat shit?"

Not realizing that the private hospitals are different than this, afraid of infection by association, no one in Juanita's household accompanied me that morning when I got sick. When Juanita discovered me dying in the yard on her way to work, she sent one of the boys running to a phone. An ambulance came for me, not a moment too soon, as I had maybe three hours left in me, tops. Juanita kept the dog but let them take me away, quite assured that I was gone forever. So I rode to the hospital insentient and alone, stretched out on the uncovered metal bed of a battered pickup, the three "paramedics" squeezed together into the truck's more comfortable cab.

Ensconced, finally, in a private room with my own chart hooked on the foot of the bed, I swelled with excess fluid, a rude reversal of the dilemma which landed me there. The IVs never suited me. My little veins duck deep down beneath the surface; the blue bulges on everyone else's arms are a sea of pure white skin on me. My veins hide when the needles seek. No easy access, wormlike ripples exist on me through which the IV fluids can course and float. Instead, the tubes dig out abstruse damaging routes and with their gush of liquid overflow my delicate blood vessels—pop!—so that the waters spill inside and swell my limbs to lymphedemic proportions. On the third day, calculating the pros and the cons, they removed the IV a bit too early to stave off the swelling and salvage my motility.

At that point, I took my medication orally, which initially caused a bit of a ruckus.

"Here is your medicine," said the sweet chubby nurse, handing me three tablets and a cup of bottled water.

"Thank you," I replied. "What exactly is it?"

She looked at me quizzically and touched each of the three tablets in my upturned palm. "It is three pills," she said.

"Yes," I giggled, "but what are they for?"

"They're for you," she said matter-of-factly.

"But why do I need to take them?"

"Because they are yours."

I changed the line of inquiry. "Why are you giving these pills to me?"

"Because the doctor said to," she riled.

"But what is wrong with me that causes the doctor to want me to take these pills?"

Here she breathed deeply and planted her hands on her hips. She spoke slowly and deliberately, as if the illness affected my brain and through force of her stance she could help me assimilate. "You are sick."

"With what?" I asked, equally exasperated.

"Your illness."

"*Precisely* what kind of illness do I have?"

"The kind. These pills. Will fix," she emphasized.

"Come here, close, for a moment please," I asked her, and took her hand, tipping the three renegade pills back into her possession. "Here is what needs to happen before I can take these pills," I said. "I need to know the name of my illness, the name of these pills, all the possible side effects, and the exact course and length of my treatment. When you bring me that information, I will take the pills."

She stormed from the room, returning moments later with four other nurses. The one in charge, with the pointy white cap, sat on the edge of my bed. "Why is there a problem here?"

"There won't be any problem," I said, "as soon as someone tells me what kind of medicine I am getting and what disease it is supposed to treat."

"There is no need for you to worry about that," headnurse murmured indulgently.

"Why not?" I asked.

147

"Because you are the patient."

"I know I am the patient," I said.

"Well, this is why," she said.

"This is why what?" I asked. This all made sense to her, but not to me.

"This is why you cannot know these things," she explained, "because they will upset you."

To clarify, I repeated, "You're saying I can't know what I have because I might be upset to know I have it."

"Correct," she said, relieved. "I'm glad we understand each other. Give her the pills," she concluded, turning to the four other nurses.

"No," I insisted, recapturing their attention. "I don't understand anything about this! I'm not taking the pills until you tell me what I want to know."

The nurse's face furrowed and she reprimanded me, "Oh, you are a bad patient!

"Do you see that woman across the hall?" she asked then, pointing through the open doorway. The woman she indicated sat shriveled in an afghan with her sunken face turned toward the window. "She is a good patient," my nurse continued. "She takes her medicine and does not bother to ask silly questions."

"Can you tell me what she has?" I wanted to know.

"Oy, of course yes!" the nurse whispered, bending to me. "It is cancer! All inside of her, very sad, very sad. First it started in her breasts and then—boom!—it took off and all of her womanliness has now turned sour." She shook her head and crossed herself, murmuring a hex against roving bad fortune.

"Did you tell her what she has?" I asked.

"Ay, *Dios mio*, my God, no, why would we do that? We tell her only that she has an infection and give her a pill so she can die happy thinking she will get better."

"Do you want to know what we do in the States?" I asked them, and all five nurses huddled in, for stories about the States are always pleasant things. "We would tell her the truth so she can get used to the idea before she dies and not feel like she was the last one to know."

The nurses exchanged horrified glances. Surely I jest. "Well that does not make any sense, that is a stupid thing to do," said the nurse at my side. "Then she does what? Worry all through the living about the dying!"

"Do I have cancer too?" I asked, certain I didn't, but spying a loophole.

"No, you do not have cancer," headnurse stated.

"Maybe I don't, but maybe I do," I said, "and maybe you are just not telling me so that you do not scare me, like the lady over there. Now I think that unless I know what my disease is and what the pills are for, something not as bad as cancer, I will just be a frantic patient thinking I will die like that woman of the breast-eating affliction." I grinned.

Headnurse directed much effort toward not grinning back. Pursing her lips to hold back a smile, she rolled her eyes and slapped my hand. "Ay, you are a pretty girl, but you are a hard kind to like," she said.

For all their talk, my hoyden spirit inspired them, I believe, and my bravura blandishments tickled them, for the room morphed into a sideshow stage. I regaled the ever-hovering staff with the horrors of ritualistic truth telling in the U.S. medical establishment and stories of the bizarre and strange culled from years of *Enquirer* and *Star* headlines involving Barbie heads and hamsters and other such titillating misadventures. The nurses pampered me, bought me treats from the store down the street to add to my hospital tray, and the next meal arrived with the three little pills and a slip of paper that read: "Flagyl pills, to treat amoebic dysentery *not* cancer," followed by a long list of side effects that I couldn't completely translate, but included liver damage, seizures, inflamed rectum, blood clots, and other equally unnerving things.

* * *

I returned to Juanita's twenty pounds lighter, in time for Christmas, my favorite of all religious festivals for the emotional/cultural spectacle it incites. While the populace at large bemoans the premature Santa piggybacked on the tail end of Halloween's goblins and frights, I have forever cherished the landscape's redress from orange and black to red and green. I look for the tinsel and listen for the sound of bells; my footsteps, beginning sometime in early November, fall to the beat of Bing Crosby and Nat King Cole while I watch the weather for signs of a white winter. As the days shorten and everyone else at long last absorbs my enthusiasm, when the world wafts with the scent of cinnamon and cocoa and pine, I think, every year, that the season could not be more glorious.

149

What a blessed idea this holiday envelopes: the opening of one's door, the feeding of strangers, the setting aside of ill will in exchange for good! This, more than the presents, I always adored, this celebration of family, hearth, and home. All the festering sour resentments slipped out the back door with the scent of cookies come December, and the eggnog drowned the guilt, so that Christmas Eve existed as the one sure night when everyone in our house loved and made certain to show it. Were it a ruse, they had me fooled and trained me well, for with childlike innocence I anticipate each year the trappings and the decorations, knowing they herald pure safety, warmth, and unsullied affection. I have no more perfect memory than that of Christmas as a child.

Christmas in Guatemala is not what I grew up with. Alone for the first time, I had no dad with whom to hang the lights, to unravel and test them, stringing them precisely through the prickly boughs. No father. No lights. I had no sisters to wrestle for the task of topping the tree with the glittery angel in a halo of gold; no one's ankles to pinch as she climbed the stepstool, victorious in her acquisition of the coveted task. No siblings. No ornaments. No mother to bundle me against the cold. No carolers. No Rudolph. No "Jingle Bells."

Tradition was subverted; the old guideposts disappeared.

All of the signs were missing, and I admit to mourning the accouterments. Were the mantel of depression to cloak me at any time, likely it would have enclothed me then, when the Ghost of Christmas Past lingered in my dreams, pointing out the path I had left behind. But I did not move away to cling to my history, nor regret my choices. Don't think for a minute Christmas desisted. I had, when I arrived in Guatemala, brought with me a daily inspirational calendar which I thought a silly going-away gift but for one saying. I kept it perpetually open to my favorite Elizabeth King quote: "It is not the circumstances in which we are placed, but the spirit with which we meet them that constitutes our comfort." I read it every day, twice a day in December, and determined to create my own new Christmas.

Minus the snow and the mistletoe, the air still crackles with electricity, and celebration springs up from the impoverished seeds of the everyday. School lets loose for a few months around the holidays, so that children run eagerly through the streets. They fashion firecrackers from gunpowder and TNT which they detonate against the walls, the roads, and occasionally their feet; cries of glee muffle any screams of pain so that the wind sounds with a spirit of joyful explosion. While the adults maintain an air of sullen decorousness until the last moment of drunken outburst, a wave of vicarious joy mounts through the young ones' well-tolerated antics. In the crescendo of that final December 20th week absolute strangers rush upon each other, cracking eggshells over one another's heads, and the unaccustomed American who shrinks from this assault, anticipating that raw ooze will cascade upon her, quickly realizes they've blown free the insides as confetti rains instead over her spared skull.

Entering a December house is to step into a stable, where hay crunches beneath your feet and the pungent scent speaks of welcome refuge. Before proceeding further, one drops to her knees upon the straw and pays homage at a homemade altar, where spicy candles illuminate the images of the saints, fashioned into paper pictures and plastic icons alike. If at that moment a donkey neighs from the street, indignant at his shouldered load, or a sheep brays from beyond an unclosed window with a hungry brawl, it is to be as close to Bethlehem as I have ever come.

In this humble reproduction I have felt closer than ever to the natural inceptions which have largely disappeared behind our modern holiday's inventions. Like Mary, Joseph, and the Baby Boy, I had traveled a long distance and needed to rest, so I settled in a strange town to give all I had to give: my natural gifts and my whole own self. It is the Kennedys, is it not?, those Peace Corps diviners, who said, "From those to whom much has been given, much is expected." While the idea of giving back to the world may be an innocent, youthful concept, it is a pure one that captivated and compelled me; is it any wonder the Blessed Mother, too, was such a young girl? In December of the year I arrived at Juanita's, and again the next year when I returned sick and needy, I lived out what I always suspected to be the true meaning of the nativity story: to share what you have with those less obviously fortunate, while recognizing that in spite of lower caste status they may own the keys to a rich internal kingdom that they're willing to share if only you will meet them where they are and ask to be invited in. My two Christmases in Guatemala symbolized every reason I ventured there in the first place.

Christmas also allowed me to forgive the cultural idiosyncrasy which vexed me the most all throughout the eleven other months. Generally speaking, commerce crawls in Central America, but for *la navidad* it stops pointedly and without exception, so that there is not a single practical element of living which can be accomplished at year's end. While this lax attitude threatened to suck from my marrow every last drop of patience under normal circumstances, complacency in the face of festivity is something I respected. A month devoted to diversion seems in retrospect a wise thing. Furthermore, this built-in societal excuse relaxed my inborn compulsion for perpetual achievement. Watching the world refrain from collapse during seasonal inattention influenced an attitudinal shift in me. I celebrate more, plan less now. I live a more carefree life in America thanks to Guatemala's yule.

Even politics paused when the great star passed overhead, and the nights yawned a temporary peace. No one renounced Rigoberta, declared a coup, killed the bishops. They waited, these army soldiers and backwoods guerrillas, perhaps in private hatching their plans, but deferring until after the Day of the Magi the resumption of their wars. Excerpts from letters to my parents, all dated shortly after Christmas that first year, detail the interrupted battle:

Now that El Salvador has signed its peace treaty, Guatemala is left as the only Latin American country still waging full-scale guerrilla warfare. And in terms of human rights violations, Guatemala, Peru, and Iraq are ranked as the three worst countries in the world. The United States no longer supplies foreign aid money to Guatemala, after the kidnapping, murder, and beheading of an American citizen living here last year by, as it turns out, Army officials. And an American tourist was shot and killed two weeks ago after trying to drive through a police barricade set up to stop cars and rob the passengers. . . .

For about a month of training, our towns were occupied after dark by guerrilla forces from the mountains. We all figured this was normal, as our families were accustomed to staying inside after dark and not opening the door to anyone. But when Peace Corps officials found out about it later, they said we would have all been evacuated if they had known what was going on. It is amazing how quickly you get used to being stopped at police and army barricades, walking past bands of soldiers in the capital or Antigua who are armed with machine guns, or being passed in the street by tanks with weaponry pointing in every direction. . . .

A Volunteer friend of mine was just assigned to a mountain town called Putepá in one of the most beautiful, but also most dangerous, parts of the country. The day we left training and she moved into her house, they found a headless body in a ravine behind her home. A week later a child discovered the head in her backyard. . . .

But oh, what a glorious mental break Christmas offered from this ongoing conflict. How quickly merriment minimized the government-sanctioned gang rapes, the kidnapped communities, the mass graves, and I forgot for a bit the civil war that waged around me when even the military forces offered a "*feliz navidad*, 'Merry Christmas'" as I passed. In December, alone among all months, the presence of armed men in camouflage gear inspired in me something less than fear. When they occupied the streets on those blessed nights the naïve girl I was, spared the scars of history, could imagine them less an occupying force and more a group of restless revelers trouping stealthily along the road toward home. From inside Juanita's house, they could have been carolers assembling outside, preparing to knock upon the door and bring us glad tidings of peace and joy.

Alone among all the poor residences, Juanita's home boasted no altar, no hay-strewn floor, no semblance of manger. She bought a tree, a real pine one from God knows where, and if she did it for me I wish she hadn't. I found it hard to like Juanita at first. In fairness, she suffered most from my preconceived notions of the exuberant, effusive Latin American woman, so her taciturn temperament failed to inspire me. I misunderstood why a woman who kept so silently to herself would choose to invite into her home an American trainee, and I additionally faulted her for not matching my expectations in appearance and dress of the long-suffering Maya. But add together her stockings and high heels, her western Christmas tree, her aloof nature, her nine-to-five job, and you see she wanted most fiercely to be An American Woman, and fancied me her guidebook to that end. Here we confronted the crux of our misguidance: She hoped I would help her become more like me, when I needed her to teach me to be more like her. The first year, I held against her the watchful way she studied me and observed without interacting, but this second year I knew more and could not fault her for aspiring to something beyond her empty house and her missing husband.

Juanita wanted desperately to be modern and sophisticated and renowned for those qualities, and her requests in light of my imposition were small. A year in the country, more sure of myself, I no longer

153

resented her diminutive desires or judged her less when she meekly asked, "Will you make pizza for Christmas?"

Delighted to see I actually returned alive and relatively well from the hospital, she said, "Let's celebrate Christmas like they do in the United States!" and that is how it started. She planned, as I came to understand, to treat all of her neighbors—and even those who weren't neighbors, but whose respect she courted—to a newfangled Western experience. She had her tree, she even found trains to run beneath it, and she had her gringa girl back to prepare a lavish feast of that quintessential American dish: pizza.

* * *

The *bombas* began their prelude at sundown, which on any other night would have meant menace, but on this Eve the explosions heralded a chaotic countdown to unadulterated exultation. We commenced cooking with the first rat-a-tat-tat, and throughout the long night wore thin a path between oven and table. One neighbor grated cheese with my Swiss Army knife, another mashed tomatoes between her palms for sauce. Juanita fried up meat while I toyed with the yeast-flour-water dough and begged it, "Rise, rise!" We pulled the toasted crusts from the oven onto our skirts, piling fixings on with abandon. The table swelled with pizzas, and the scent of garlic and warm bread burst from the house and tore through the streets, bidding the townsfolk come, the food is ready!

They appeared shyly at first, knocking softly on the door, unaccustomed to holidays in a place other than home. But the lure of pizza proved strong, and the rum materializing from shirtsleeves and pockets hijacked their fears, so that soon the neighbors not only packed the house, but they began to speak, too. First the compliments rolled out: for the food which all admired but no one dared touch, for the house, for the hostess who beamed magisterially from the corner and who finally broke the spell with a toast and a bite of pizza. For over an hour everyone ate reverentially while the men took their turns raising a glass to Juanita, to me, to the Italian-American tradition of cooking, to the powers of yeast, and on and on until finally, sixty minutes later, we clinked our cups to Jesus, who thank heaven was born and died and reigns with God, providentially providing us with a reason to congregate and devour pizza in his honor.

The murmur of voices and the breadth of conversation escalated in direct proportion to the ebbing volume of liquor in the twenty or so Quetzalteca bottles scattered and toppled among the vanishing pizzas. I continued to cook, passing pies to Juanita who proudly placed them on her table. As midnight inched toward us the detonation of firecrackers and *bombas* achieved a concussive climax, blasting at unrelieved intervals outdoors and, finally, indoors as well. Sparklers ricocheted off the ceiling in the front room and one poor old woman screamed when a pop!pop! issued from beneath her skirts, coupling the room's rancid scent of beer burps with the acrid odor of scorched hair. The whole house shivered with excitement when the late night became the early morn, and the men stampeded drunkenly into the streets. Brandishing revolvers, every one, they culminated the boisterous blowout with a rash of gunshots and tears of pure joy.

The town slid through the rest of the night with diminished intensity; a burgeoning melancholy settled in.

The best night of the year had come and gone.

But inside the party roared on. Minus the general hullabaloo and half the guests, with the men lost in the streets to inebriated unconsciousness, I sat finally with the tipsy female stragglers and talked until dawn. The edge of my sobriety made their garrulousness more gay. There was a time when I drank—in high school, of course, before it was allowable. By the time my twenty-first birthday rolled around and I could do it legally, the desire had left me. I never did like the taste, and my demeanor drunk came to appall me. The day I realized I imbibed only because everyone else did I stopped, having identified for myself the poorest excuse for bad behavior and the surest route to the alcoholism that plagued my ancestors. I never drank alcohol again, and Guatemala allowed me not to, seeing as how I am a woman with strange red hair that surely inclines me toward odd tendencies. If I had been a brunette or a man it would not have been advisable to turn down a proffered drink and if, as some Volunteers did, I drank every time someone invited me to, I would have returned home two years later a veritable lush. Such is the habit in these countries where only one pastime exists.

The women left behind huddled around the table passing the remaining Quetzalteca bottle from hand to hand, furtively at first, then deliberately. Someone lit a cigarette and someone else hiked up her skirt as a comfort measure; their eyes grew wide with ribald rebellion at the masculine nature of their impromptu soiree. They started to swap

155

salacious stories chastising their men, which set the whites of their eyes to glittering with a sheen I never before noticed and never saw again. Someone belched. Two laughed so hard they fell to the floor, and one leapt up with her hand pressed to the crevice between her legs and waddled toward the latrine.

In the middle of the night the radio stations switched back to secular music, and I dug out my tiny clock radio and climbed atop the table to plug it into the dangling ceiling socket beside the bare light bulb. It took some time to tune, but a mariachi band finally rewarded my effort, followed by the ever-popular pharmacia song, wherein a man with a squeaky voice bolstered by a tooting tuba recites a lyrical litany of items available for sale at the apothecary. (To this day I can't reach for a bottle of painkiller without hearing ". . . aspirina, penicilina . . ." set to the rhythm of a brass band in the back of my head.)

The party, to a woman, leapt to their feet and began to dance. All unashamed partner pairings, a waltzlike trot, with our left hands clasped in a straight-armed salute to the side, and our right hands snuggly cradling each other's necks and shoulders. Some were rather schooled gambolers, skilled at the dips and spins which left their comparatively more tipsy partners staring up from the floor. At them we laughed, but mostly we frolicked with disregard for technique. All participated, for no one was watched and the men who imposed self-critique had departed. I danced until my feet hurt, switching partners like the belle of the ball, spinning in dizzy circles to make my dress fly high, and wiping the trickle of sweat away from my forehead.

By the time Juanita picked me her workaday world was eons away. Her laugh echoed mine, her eyes shone, and I thought, "After all this time, I am finally introduced to the girl in her whom I could enjoy." When she threw back her head and laughed from her belly at our misplaced footsteps, I really liked her. We twirled each other with abandon, her pendant breasts volleying boisterously off my chest while the radioman crooned a jolly tune extolling the virtues of the potato.

By the time we all tired of the dance and settled again into our chairs, the group's besotted manners had fully infected me with a vicarious punchiness so that I might have become more involved in the subsequent banter had I been better able to understand the content of the conversation. As the last remaining bottle drained they spoke more rapidly with an elided diction, dropping the tail syllable off every other word and running their thoughts together. Had they spoken with Queen's English I still would probably not have understood but half.

Juanita had to repeat the phrase three times before I could fathom the meaning: "Tell us about the car your father bought you for your sixteenth birthday," and even when she nailed the pronunciation I remained a bit baffled.

"What car?" I asked.

"*Tu carro*," she slurred, "your car."

"I don't own a car."

"Yes you do," she said with enough conviction to make it true.

"No, I really don't own a car," I reiterated. The contradiction made everyone jolly.

"She owns a car," Juanita said to the other women. "Her father bought it for her on her sixteenth birthday."

"No he did not," I said, laughing. "You are so drunk—" and at this she giggled ceaselessly "—that you have me confused with someone else!"

"Just tell me what color it is," she begged. "Is it red? I love red cars!"

"What on earth makes you think I got a car for my birthday?"

"Because all rich *americanos* fathers give their gringo children a sporty car on their sixteenth birthday." The falsities she accepted as fact could put a charlatan to shame, and although her sophisms made little sense she spoke with such authority that everyone believed her.

But I burst her bubble and shook my head, No. I crushed her; her look turned to one of profound disappointment. "What a bad father you have!" she whispered, and I couldn't tell if she was more disappointed for me that I didn't get the car, or more disappointed for herself that she didn't get the story. "There is just something wrong with her family," I made out as she explained her error to the gang by pointing the finger of blame squarely at me.

For what was left of the night their conversation swirled around me, occasionally picking me up and pulling me in, but after I refused to play the gringo game it no longer tottered in the direction of my privilege. Mostly, they treated me like one of them and paid me no greater mind than any other neighbor. We talked and laughed until four o'clock in the morning, and as the liquor wore off they shared only friendship. I discovered that Juanita's cousin's husband lost the equivalent of twenty dollars, their entire life savings, in a drunken game of cards. I learned that the quietest, most refined woman stopped menstruating five months ago when a blue-eyed blonde gave her the evil eye on a bus. The fattest woman had recently been to a shaman to level a curse on her unclean neighbor whose filthy pets gave her rabbits pinkeye. The young girl beside me said, quietly, "I met a man. . . ." I admitted aloud my fear of chickens.

As I look back on that scene now, I am only one of nine, no better, no worse, in my careworn dress, choking on laughter, sharing sexy secrets of love and foibles with women who would hold me exempt at dawn.

Necessity creates intense bonds, and family is not only what you're born to but also what you cultivate. Thousands of miles from my own country, I have always been home for Christmas.

8. Juanita's Story

When at first I tried to think of how to describe her to you I thought I would say that she was a disappointment to me, but no, that isn't the way to say it, because there were many things about Elena that I liked, and when she came back to visit after being gone for a year, and I walked in and she was standing there in my house, I realized right at that moment how happy I was to see her again. So calling her a disappointment isn't the right way to describe her, but instead maybe I should just say that the first time I met her I was disappointed—yes, *I* was disappointed, not that *she* was the disappointment. I was disappointed because at the beginning she just didn't seem to be at all like the kind of *americana* that I was thinking I would like to get.

I know all about *americanos*. I have watched *Dallas* every week since the very beginning when the show started, on the channel that comes out of Mexico. Even on days when I am sick I still go to work so I can see it on the television in the breakroom. I watch *Dallas* to learn about the United States and how to be a real *americana*. So that is the way I know all about the clothes to wear to be a real *americana*, and the kind of houses that everyone lives in on their ranches, and how the cars have drivers to take you places. I really like the hats that the men wear in the United States and I find it interesting how there is a rule that you can sleep with many different men who are not just your husband and that is okay there.

I have been trying very hard for many years to make myself into the kind of woman that would come from a place like the United States by wearing shoes that have high heels on the bottom of them and skirts of the same style that they wear in Texas, which is the heart of America. Also, I save my money so that two times during the year I can go to a shop in the capital where they perform specialized U.S.-style hairdos and get my hair cut in the way that Miss Ellie's beautiful hair is cut. I have a job that I go to every day like a liberated feminist American woman with her own money and independence which are words I learned from a pamphlet that a white woman in a long skirt handed to me on a corner in *Zona 9* and a woman at work read and explained to me. I have invented myself into the person I always wished I could be, and that is probably why Elena was disappointing, because I expected her to at least be better at being an *americana* than I was!

There is an organization called "The Group of Peace" that has a training camp in a nearby town and they bring people from the United States to stay there and pay Guatemalan families to let them live in their houses for three months before they send the gringos off somewhere else to work. I always thought it would be wonderful to get my own *americana* person to live with me but so does everyone else. Everyone else wants *americanos* for the money, but I wanted an *americana* that I could observe. It is very hard to get picked to get an *americana* if you haven't had one before though, because they always send them to the same houses they sent them to the last time. But one day, when I was walking past the store on my way home from work, there were two women sitting on the step talking about how the one lady's *americana* was taking up too much room and she needed the extra bed for her own children, so I told her what my name was, and that I lived right here, on her street, and that I would be very happy to take the next *americana* that was coming. The next day I took a day of vacation from my job so I could go with her to the training camp and make the arrangements to have her next *americana* delivered to my house instead.

It was so exciting to think I would be getting my own *americana* to live in my house with me! At the training camp they told me the rules that are these:

1) The guest needs to have her own room to sleep in.
2) The room must have a bed that is not made of straw.
3) All meals must be made for the guest including lunch to take to the training camp every day.
4) Nobody in the family should take the gurst's things without permission.
5) The guest must be spoken to in Spanish only for her learning purposes even if someone in the family is trying to learn English and would like the practice.

In addition to following all of these rules I also took some extra care to get ready by making my daughter move out of the bed in her room into my bed in my room with me, and by buying a dresser to put beside the bed in the room that we prepared for the *americana* where all of her clothing and beautifying items could be stored. I bought the dresser from out of the window of my favorite store that I gaze into while I wait every evening for the bus, the store where they sell special things like a tall storage cabinet for Chinese plates, and a sofa with cushions that are attached and filled very full with a soft and squishy material, and a gold lamp that lights up when you turn a switch near the head of the woman on the stand who wears a long flowing dress and carries grapes. Many years ago I picked out all of these things for myself to make my house beautiful. Even though these things are still waiting there in the store for me to buy someday, I already know where they will go when I bring them home. I have thought about their placement for so long that in the evening when I walk through my door I can actually see these beautiful things of mine there in my rooms. But the dresser is the first thing that has ever come home with me and even though it took all the money I had, and also an agreement to pay more money every two weeks for the next year, I knew it would be worth it so that my *americana* would be pleased with my home and happy to live with us.

So the room was ready and I was ready for my fancy U.S. guest many days before she arrived. I had all the time in those days to picture her lovely look, her special clothes that we could share, her makeup that she could put on my face, her green dollar money that we could spend on special treats, and all her good stories about her cars, her drivers, and her ranch with horses to entertain me. Then what happened is just this: Elena arrived without any of those things at all.

A Guatemalan man from the training camp, driving a pickup truck full of young *americanos*, pulled up and walked Elena to my house. He said that she came on an airplane the day before and so maybe she was hungry but who could tell?, because she didn't speak any Spanish that he could understand. She only smiled with nice straight teeth and shrugged her shoulders when you tried to talk to her. He left quickly and I was a little bit confused, so I tried to ask her if she was sure she was the *americana* that was supposed to come to me, but he was right that she couldn't understand anything. Then I was confused and she was confused too, and we just stood there for a little while in the street looking at each other while I tried to figure out what had gone wrong because aside from having hair almost the same color as Sue Ellen's, in every other way she was nothing like the *Dallas* person I had planned on getting. Her hair was just in a plain knot on the back of her head instead of in a beautiful style, her things were in a bag tied to her back instead of in the lovely leather suitcases I was hoping to borrow, she wore big ugly man boots for heavy walking instead of pretty girl shoes for sharing, and even though she wore a nice dress that I liked very much it was in a size that was never ever going to fit on me. She didn't bring a purse made by a special designer or any money with her, she didn't wear diamonds or even any other kind of jewelry, her fingernails were just the plain color of regular nails without paint on them, and without speaking Spanish she wasn't even useful for the purposes of being entertaining or amusing. The only good thing she brought was a bag of candies, and since that is the only good thing that came with her I decided I had better save it for awhile.

Finally, I just led her to her room with the bed and the dresser, and I waited to see all the things she might take from her bag and put inside the new furniture, but she just waited too, so we waited and waited until finally I got tired of just sitting there on the bed with nothing to do or say so I left the room and it wasn't until I was gone that she pulled closed the curtain door and I could hear her in there moving around, opening and closing the drawers. I had to wait all through the night until she left the next day for the training camp to open the dresser and look inside and remove all her things to see them and practice using them. Only then could I finally brush my hair with her hairbrush, put on her makeup, and lie inside the blue sack she put on the bed and slept in instead of under the blanket like a normal person. (I found this out when I peered through the doorway at night and saw she did not sleep at all like a real lady from Texas is supposed to sleep—Elena was on her back, with her mouth open and snoring, in green and black striped shirt and pants! Where was her lacy soft nightgown? Where was her beauty cream to soften her face and delicate skin?) I soon discovered that in addition to her sleeping habits there were many other unexpected things about her which is why, like I said before, I felt so disappointed, thinking that I had the bad luck to get a not really right *americana* by mistake. She was nothing like the real *americanos* they show on television.

The thing is, I realized very quickly that it was stupid of me to have thought it could have been any different from how it turned out, to have thought that this one time I would have gotten just what I wished for. Who has that right? If I were less of a fool I would have expected not to get what I wanted, because the way my life has always gone is that every time I expect better, the person I think can help me fill out all my hopes and live the life I dream of disappoints me. I am thirty-four years old, an old woman with a long life of living, and so you would think I would know better by now than to believe that my luck or my fate might have changed after so much time of everything being the same. After all, I started out with a disappointing life, and when the beginning is bad and the bad luck is inside your very own blood, what hope is there of everything changing just because you want it to? Why do I keep letting myself believe that can happen? It is a long time since I left behind my ragged clothes and cut my hair, such a long, long time since I left the box I got born into, but still no matter where I go or what I try to do I can never get away from the truth that is this: I will always just be a grown-up version of a girl who came from trash.

There, I said it. Now you know the secret I have hidden all these years, the secret of whom I started out to be.

* * *

Sometime in the year 1957 or maybe 1958, I got born in Guatemala City in the one place that guarantees you the worst of all the lives a person could possibly get born into and proves that the gods have no favor to shine on you. "The dump kids" is what everyone called us and we knew it meant that even the mangy dogs picking through the scraps that the trash trucks unloaded would be better off than we would be, because at least they had somewhere else to go at night. If we were lucky, it meant that our parents had found a cardboard box big enough for all of us to sleep under and that maybe someone had found a good bag of new restaurant trash with plenty of uneaten food parts so that no one would be too hungry or have to eat from a bag that was older and had begun to stink. I was pretty good at recognizing the trash trucks that came from *Zona Viva*, where there are nice restaurants and where the people with money to order good food but not finish it all live, and I got skilled at climbing the piles fast to get to the good bags before the other kids reached them. I was a good fighter so I could usually keep the things I found and not lose them even to the older kids or to the boys. I also knew better than to move in too quickly after the truck dumped its load

163

because sometimes the end of the load stuck and would drop out late and I saw a girl die that way buried under the trash.

My family and the other dump families kept our boxes and the shacks we built with the thrown-away construction materials close together at night on the south side of the trash field for greater safety from the street people who came after dark to raid the trash piles and were often drunk and had knives. They looked at us children in frightening ways. So at night we stayed together, but during the day we all spread out looking for things to trade or sell, some candles that weren't all the way burned down or if we were lucky a necklace with a shiny stone. From the time I was five or six, I would spend the afternoon sitting on the city corner where my parents put me, trying to talk the people who passed by into purchasing my objects. When I was especially little, I could easily sit with one leg tucked up underneath me and the other sticking out so that it looked like I was a cripple, and that way even if people did not purchase my items they would often give me a few *centavos* as they passed because they felt sorry for me and so I earned some good money. But the older I got the harder it was to hide my good leg, and one day some passing nuns noticed what I was doing and they stopped to yell at me for lying, which they said the Bible says is wrong, and for being a beggar, which a man named Jesus does not allow. Sister Santa Rosa—whose name I only learned later, of course—the tall one, the one who ran the convent and organized all the sister's good works, grabbed me up and shook me to give me the fear of God. When she yelled, "Where are your parents?!" it was due to fear and also the shame of telling the truth that instead of being honest I said quickly and without much thought that they were dead. So that is why the nuns took me with them off the street that day and that is how I wound up living in the orphanage run by the sisters.

To me, this was not a bad thing that happened; it wasn't, I swear to it. The orphanage was a real building that kept the rain off and the cold out. There were beds, one for each person, and I got my own with a blanket too that kept me warm. Every day I got to eat food served hot or cold, the way it was meant to be, not the same temperature as the air outdoors. I had chores to do, and the work was hard, but it was safe and so it was better because no one tried to touch me or knife me or spit on me. Only at night sometimes did I get lonely for my parents and my family, and I wondered if they thought of me or even came to look for me when I did not return, but then I would stop thinking of those things that made me sad. I would think instead of the pictures in the lovely shiny magazine I had found one day in a trash sack many months before, pictures of big California houses in the states with fabric hanging from the windows and all the walls painted different colors inside that were so beautiful, and I would remind myself that I was getting closer to having the magazine life I had been dreaming of ever since I found those pictures. As I lay in my bed every single night, for many years, I would imagine myself walking in those houses and they became mine. I touched the window fabric and could actually feel its softness, and then I sat in the sturdy chairs with the wood slats that made real dents in the skin of my thighs. This became my own real world, the one I could go to whenever I wanted by only closing my eyes. It made me happy and that is how I replaced the thoughts of my missing family. Even many years later, when I was out on my own, and I could have gone back as a grown-up person just to visit, I never tried to find my family again, and I have ever since blocked the thought of them from my mind, because that makes it easier to keep on believing I have also left behind the person I started out in life to be. I was never meant to be that person; I have forgotten who she was; I live the life I imagine. And that is all I will say of that.

* * *

Elena behaved most oddly with her dog. Then again, she behaved oddly about all animals. She would scream and run into the house with her clothes pressed against her naked body if a chicken came too close to her while she bathed from the bucket in the yard. She refused to eat any food that had an animal part in it, which is all of the good food that I know how to make, and so I was only able to feed her pancakes with jam or fried cauliflower and chamomile tea at every meal. And you should have seen the way in which she sobbed like a confused child when she noticed that the rabbit she gave me for a Christmas gift that first year was boiling in the cookpot on the stove one night. By then she had been living here in Guatemala for only two months but her Spanish was improving greatly and she cried: "You killed the bunny?!" But I told her that no, it had eaten some grass that must have had pesticide on it and it shook for a couple of hours in the yard before it died all on its own so I didn't have to kill it, and for some reason this made her even more upset. But like I said, the oddest thing of all is the way she treated her dog, like it wasn't even a dog, like it was a baby or something but

165

even more spoiled. When she got Calixta at Christmas that first year, she bought special food in a bag that was for the dog only, not to be shared with the rest of us. She let the dog sleep on her bed even when I told her it would give her fleas. Despite the fact that Elena got scabies bugs living under her skin and had to rub on a special medicine, she still didn't make the dog sleep outside. She even talked to the dog—private conversations in English only for her and Calixta that no one else could understand. And she carried that puppy around in her arms for such a long time every day that I warned her it might never learn to walk on its own four feet! I told Elena that she was going to wreck that beautiful dog and make her spoiled and weird, but Elena would only reply that something cannot get spoiled by love. Of course, I was right and Elena was wrong, because the next Christmas when she and Calixta came back for a visit, and I had to watch over the dog when Elena went away to the hospital, I discovered it had many of the strangest and not very doglike habits. If I put her in the yard, Calixta would howl and scratch on the door until I let her in, and every night she would get in the bed that had been Elena's and growl if we came near it. During the day whenever we ate our meals she would sit beside us at the table as if she expected to share our food instead of going out and hunting down some of her own! In some ways, it reminded me of living with señora Chavez's spoiled yapping dog, except that Calixta was bigger and not all white.

Of all the animals I have known, I hated señora Chavez's dog the most, and of all the people I have known, I hated señora Chavez more than any other. Señora Chavez had a little white dog that she carried around and cuddled and hugged and fed the good food to and put to sleep in a soft safe place while I—a real person!—got the scraps, the damp room, and no attention at all unless it was to tell me what was wrong with me and what I wasn't doing right. She even had that stupid dog with her when she came to the orphanage looking for a maid, when I was around thirteen and considered grown. The nuns decided that taking care of señora Chavez and her house would be the perfect job for me. In the car, as she drove me away, I sat in the back and the dog sat in the front, and señora Chavez talked to it all throughout the entire ride, saying to the dog how I was dirty and smelled worse than a stable. The whole time she never said one single word to me. It would have bothered me more, the thought of living with this nasty woman, except that when I saw the house, locked behind a big iron gate with flowers

166

coming over the top, the most beautiful house I ever saw in real life, not just in a picture, I felt so important and lucky that I figured it didn't really matter after all who I had to live with as long as I could call it mine.

And most of the time, that is just how it was. I could ignore her and be happy enough. There were some things that were difficult to get accustomed to, of course, like having to wear shoes which I had never had to wear before and which caused me often to slip on the shiny floors and fall off the steps. It was especially hard having to wear white gloves on my hands all during the day, but fortunately that did not last too long because the gloves caused me to drop everything I picked up to dust and finally señora Chavez decided to make me keep wearing the shoes, but not the gloves anymore. I owed her a lot of money for all those things the gloves made me break, and even though I was supposed to get five *quetzales* a week for my work—that is what she told the nuns I would get, I heard her say it, even though later she said it was too generous given all the food I ate and all the space I took up—she added up the cost of all the money I owed her for the broken things and said she would keep my five *quetzales* each week until I paid her back. I must have broken some expensive things, because I never did get any five *quetzales* ever.

Anyway, some things were difficult to get accustomed to, but mostly I kept to myself and did okay. During the day, while I worked, señora Chavez often had places to go to so I was alone (because the cook always stayed in the kitchen and the gardener always stayed in the yard) and I could think that this whole beautiful house was mine only. The stairs that I scrubbed were for my feet to step on, and the silver that I polished was for me to drink tea from, and the furniture that I dusted was for me and my husband and my children to sit on and be comfortable. All day long I thought of the family I could have in this house, and the things we could do, and because it was mine I treated everything with great care and loved the house very much. On the other hand, I found it easy enough to ignore the people who lived there when they returned at the end of each day, señora Chavez and her husband, especially because they spent so much time ignoring each other. For the most part I kept very busy, and if ever I got lonely from working all day alone with no one to speak to I just pictured the family of my imagination using the space I cleaned so carefully for them, telling me over and over what a fine house I kept and how much they loved me for it, and I fell asleep content enough at night.

I would say the only real problem during those first months, once I learned to ignore señora Chavez and her dog, was my hunger. I was hungry all the time, more hungry than I had been in some years. Every time señora Chavez and her husband ate a meal the cook would scrape anything that was left on their plates after they finished onto a plate for me, which I could eat on the kitchen step outside the door, but they liked her food and it never seemed as if there was very much left over for me. At first it wasn't too bad, but every day it seemed like I just got more hungry than the day before, so that sometimes when I fell down the stairs, I wasn't sure anymore if it was still the fault of the shoes or if it was the fault of fainting from all that hunger. Eventually, on days when my hunger caused me the most pain, I began to spend a lot of time cleaning items in the dining room, and if I saw the cook leave the kitchen I would sneak in there to spill some extra pepper into the cookpot or spray some of the cleanser onto the meat in the stove. That way señora Chavez and her husband would complain about the flavor and refuse to eat it, and I would get a more full meal. But my chances to do that got fewer and fewer once the cook got in trouble a few times, got suspicious, and started to keep a better watch over her work.

So what I did finally is that I waited until everyone was asleep and I would sneak down the back staircase and hunt through the kitchen to find something to eat. I was careful to observe everything, even in my great hunger, and not to eat until I was sure that the cook would not notice what was missing in the morning. If there were two ripe avocados but they were uncut, with their skins on, surely she would see if one was missing or peeled so those I would not touch. The bowl of soup though would not show a few spoonfuls missing, and the chopped up papaya pieces would still fill the plate if I moved a few slices around after eating some. After that, I found a cake under a lid on the counter, a chocolate cake with creamy frosting, and I thought that if I used a knife to take off a small sliver from the side where pieces had already been served from no one could tell. I was just about to cut the slice when a voice behind me said, "I see we have come for the same thing."

It was señor Chavez, the husband, and he scared me so much that I dropped the knife and it hit the floor with a BANG. "Shh!" he said. "We must be quiet or else the señora will catch us and we will both be in more trouble than we need." Then he winked at me, smiled, and handed me the knife he picked up off the floor. Only then did I breathe again and close my still-open mouth. He said I should cut us each a piece while he warmed the café, and I realized that he meant to eat with me instead of punish me. When I came toward the table with a slice held in the palm of each of my hands he laughed and said, "Plates would work well in this situation." He then wrapped all the fingers of his right hand around my wrist and turned my own palm gently so that the cake fell onto the plate he held. Without ever letting go of me, he put the plate on the table and took one of my fingers into his mouth, sucking off the chocolate, and sending a shivery feeling all through me that was good and warm. "The frosting is the best part," he said softly before he let go of my wrist and sat down to eat.

We talked while we ate, but I do not remember much more of what was said that first night after his mouth touched my skin, except I do remember some feeling of embarrassment when he asked me why I was wearing my uniform in the middle of the night and I told him simply that my uniform is all the clothes I had to wear. He wore pajamas of a beautiful texture, which I said I liked to change the subject. I did not tell him the details of my two uniforms (which señora Chavez added to the list of the things I owed her money for); how every day I wore one to work and then to bed, washing it out the next day while I wore the other and ironing it at the end of the day when it was dry so señora Chavez would not have to see me in wrinkles which bothered her badly. He laughed when I mentioned his pajamas, but a kind laugh, and then he looked at me silently for a long while before he wished me a very good night and returned to bed. Myself, I sat there for a long time thinking: "Who would have guessed such a wonderful man could be married to such an awful woman? How had I not noticed him before?"

The next day I did not see him at all, but I thought of him, of the shape of him beneath his clothes, of the kindness in his voice, and when at the end of the day I went to my room full of these secret thoughts he had been there and left behind a box tied with a red ribbon on my bed. I knew it was from him, who else would it be?, for inside the box was a beautiful gown for sleeping made all of white, with lace at the neck and the wrist, where his hand had held me, and the fabric felt softer against the skin of my body than anything had ever felt before. Wearing his gift, I went to the kitchen after dark, and waited in the chair for him there. When he arrived I did not hear him, but only felt his hand on my back, and I jumped in my seat and smiled at him and he smiled right back. "I brought you a special treat," he said, and fed me cookies, placing them one at a time into my mouth, gently. When he put the last bite on my tongue, he licked the crumbs from the edge of my lips and closed his mouth over mine. "Goodnight," he said, and before I opened my eyes again he was gone.

That is the last time I went to the kitchen in the night, for after that he came to me instead, and my hunger disappeared. He touched me as no one has ever touched me, and kissed me in places I did not know were for kissing, but his lips felt warm and wet and good and gave me such sensations that I shook all over, my body hot and moist as I bent it to him. When he pressed against me and put himself up inside of me, rocking me back and forth beneath him, I knew finally what love was and thought that never again could I be so happy. He came to me every night without fail, and though before then mine had been the ugliest room in the house, at the top of the highest staircase where the wind blew in and the rain made it smell wet, with him there it was a cozy, wonderful place. I wanted to be nowhere else ever again.

After that the days became for me only hours to get through until night fell, and I passed the time at my chores with a new vision: of him and me in this house of ours with our child that I was waiting for him to put in me so that then we would be a family and he would have reason to send señora Chavez away and I could be his wife. Every night when he pulled me to him I thought, "This could be the night it happens!" for having lived on the streets I knew that babies came from our actions and that this is why he came to me, to make me the mother of his child and the woman of his house whom he could love as he never could love that other, mean woman he was trapped here with. Then, after many months it occurred as I expected, and my belly swelled with the child of him inside me, and even though our purpose was achieved he loved me so much that he still came every night to lie upon me. Even when my belly got larger he loved me so much that he could not stop and would roll me over and give me his love from behind.

I know he loved me! When señora Chavez found out about us and about our baby he sent a man to help me, his own personal assistant, and a man who didn't love me wouldn't have done that. I thought she was going to kill me that day, when she pulled me out of my bed and ripped my beautiful sleeping gown right off of my body. I screamed, "You can't do that! That's mine!" but she only she kicked me in the belly over and over.

When she screamed, "None of this is yours! None of this will ever be yours!" I ran from her without thinking, out through the door and through the front gate, and I was on the street holding my belly before I realized I was naked and climbed into a neighbor's bush to hide.

That is when the assistant came and found me. He gave me his coat, put me in his car, and said señor Chavez had sent him to take care of me. The assistant left me in a hotel where I stayed for two nights. Then he came back for me and drove me to a house in a town near the capital and told me that señor Chavez had paid the rent on the house for two whole months for me, and gave me some clothes that were bought for me specially. Then he took me to the job señor Chavez arranged for me in the mailroom of his company. The assistant said, "It is better if you do not try to contact señor Chavez; he will come find you," so I obeyed.

I learned to ride the bus between my new house and my work, and spoke sometimes with an older woman there who showed me how to recognize the names of the people the mail went to according to the shape of the letters on the envelopes, and one day because I thought we were becoming friends I told her that señor Chavez himself had given me this important job in his business. But she only looked at me and at my big belly for a long time before she began to laugh in a cruel manner and said that this business belonged to the father of señor Chavez's wife, and that if I wanted to keep my job I had better not tell anyone else how I got the work, especially since señor Chavez himself didn't have a job there anymore.

When I heard that, even though I had been told not to, I immediately went to find him and although I looked all over the city, walking through the neighborhoods for many hours every day after work, even when I had to do so with my daughter tied to my back, I never could find again the house where we lived together. Finally, instead, I just stayed late into the evening at work, where he might think to come for me, and went home every evening to the house he arranged for me. Even though, at many times, the rent here has been very hard to afford, I have never left and I live here still, because on the day when he is free of that señora Chavez, when he can escape from that horrible woman who prevents him from loving me and finally is able to come looking for me as he desires, he may return to this house, where I have hidden a key in a usual place outside the door, and here I might someday be found.

* * *

171

My daughter, who is nineteen, lives a much better life than I ever did, and that is my gift to her. She will have all the chances I never had. Although most of my life is gone and the hopes I had grow smaller every day, for her there are still all the possibilities ahead that have not come true for me. Maybe she will be the one to live a lucky life.

I tell you the truth when I say I am every day full of confusion, for on the sunny days I still imagine possibilities and dreams for myself, but then like the rains coming I am surrounded by darkness and by clouds that soak these thoughts and send them floating away. I feel like a fool to have kept up my hopes. From day to day I go between these feelings, some days more than others. Like when my *americana* girl Elena, whom I really was so happy to see on her return this year, left me to go die in the hospital; I went from high to low so quickly. This is how the fate of my life has always worked. But I will tell you, what a surprise I got when she returned—a real wish come true—the first person I have ever known to return alive again from the dead! On a day such as that, who would not be left to wonder: "Why are there not things that I can dream of still? Might it be possible that there are a few dreams left that might still come true?" Even Sue Ellen, in spite of everyone plotting against her, still got Bobby. It is this little bit of a possibility, this seed of a hopeful idea, that helps me every morning to get up, and to make it through to the end of the day.

After Elena's resurrection I thought, "Perhaps some of Elena's luck will rub off on me," and I decided to try for something I always wanted. I wanted to have a Christmas party like they have in the United States and invite everyone in the town, so that people would come and see my large attractive house and watch me walk in my most expensive high-heeled *Dallas* shoes, and I could tell them about my job in the capital and introduce them to my *americana*, my friend. Then maybe, even just for that one night, they would all think of me as someone special, someone not plain like everyone else, and I would be the person I always wanted to be: the person everyone else wanted to know.

And will you truly believe it if I tell you that after all these years, I finally got exactly what I wanted? Elena made the food and so many people came, even people who had not been invited, that there was hardly room for everyone inside my house. People laughed and were happy. They admired me and my home and my things and my gringa friend, and I was proud. *I* was proud! When they made their toasts, it was to compliment me!, and even when it got dark and the day turned to another day, still the women lingered in my presence and treated me as a friend!

It is hard to find special enough words to say how wonderful this day was for me. I finally became the woman with the long table in her own beautiful house, serving pretty food to her happy guests just like in the pictures from the California magazine, the one that I rescued from the trash so many years ago. This must be what they call the American Dream, and here is what I think of it: Perhaps the memory of just one day, of one dream realized, is enough to cut through the coming of many clouds and give you a reason to keep getting up out of bed every morning. A single American Dream come true might just be the thing that gets a person through to the end of many other darker days.

9. Elena's Story, Spring 1993

It took some cajoling, but finally we boarded the bus. I paid for one whole bench seat for just the two of us. We stole off in the middle of the night toward a destination west, where the sun sets over volcano peaks and the chill of her dark departure causes bones to freeze, turn brittle, and occasionally crack. I had waited just long enough for the vertiginous feeling of fever and dehydration to ebb, and then we left. We moved again.

Cali and I departed Juanita's as soon as I was healthy enough to travel, heading into the indigenous region of the Quiché Indians toward the Pacific, deep inside the Sierra Madre range. We rode the 3 AM bus with the sunrise at our back, so the future of the whole trip angled us always into the night. We aimed for the little town of Zataquepeque, which my traveler's guidebook called "the gangland capital of Guatemala," where legend has it the Xequijel River ran red with the blood of Quiché warriors in 1523 during the first great battle of the Conquest. The native priests had predicted the coming of the white man with his government, God, and germs, but no one listened. They are unprepared still.

The windows of the bus, shut tight against the frost, hid most of the outside world, revealing only the smoggy, condensed breath of almost ninety people and assorted fowl chugging through the mountain passes, crammed into a space which clearly said "Capacity 45 Passengers" in English at the front of the aisle. Guatemala's public bus system operates discarded U.S. school buses, long past their prime, unfit to pass rigorous testing requirements in the States and sold for a pittance across the border. Few remnants stand more ridiculous sentinel to the vehicles' previous use than the capacity sign, followed by a list of conduct rules for grade-schoolers including such niceties as, "Do not stand while the bus is in motion," and "Do not open the rear door except in an emergency."

Passengers crammed three wide adult butts into every bench-seat-built-for-two with the overflow standing sandwiched in the aisle, while at least five men hung in a one-armed death sling out the open emergency exit, suspended over the roaring-past asphalt highway in a half doze, accustomed to the position. An old woman split the standing-room-only crowd with her gangrenous leg, perched on the knee of a stranger across the row. A pus puddle collected on the floor.

I paid for the privilege and meant to keep one whole seat to ourselves. (This came to be my dream, living in the highlands, a bus seat alone, nothing more.) But I caved, as always, when we breached capacity and the woman with the soulful eyes and the baby and the other child stared at me and I heard her thinking, "Who will the gringa pick, my family or the dog?" Guilt squished me and gave her space. So instead of two we sat five to the seat: Cali pressed against the wall by the window—part on the seat, part on me, part on the floor with her head hanging over the seatback in front of us—the woman whose clothes smelled of smoky fires in cramped mud huts with a baby on her back and another standing squashed between her knees, and me in the middle of it all. We breathed in each other's humid air, and when the baby peed it oozed through the blanket onto the mother's skin and mine, so the scent of pus and piss and unclean teeth soaked us all with a fine misty dampness.

I smelled her hair, too, pitch black and pulled tight in a braid slung down her back like a horse's mane. It smelled like her skin looked, wind-whipped and too-long cooked by the elements, a stale mulled wine. Every time we took a turn fast we lurched together, cracking our skulls against each other's temples, and she'd mumble a "*Disculpe*, 'pardon me please,'" but didn't care that her sleeping son drooled a long wet trail of mucus down my thigh.

We stopped in village after village as we climbed, and in the more populous ones the vendors rushed us with their goods. "Coca-Cola! Coca, Coca, Coca-Cola!" screeched the men who hopped aboard and scooted along the seat backs, clinging to the overhead schoolbag racks for balance. Coins passed in one direction and syrupy *bolsas*, bags full of Coke, in the other, with striped straws protruding from one end for sucking. They sold mangos too, green ones, and barbecued corn on the cob—not the sweet kind. When the bus pulled away, full of more passengers, the salesmen hopped out as it hit the road, but often clung to an outside window for that last bit of cash until they got dragged a bit and, risking injury, finally let go. I never bought road food except for the *mariñones* and the newspaper cones full of peanuts. Their roasted aroma seduced me so that I'd hurl my body halfway out any open window, in direct defiance of the conduct sign which preached, "Keep hands and other body parts inside the bus at all times," and I'd pay much too much money to the jogging salesman who always kept pace with the bus long enough to take my cash, but never long enough to make my change.

The woman beside me, with the smoky hair, bought a paper satchel full of fried *lengua*. All was well, I swear, until the moment she started gnawing on that bag full of tongue.

Cali retched in direct response to the woman's first mouthful of mouth, and I empathized with the reaction. Poor dog, she had ridden well initially, as I promised the driver she would. He looked at me queerly when I asked to purchase a ticket for her, and he had good reason. Only a gringa girl would bring her dog on the bus; the other poor folks would never actively choose to be near their dogs, and the rich people who might coddle their pets would never permit themselves to ride a bus. It took some convincing for him to give the dog a seat. Not that plenty of other animals didn't ride the bus: Chickens in mesh bags bumped along the overhead rack, piglets tied up in canvas and rope screamed from beneath seats, and the occasional sheep got lashed to the roof for the long trip toward market. But only Cali sat as a human, untethered and unpackaged, beside me on the seat. I bribed the driver into it, which is why we took the 3 AM bus, part of our agreement, so that no one of merit might see her through the window of his vehicle and chastise him for it.

In preparation for our trip to our new home, knowing we'd be removed from good food for some time, I bought a pound of mozzarella at the cheese factory and made us each two huge grilled cheese sandwiches before we departed from Juanita's house. I used lots of butter and bartered away a sundress for some leavened white bread. The cheese oozed a delightful oily goo between the slices. Cali ate hers fast but I savored mine, letting the warm melt sear the roof of my mouth just a touch before swallowing. We'd been deprived for a long time, and the fat felt so fulfilling going in.

You see, it wasn't the tongue that made Cali sick.

The first retch on the bus I took to be an isolated incident, but then the bad gas followed, redolent of grilled cheese, and I suddenly realized the depth of our predicament. Jesus God, the odor coming from her bullied every other smell on the bus into oblivion. She scrambled rest-lessly to escape through a door or window, to get herself to a proper place for defecating, but we were so crammed together she only man-aged to scratch me with her nails, drawing more attention. I tried to make her more comfortable, pull her onto my lap a bit, and in doing so realized—as my hand smeared right into it—that the seat was covered with a creamy brown mush that escaped her bottom with every loud fart.

It got worse, and I won't go into it, because the depth of how dis-gusting the morning dawned still distresses me. We couldn't move, and she couldn't stop. I had some pantyliners in my pack, but they proved as utile as the proverbial finger in the dike at mopping up our storm. I tried ripping pages from Dostoevsky's *The Brothers Karamazov*, cup-ping them in my hands beneath her before hurling the whole mess out the window, but my little bowls filled too quickly and I couldn't tear fast enough. It kept coming.

The woman with the baby and the child somehow wiggled her way away from us. Windows opened, heads hung out, and men tied their shirts about their faces to sit barechested in the windy cold breathing their own perspiration instead of the scent of us. Everyone glared and though I did everything I could it made no difference. I finally even prayed to the saints whose Mass card pictures plastered the windshield and the roof beside the buxom truck-flap-lady stickers, but the saints ignored me and helped Cali not one bit. It was the first time I wished her away from me, so I ruefully rode the rest of the way covered in equal parts guilt and diarrhea.

The fleeting sentiment spooked me; it reminded me too much of our familial tendency toward dogs. Pets were beloved foreigners in my childhood home, who most frequently failed to assimilate in spite of our highest hopes. My mother was an avowed indifferent who birthed three animal aficionados, which estranged her from her children at times, so in moments of weakness she routinely allowed us a pound-picked pup but returned it a few weeks later when it chewed holes in our socks and teethed on electric cords. Her best intentions bruised us, and the greatest torture of my youth was watching my mother haul the endless retinue of unpopular puppies, with their abominable behaviors, away from our home and back to the pound so they could become someone else's problem.

Whatever happened now, I would stand by my dog.

And, oh!—did I ever take it for her! When we finally stopped, the whole lot of riders sprung from the bus, sliding and slipping on the sewage that had seeped across the floor as we inclined up into the mountains. A few women fell and came up wet. Two bags of fruit for market sale dripped brown liquid waste. I was the last one off, Cali behind me, but the whole group ganged me before I hopped down and screamed execrations and shook their fists. I threw my body over Cali's thinking we'd be stoned. (It happened, you know, to an Alaskan tourist in that very town a few years later, when someone's child disembarked a bus unnoticed and the mother insisted the white woman stole her.) I screamed out frenzied apologies and tried to be strong, but their fury terrified me and I started to cry. When I swiped at my tears and left a swathe of shit across my face perhaps they realized I was the worst off, for then the driver spoke in my defense and the crowd backed off, leaving us to dwell on our own ignominy.

So it is we came to live in Zataquepeque.

* * *

Had I my druthers, Peace Corps would have been a club and we would all have lived in the fort together. It would have been like an extended sleepover, which I've always enjoyed, or a delightful camping trip without the tents. This would have been pure fun. Instead, I went to my home alone and the house rattled around me and did not make me welcome.

Being alone at night has always scared me—perhaps the night part more so even than the aloneness. If something is coming at me I want to see it approaching, and rest confident that I can either handle or avoid it based on my ability to discern its presence. But night steals sight, and shadows envelope, and even a daisy might become some other pest hovering at my ankles. I always sleep with my whole body contained on the mattress, with not an arm, a leg, or even a toe dangling off the edge, for who knows what can move and hide in the dark that would never dare appear in the light of day?

As a wee child, before slumbering in my Philadelphia row home, I always pressed my hand to the wall that connected our house to the next and imagined those other people moving about inside. It brought me comfort to think that if something happened, and we needed reinforcement, I could kick hard enough on that wall to summon help. When we moved to our Virginia stand-alone house, and my sisters and I finally had our own private rooms, we nonetheless dragged our sleeping bags up next to one or another's bed and cocooned together for many years. College brought some reprieve: I am the only person I know who truly liked dorm life, for I could once again scrunch my pillow up against the shared partition and think, "There are more people, right on the other side of this wall, and someone else's sleeping head is so close it almost touches mine."

In Zataquepeque, my new cavern of a house touched on nothing and dwelled in shadows exclusively; my days in it always verged on the uneasy.

I have always been the one to pick the tiniest space, to cozy into a corner where my surroundings acquaint themselves with me and I can trust in the familiarity of that which encloses me. So the house I moved into is not the one I would have picked had there been any other choice. Because the only other vacant property opened into the neighbor's pig sty, and the pigs were a vicious lot, I moved into the huge house on the corner at the edge of town—the never-ending house. That is how it felt. The rooms were vast and hollow, good I suppose for entertaining (so when my American friends came to visit and we filled the house with celebration it finally felt warm and full and right) but for a party of one I could not stop the drafts and the wind spun through the mawish space sounding windy sounds and I could have been adrift inside and no one might have ever found me.

To mark off the paces of the enclosed courtyard was to stroll the length of a dusty, weed-crusted soccer field. The perimeter wall of thick mud brick reached high, embedded all along the top with shards of glass to keep out the pests and the thieves and the gawkers. It kept me in, too. I couldn't see over, and you may think it sounds like a jail but the benefit was privacy at last, a space where no one could see me, and I relished it, false though it was. Without the wall, life as a foreigner in a town not your own is to always be an attraction. I no longer think it matters, although once I suppose I did, how many years one stays or how deeply embedded one becomes in the fabric of a community. To be white where no one else is is to always be that flash which catches in the corner of people's eyes, and they turn and stare as if something odd has happened only to realize it is that bright skin of yours which captured their attention.

There is a white woman who lives in Zunil, the town of the eternal hot springs; she has lived there for twenty or thirty years. I do not know her name and have no association with her, yet once when I stopped there to visit the baths, as I stepped from the bus the townsfolk swarmed me and offered to take me to her, as if reuniting two accidentally separated pieces of one whole. Even she, so long integrated in that town, could not hide from the fact that her neighbors of decades thought a skin-same stranger a better companion for her than themselves. For this reason I liked my wall, because it hid the color of my skin and left me alone to my own normalcy. Often I closed the big wooden doors leading into the courtyard, which open allowed all the folks crammed at the front window to watch me for hours, and rested alone in the privacy of my yard. I trusted that wall, which is why its betrayal felt so personal, as if a close comrade led the sniper right straight to the door of my hiding place—but that is a story for later, as I have not yet finished describing for you the whole rest of the house.

Four gigantic rooms lined up in a row, each one with its own door onto the covered porch adjacent the courtyard—there you have it. Nothing special, adobe walls and a cracked tile roof . . . except for the third room down the row packed tightly with religious relics and icons, an altar and life-size plaster saints. The room had no light (well, none of them did . . .) but it felt more dark and more damp than the others, and although I am not a superstitious person all those sentinels to the dead and maimed had a palpable presence. I don't know what they were doing in the house, but they seemed to want me to know they'd been brought there under duress, and the first thing I purchased in Zátaquepeque was a chain and a padlock to contain the room's distress. So as I recall it, ever more avoiding the haunted chamber, my house had only the three more-than-sizeable empty rooms and a latrine out back.

I did my best to carve out little corners of domesticity. Built shelves, sewed curtains and matching bedspreads, used my hands to paint colorful dancing chair rails along the walls. Paid a king's ransom for the privilege of stringing a slew of extension cords from one of the downtown houses over the roofs of all the homes along the block, which ended in a dangling array of light bulbs and hand-rigged sockets, one per room, snaking along my ceilings. When the lights stopped working, as they did once every month or so, it less frequently implied a problem with the extension system than a feudal-forced increase in the electricity rent. The old bugger who owned the energy took full advantage of my addiction to an electric blanket.

Whereas the east's desert eves brought reprieve from the sun's daily badgering, the west's temperate days were swallowed into the gale of frozen night. With the sun went all comfort. Darkness brought the cold of stinging nose and numb parts, cold that cracks the corners of your lips and settles on you a sore throat and a cough that only abates between noon and three o'clock. The frost taught me to brush my teeth without water, for cracking the ice off the *pila* took much effort and though I did it once, the bracing rinse pierced my teeth terribly and required twenty minutes hovering over a fat candle flame to thaw and recover. I considered the electric blanket pure salvation. It was a luxury, yes, but one for which, had it been required, I would have eagerly sliced my own wrist and traded a pint of blood. The blanket kept me sane, and I spent all the dark hours, from early evening to late morn, buried in bed with a book and the dog making frenzied plans for all that must be accomplished in the short hours of sun-baked warmth.

In the afternoon is when everyone moved and shook to life, shedding the piles of blankets and sweaters and shawls which otherwise cloaked us all in a heavy darkness. Chickens scratched and laid all their eggs at 1 PM, which is when babies nursed and dogs fought, for the blinding smoke of crepuscular fires that otherwise kept us all defrosted abated with full sun. All of life happened after noon when we could see clearly and move freely.

The market took advantage of the fine afternoon weather and assembled itself in an open arcade two blocks from my house every Tuesday and Friday. I regularly ventured there. Market managed, in spite of its frequency, to be touched by celebration; at least for me, for whom the whole affair blossomed fresh with each incarnation. It represented a vital smorgasbord of sensation and a feast of human interaction—what with everyone focused so exclusively on taking in money I could often become just any other shopper to the equally homogenous peddlers. I might set forth to the emporium in ragged shoes and a mended sweater, but with the sun on my face and money in my pocket Tuesdays and Fridays were always good days. My belly would be full and my mind entertained.

The noise of every individual voice yelling out a sale, a bid, an enticing come-hither, built into a low roar that picked me up and sucked me in so that I could never pass an active market anywhere without popping in. The entrance typically ran a gauntlet past the poorest women selling *paches de papa* and tamales and any other hardened mush of corn and vegetable rolled into a maize leaf that could be fashioned fast and cheap for sale. I always bought a potato loaf from fat Lucinda, for although I plucked it out and fed it to the dog, I appreciated her gesture in always surreptitiously slipping me the one *pache* that had the bubble of pork fat bouncing in the center. She sat on the entrance ground with a few of her many children, surrounded by other women sitting, standing, kneeling, around whom I had to tread. I bought from Lucinda because of them all she never grabbed at me when I walked past. I thanked her daily with my purchase.

The women meant no harm, of course, grabbing at me for my attention. Only the men loitering on the streets meant disrespect, not just touching my hair and skin to test their reality but lunging for my crotch or my breasts to taunt me. The less ballsy ones, but nonetheless still crude, would call to me sick sexualisms as I strolled down the street. Once, in an effort to gauge the precise frequency with which this occurred, I counted the tally of crude gestures in a seven block round trip walk to the store. Fourteen different men assaulted me either verbally or physically (but this is only because I left Cali behind to get an accurate count, for no one would have dared touch me with her along). I understood this would happen, and it always did, when traveling outside my own town, but Zataquepeque surprised me in that it never ceased there, not even when I became well-known and liked. Except at the market. Such an affront never occurred there, for the market is the women's domain.

As such it swells with color, awash in the resplendent cloth *telas* for which Guatemala is famous, wrapped and wrapped and wrapped again around every indigenous woman's waist and tied tightly there with fabric belts. The colors announce the village in which her mother birthed her, and the bosom-embroidered *huipiles* tell the story of the town in which she lives. The shirts of Zataque grow a profusion of flowers, blue thread rimmed around a jolly burst of pink, yellow, and green. (If you consider Zataque to be no more than the cluster of dirt roads and decrepit storefronts, the whimsical design belies the general nature of the town; however, just out of town, where the pastures grow the deepest green and roll right up to the toes of the nearby mountain ridge, where the river sings as it saunters by and the trees curtsy and drink from its brook—this is where one might imagine the motif for the floral shirts rose from the bucolic land.)

Every woman has a special something to sell, on a table spread with another day's skirt fabric, and the aisles of booths brimming with edibles and material goods stretch long and far. I bought food for pennies, plucked from the ground that morning, and if I had been robbed recently I could often find my things at the market where it was easier to buy them back cheaply than to argue the nature of their origin. But I always waited to purchase these things to carry home until after I had strolled through the animal market, for this area most truly intrigued me. Out back, on the river's bank, the women held tightly to their tethered possessions. Donkeys brayed and pigs squealed and sheep and goats and cows stamped their feet and whined their fury. To wend my way through the melee was to always be stepped on or bumped by an indignant creature. Chickens, geese, and turkeys flapped like boomerangs through the air, flying for freedom only to bounce back to earth at the end of a length of restraining rope. I found most cruel, but also infinitely compelling, the sight of a woman wrestling a swine to the ground, where she would pry open its mouth with a stick so I and the others could ogle its orifice and judge its health and age by the nature of its molars. I hardly know what enticed me back there, where the animals trampled the riverbank and the refuse of the day got poured into the water's depths, except to say that the pungent bouquet of offal and discards and rot smelled real— not tampered or toyed with for my benefit—and so in the filth of the backyard market I felt nearly Guatemalan and very much alive.

"How much is this head of garlic?" I asked the shrunken old woman behind the table. It was my first market visit, and I had returned inside for food after inspecting the pigs.

"Ten *centavos*," she said. I fished for the coin and, finding it, placed it in her outstretched palm while reaching for the bulb with my free hand.

That quick she slapped it from my grip, knocked the garlic to the ground, tossed back my dime and leaning over the table screamed, "No!" in my face.

I spun to leave, thinking her a freak, when she climbed up onto the table, grabbed the back of my shirt, and detained me there saying, "That head of garlic is not worth ten cents."

"But you said it cost ten cents," I said indignantly.

"I know."

"So I paid you ten cents!"

"I know."

"So what is the problem?"

"You have done everything wrong," she said. "You were supposed to say: 'This is a rotten head of garlic!, the most rotten head of garlic I have ever seen. It is not firm. It is not fresh. It is not worth half what you ask for it!'"

"But it is a fine garlic," I said, concerned.

"This is of no importance," she said. "You must tell me I am a thief to think I can steal from you ten *centavos* for this lousy garlic, and then full of disgust walk away."

"But I don't think that," I said. "Your garlic is beautiful and I want to buy it."

"Just do what I say," she insisted, her voice full of impertinence.

So I said, meekly, resignedly, "Fine, I don't like you or your garlic very much and I guess I don't want it," and began to stride away.

"Agh," she moaned, "you are not very convincing, that is not how it is done, but nonetheless, okay, I will give you the garlic for eight cents."

Flummoxed, I reached for smaller coins, but her glare stopped me.

"*What* are you doing?" she asked.

"I am getting your eight cents," I said, frustrated.

"No!" she screamed again, leaning over the booth. Her eyes got big like she expected something more from me, and then she cocked her head, gesturing to me with her hand: Come on, play the game.

After looking at her quizzically for a moment I said, "Your rotten garlic is not worth eight cents." She smiled happily and I said, "I will pay no more than six cents for it!" At that she glared again, furrowed her brow, shook her head, and I said, "No, wait! I will pay no more than five cents for this measly garlic!"

At this she bounced back off the table gleefully and, turning to her neighbor, feigned a frown and bemoaned, "This gringa is trying to steal from me!, a little old lady who toiled all morning in her fields. She is criticizing my produce, how dare she!, I who have so little!" Her lament manifested such a heartfelt pitch that I became frightened for a moment, but mid-refrain she winked at me and set me at ease. She continued to point out to me my corrupt nature, finally admitting that she could part with the garlic for seven cents. I raised an eyebrow and reached for my pocket, but she glared, so I said, "Six!"

At that she shouted, "Six?!" and clutched at her heart, but ultimately said, "Fine, if this is how you are, and are willing to rob an old woman of a few pennies, then if I must I will sell you the garlic for six cents."

"No!" I yelled out, finally fully immersed in the process, but she waved her hand in my face, a friendly warning.

"Don't be greedy, girl," she demanded. "Give me the money." I waited for her to admonish me not to, but she nodded and reached for my coins so I gave them to her and she passed me my purchase. Placing it in my hand, she tugged me close, grasped my face in her hands, pulled me to her and whispered in my ear, "There, dear, now you have learned the proper way to buy garlic!"

* * *

I was the weekly attraction, don't you know?, and I am not so vain as to think myself more. I measure this by the hordes of children who awaited my arrival, by the general disruption which announced my appearance, by the farmers and housewives who ran to wave at me as I strolled past their farms. Even the young ones, too wee for school, chased after my path and screamed in high-pitched newfound voices the one English phrase everyone knows, "Goodbye my lover!" as I disappeared from sight beyond a hilly bend, a cornfield, or a patch of fog.

Each weekday I hiked to one of five outlying village schools and turned the world on its head. I arrived at noon, when school let out, for I could not bear to be part of the rote routine of the regular classes and I think it is not a bad thing for children to spend more than three hours per day at school. Arriving at noon allowed plenty of time for our group's class and some socializing before I turned for home at 3 PM when the spring storm clouds moved in. With luck I got inside before the rain came so I did not have to walk both cold and wet.

It did not take long to realize that more than a scholastic lesson would be called for should I hope to make any lasting impact. My mission, if you want to call it that, the thing I got sent to Guatemala to do, bore the lofty definition "Youth Development." My assigned task: to teach a generation of children the skills that might elevate their station in life. My assigned method: 4-H clubs, complete with parliamentary procedure and proscribed leadership tiers. My assigned accomplices: local representatives from the Department of Agriculture (the original one, in San Marq, I fled from, remember?, after he tried to attack me in the storm; the one in Zataque was newly arrived in town, like me, freshly deported from a stateside visit after being accused of rape).

The proscribed method never really worked for me.

185

Here is the thing with the Peace Corps, and success depends entirely on figuring it out fast and not being bothered by it: It will never be what you expected originally, and what you were trained for may not be what anyone needs, and if you can't adapt and learn to make it what you want for yourself then it will be nothing and you will not last. It is this disillusionment, I believe, that causes so many to leave, and resolves a few who stay to hang too long in hammocks and drink too much beer and turn the slogan "The toughest job you'll ever love" into a critique: "The easiest job you'll ever hate." But here is where things worked out perfectly for me, for I have never had a problem defining my own terms. Send me away, leave me alone, let me decide what I want and put me to it. Do not watch me, I do not need the guidance—I will set to it myself and like it better.

Even as a youngster I did not color most frequently inside preset lines; I preferred a freehand style or, even better, to construct a thing of my own imagining. There is a closet in my parents' house, full of pictures and albums and mementos, and attached to odd little contraptions are notes in my mother's handwriting that proudly say, "Ellen made this," stuck on with aged yellowing tape to a carousel built from a refrigerator box, to a spooky scene cut in a child's hand from dress scraps and reassembled with glue and a stapler into a Halloween decoration for the front window. I've always preferred to devise a way of my own invention.

So when I found it nonsensical to impose parliamentary procedure on a gaggle of children too shy to run for club office, too excited to sit still and read a recitation of the minutes, we dispensed with that notion and worked as a joyful gang. As for elevating anyone's station in life, that was not for me to accomplish; is this not more of a mindset than a talent? I might manage to teach a boy to sew a fine *bolsa* bag, which at market could fetch twice as much money as a corn or a lettuce. But unless I could teach him to think beyond the routine of rise, till, sow, sleep, rise, till, sow, sleep that has been the perpetual pattern of his history, I will never make a *bolsa* manufacturer of a farmer. This is where the children's needs and my own natural inclination bumped right up against each other and aimed us down a propitious path. I wanted less to make them master a task than encourage them to think creatively, trust in their strengths, take pride in their abilities, and invite initiative. Art had always done that for me, and it served me well.

Fearing reliance on devices that would not be available after I was gone and forgotten, our after-school art group made, found, or salvaged everything we used. Crushed berries became paint, the hard soil that plagued the fields (kneaded ceaselessly and mixed with just the right amount of water) became clay, and the borrowed ends of horses' tails—snipped surreptitiously while someone held out a lump of sugar—transformed into paint brushes tied with twine to the end of a tree twig. Yarn, widely available and very cheap, took on a thousand nuanced faces. We painted a map of the world, three people tall!, on the exterior of the schoolhouse wall. (While generally well received, this did cause some grumbling. "How can it be that Guatemala is not in the center?" they asked. "And why is it that you accidentally drew it so small?")

We staged art shows complete with prizes for most creative, most innovative, most of any and everything so that each child remarkably earned laurelled recognition and the reward of one plastic jar of U.S. bubbles, which brought endless delight and spurred an impromptu science exhibit. Parents began attending these festivities, lured by handmade invitations bursting with pride, and they all arrived dressed in their finery best, prepared for quite a momentous occasion. This we gave them. Those children who would not be club president vied for the honor of rising first to formally speak of the intent behind their artwork. They led their parents prestigiously through the drawing room, where pictures hung suspended from strings stretched from wall to wall, to the fabric room full of knitted scarves and yarn animals, to the sculpture room which held a collection of hard brown mud-made corn cobs, a holy and venerated symbol for the Maya. The children told me the story of God taking the corn and molding a man as they used their own little hands to reverse the process.

One of these exhibits corresponded with the week of my birthday, so the children surprised me with a cake. It is the only time I doubted my influence. Banking on what I taught them of innovation and unbridled thought, they made me a cake of their own design. No recipe-dictated confection for me! The result, which of course I had to eat, consisted of white bread cut into cubes soaked in cherry juice and mushed together with a dozen dirty hands. Spread in a pan with red Jell-O cementing the top, it would have been plenty disgusting even without the red gummy worms, bought for too high a price in Zataque, burrowing through the viscid creation. "Please share," I invited everyone, terrified of consuming the whole thing alone, so the parents and I all ate and smiled false smiles at the charmed children.

At the end of these events the fathers stepped forward and made elaborate, formal speeches about all the vast possibilities their children might aspire to, and I thought, "They get it!" The last man typically spoke too long, but we could not stop him for that would be rude, and besides he was invariably drunk and therefore forgiven. One ended his speech by somehow tying the yarn dolls to the establishment of world peace, and I thought, "Glad you got it, but now we're going overboard." Nonetheless, it was an uplifting, if unverifiable, sentiment to end on. As I walked the road home, alongside houses with paintings and models and handmade paraphernalia brimming from the window ledges, I knew there lived a happy child, full up for now with his own potential.

It was on these walks to-and-fro that I first saw Hermilda watching me from the windowhole in her wall, hovering almost out of view, her hawk eyes glued to me.

Her house sat just beneath the schoolhouse, on the lower part of an incline marked by craggy outcroppings of basalt and stone over which one could gambol on the marked paths, but which dropped precipitously otherwise. This intervening rock face bordered on disguise and enabled her to stare up at me with abandon. For the first number of weeks I might look up from a task in the schoolyard to catch a snatch of black-top-of-head bobbing below a boulder's rim, or a snippet of skirt whipping secretively behind the back wall of her house, and if I felt eyes on me I knew from where they came although I never responded fast enough to catch and hold them in the act.

While I became inured to the general stares of all others, the dozens of eyes that at every moment monitored my movements, Hermilda's spying spoke less of amusement or interest than stealthy subversion; she stalked me like a squirrel who has only her eyes to protect her from the loose dog across the street. This is unnerving, as you might well imagine, and I see now why the squirrels get chased. In fact, it is the very sense of imbalance which her ceaseless stares caused in me, the vertigo induced by my spinning to look always over my shoulders to try to catch her in the act, which likely tripped me up and caused the fall.

The kids and I had been dyeing Easter eggs, an activity new to them and cherished by me, which allowed for an exploration of cultural traditions and differences as well as a great deal of fun. Divided into two groups now, we initiated the hunt, one gang hiding, the other seeking, and then with all the eggs repossessed switching sides. It was my turn to seek. I led the giddy youngsters in a run through the schoolyard, plucking dull-hued but flamboyantly patterned eggs from beneath decrepit desks, out of cracks in the wall, from within the folds of leaves and the limbs of stunted trees. We came up one egg short, and searched for some time, until I saw it perched on a little rock ledge just over the side of the sheer precipice. The children yelled their triumph as I reached to retrieve it: "*Seño*, hooray you have found it!" and they clapped and their little bare feet ran to where I stood, but in spite of the hullabaloo and the pounding and the glee I felt a shiver and looked up and there she was!

Bent in half, leaning over the rock face, I saw straight down through her windowhole, where she stood on a stool to spy on me. Seen in full, she had a shrunken head look, like a face carved in an apple and set to wither, full of wrinkles, pinches, and sucked-dry skin. She yelped when I saw her, a tooth-free scream. Her shock shocked me and over the cliff I went.

Okay, so to call it a cliff is not entirely accurate because I probably only fell fifteen feet or so, but it was all hard rock going down and I am all soft skin, and the two were not meant to crash upon each other so fiercely. I landed on my back with nothing broken, though everything hurt and some spots bled. From below, looking up, the children's faces seemed so far away. Their heads hung over the edge of the bluff and their black hair waved softly in the breeze. Finally, one incredulous young boy spoke: "Miss, you must be more sensible. It is not a good thing to leap off this cliff. You could get hurt. But now that you have chosen to leave the game, may I have this egg you left behind?"

"Take the egg," I told him, and peeled myself up off the ground.

I landed right on Hermilda's doorstep, where I now stood. Because I presented myself at her home, however accidentally and indecorously, she had no option but to offer me food. "Would you like some chicken soup?" called the hidden voice from within the dark recess of the doorway.

Visions of chicken feet soup still haunt me. "*Fijese*, no thank you," I replied. "I am a vegetarian."

"What?" she called out.

"I am a vegetarian."

"What is a vegetarian?" she called out, again, still hidden.

"A vegetarian is someone who does not eat meat," I said. "I cannot eat meat of any kind because I am allergic to it and will get hives," I lied to avoid the feet.

At that her head dashed out from behind the wall, her body still hidden, her hands clutching the doorframe. "You don't eat meat?" she asked.

"No."

"You don't eat meat of any kind at all?"

"No, I don't," I said, afraid of offending her, "otherwise I would gladly share some of your soup, which I am sure is rather delicious."

"You don't eat meat!" she shouted with pleasure. "You are a vegetarian!" With this she clapped her hands and said, "Why, this changes everything! Come in! Come in!"

She tugged on my hand and pulled me into her cramped, dark room. "I am Hermilda," she said formally, "and it is very good to make your acquaintance." From behind her skirt she produced a tiny girl. "This is my daughter."

"Hello," I said, bending to the child, "I don't think we've met before," which is odd because I know all the village children from school.

"No, you've never met her," Hermilda said. "I kept her home from school every Wednesday when you came to teach, because I didn't know you were a vegetarian."

"Pardon me," I questioned, "*why* did you keep her home?"

"So that you wouldn't eat her," Hermilda said succinctly, then turned and headed off down an unlit corridor.

I trailed her past a rather large kitchen, with a raised cookstove and a sturdy table, into a narrow, confined room, a closet-sized space with a disintegrating adobe firepit that drafted through the sparse thatch roof. Soot stained the interior an oily black smear which slicked onto your clothes if you touched a wall. I ducked a bit to keep my hair from catching in the ceiling reeds as the dying fire coughed a sputtering poof. "Make yourself comfortable," she said, though I didn't know how until she removed a pot from the table-for-two, allowing me to take a chair. As long as I didn't move in any direction but forward I could rest my elbow on the table edge with my chin in my hand and talk with her as if we were not in a dungeonous den, as if we were sharing small talk, having a standard how-nice-to-get-to-know-you interchange.

"Hermilda, what would make you think I wanted to eat your daughter?"

"All *americanos* eat Guatemalan children," she said, shuffling around with the pot, whipping out a handleless knife, stepping on her own toes as she bustled about. "But not you, you no meat eater!" she smiled, "so I will make you guacamole."

"What makes you think Americans eat Guatemalan children?" I wondered. "Have you ever actually witnessed an American eating a child?"

"Of course!" she replied with verve as the avocado peel flew over my head into a corner. From nowhere a dog half covered in hair, the rest a scabby red crust, shot through the door, beneath my chair, and out again with the green skin without stopping for so much as a sniff at my feet.

"Now wait a minute," I said, and held my hand up in the air as if my extended palm could stop the nonsense. "You're telling me that you have actually seen, with your own eyes, a U.S. citizen chewing on the body of a Guatemalan child?"

"I've not seen it like that," she acquiesced, "but I've seen them eating body parts in a can." I wrinkled my forehead and shook my head, for it was too early in our relationship to contradict her verbally, but she saw my mistrust and so continued: "I went to Xela once"—a town not far away, renowned for its Spanish schools, which draw flocks of U.S. and European students—"and there I saw a white man, and a woman!, take two cans out of their packs and open them with a device, cook them on a little stove in the square, and then eat the canned body parts!" Some hippie travelers, too cool for the local fare, importing their own organic pesticide-free peas and eating them in front of everyone who couldn't afford them, I'm sure.

"Hermilda, lots of people all throughout the world eat food out of cans, but the cans are not full of children's body parts. The cans are full of fruit, and vegetables—and sometimes soup, like yours."

"That does not make sense, and you cannot fool me," she said. To prove her point she asked quite logically, "How is it that this guacamole"—which she placed in front of me—"that will be brown if you do not eat it quickly, would stay good in a can?"

Lest you think her a lunatic (lunacy being an issue we will shortly address), you should know her perception of cannibalism was not an isolated belief but one ascribed to throughout the years by many indigenous.

It all began, if my history is correct, with a kindhearted but misguided group of nutritionists sent on behalf of a U.S. charity to a mountain village not far from the town in which I first lived. Oblivious to indigenous customs, they offered a basketful of glorious food to each family once a week—meats and delicacies no one could otherwise afford—and asked only to draw blood from every child once a month to run labs and see how quickly nutritional deficiencies could be reversed. Grateful initially for the food, but soon misunderstanding what possible motive the foreigners could have for being so generous, some wise chap determined that the food was intended to fatten the children and the blood draws meant to slowly kill them (for blood that is taken is never replaced, you know, and if you lose too much you will never recover). The only possible reason to fatten a child you're planning on killing, like a pig intended for slaughter, is to eat it. Hermilda's creative addition of the canning process only built on a rumor long circulating, and a belief system forty or fifty years in the making cannot easily be dispelled over guacamole in one afternoon. "But do not worry," she said, "you do not need to make excuses for all the rest. I know that *you* do not eat children, and so now you are my friend."

Who would have guessed my simple distaste for chicken feet soup might someday prove so useful?

* * *

When I first met Hermilda she seemed a nebbish soul; by then she was no longer who she had once been. Life sucked her from herself. But like a child she was eager for new experiences, as if to replace all she had lost. In truth I had no better pupil.

She expressed great interest in the after-school class I taught, her curiosity and watchful eye obviously having extended beyond just me. "I would like to *learn*!" she said with gusto, and so I invited her along but, egad, No!, she could not do that. "My husband," she said, with a swooping gesture, as if to indicate he could be around, anywhere, omnipotent.

"What about him?" I asked, and she replied with a whisper that he would never let her leave, and so it is that I discovered her confined to the house.

"Then I will write instructions for you," I said, "and you can do the projects here at home." But, egad, No!, she could not do that, and so it is that I discovered she cannot read.

"Then I will stop here before I return home every Wednesday, and we will work on something together." Here, finally, we hit on a plan that worked.

So I started first at the school and then worked my way to Hermilda's home. We sat always together in the cramped kitchen corner, which she explained belonged to her, and the other, larger (nicer) kitchen, to her mother-in-law who lived with her. To my practical question of why they did not share a kitchen she responded with incredulity: "She would never let me work in her kitchen, and since this is her son's house I do not deserve the better space. This is because she hates me, of course, and I am very scared of her. But she won't come into my kitchen, because it disgusts her, and so I am safe in here."

Safe inside the gloomy and incommodious space, we spent our Wednesday late afternoons. I taught her first to spell her name and then to draw, to knit, and to crochet. She taught me to make her glorious guacamole, the ingredients for which are simple and few, but—as with my grandmother's mashed potatoes—I can never seem to mix them appropriately enough to replicate the taste of the original. I introduced her to the traveler's dutch oven, a big pot with a pan balanced on a rock inside that, covered and put to flame, yields a biscuit or cake or cookie, and at this the chef in her escaped and never disappeared again.

From the single pot on the chintzy flame came this insurrection: aromatic stews, roasted squash, pasta, a pie! (All these things you may not think exciting but trust me, they are!, especially in a land with no cuisine. Anything not involving a black bean and a brown egg is a revolution unto itself.) Hermilda blossomed at the end of a wooden spoon.

At first she wanted me to instruct her in this private rebellion but after a few simple lessons I left her entirely to her own devices. Her original confections so pleased me, and my enthusiasm so pleased her, that soon she set her full creative energies to the design of self-inspired meals for our pleasure. I stopped teaching her my artistic crafts, for what sense is there in diverting such bountiful potential? Instead, I kept her company while she worked and then ate and departed. Hermilda knew when to shoo me from her home, shuffling me out with an eye to the sun, so she could cook the beans and tortillas her family required. This left her time to finish her mundane chores before her husband or mother-in-law returned from their day out to cause her trouble.

One day when I arrived on schedule, the cookfire was only dying embers, and she greeted me with a parcel, a hand-knitted cozy covering a steaming and fragrant edible bounty. She had an idea. "My mother-in-law, she is at market in Xela today, and my husband is working in a field four kilometers from here. I think we have time to sneak over to the neighbor's and share with her some of my food." She meant to furlough herself for an afternoon, and took me to be a fine accomplice. We stole off on a back path through a cornfield, so as not to be spotted by spies and reported to her spouse. The storm clouds rolled in as we walked and offered some cover, for the light dimmed and shrouded us in secret. The cornstalks, too, bent to our service, and gathered behind our backs to shield our path. Only the bouquet of cooling zucchini wafting up from Hermilda's arms threatened to betray us, but the crows laughed a cawing appreciation for our escape and flapped in the air above our heads so that the scent drifted and scattered away. We moved undetected.

The neighbor I took at first to be an elderly woman, but she and Hermilda gushed so convivially that they had to be peers (and we know already I am not a good judge of age, for life in the highlands robs one of youth). They sat right on the ground outside her hut, for she was clearly poor and likely had no table and the ground in these cases is a fine substitute. Her clothes hung from her in tatters, sewn, resewn, and sewn again, but her face was pleasant and her hair combed. Hermilda uncovered the zucchini bake, and the woman's gaze said she had never seen anything so scrumptious. "I have a spoon we can share," she said, but not wanting them to lose even a moment of their furtive meeting, I jumped up and stepped into the hut to get it.

"No!" they both screamed and reached to restrain me, but I had moved with much zest and crossed the threshold before they could stop me. They lunged at me from behind, futilely, while a man lunged at me from inside but also, fortunately, without success. The chain, wrapped many times round his bloody ankle, snagged his foot and he landed naked facedown on the dirt floor, his fingers clawing at the earth. Only a foot or so prevented him from reaching me. Can you hear me screaming? Might the frenzy in my voice still echo off the mountain?

The neighbor woman brushed past me and said calmly, "I will get the spoon," as Hermilda explained away the human-beast chained to the bed with a single word, *loco*, "crazy," as if this would clarify everything for me. I repositioned myself in the security of the open air, and sat stunned. For her to call him crazy was a scary thing indeed, for

194

Guatemalan crazy verged on raging psychopath, the upper echelon of loony, many degrees beyond what I had previously considered nuts.

I first encountered this discrepancy one day at the butcher's when, in the course of pleasant everyday conversation while I waited in the store for a dog bone, the owner offered a solution to my rat problem. "Here, take this," he said, soaking a piece of bread in rat poison retrieved from beneath the meat counter and passing it to me wrapped in a sheet of newspaper. He said to stick a few pieces of the bread in the cracks in my walls, and all the rats would die, but I countered that there were many rats and perhaps he did not use sufficient poison. "No worries," he replied, waving away my concern. "I once killed two grown men with less than half of what is on your bread. Do not fret—it will work," and this he said in a store full of people who thought him neither wicked nor crazy, but only industrious.

There is also the tale of the man who needed to dispose of a dog who had begun attacking chickens, and pigs, then finally small children. He took his three *quetzales* and went to buy a bullet, but, overcome by guilt and fear of blood, he drank the money instead. He subsequently tried the rat poison route, which was in this one case ineffective, and in frustration he walloped the dog on the head with a piece of firewood when she meandered by as he was collecting fuel for dinner. This he thought had done the trick, for she remained unconscious in the road for many days, but then she walked through the yard one morning skinnier but alive. As a last resort he took the dog, a length of rope, and walked to the largest tree in the town square. I will always regret I did not see him coaxing the dog to climb up onto its limbs, for here he finally did encounter success. Aloft, he noosed her and slung her from the tree where she swayed before the assembled gawkers and died a hangdog death. This part I am obviously glad I missed. I think the whole affair insane, but while most would agree his methods seemed odd, the majority of the townsfolk thanked him simply for a week's amusement and never thought to consider him crazy.

Finally, there are those who, outside the course of regular everyday oddness, are recognized by all as not really normal, but still not crazy. There is an elderly woman who hikes out to the highway once a week and there strips naked and chases all the vehicles, until finally someone from her own town passes by and returns her home. There is a one-toothed man who lives at the local pub, smoking nasty cigars and telling stories about his conversations with women who morph into owls.

There is a woman who talks in a perfectly appropriate way if you stop on the street to chat, but who will reach into her pocket and hurl a slew of stones at every passing bus, chasing, cursing, and pummeling it until it disappears from view. Then she will walk back and resume her normal conversation with you. Everyone, of course, recognizes the special nature of these people and guards them more carefully because of it, but they are not confined at home nor chained to bedposts.

Hermilda's neighbor was still inside retrieving the spoon, so I inquired, frenzied, "Good God, what is going on here?"

"He's *crazy*!" Hermilda said again, as if I didn't understand the first time, which I didn't exactly.

"*How* crazy?" I asked, meaning, what has he done that would indicate he's crazy, but she replied:

"Very crazy." Spooky crazy, said her voice.

"Then why isn't he at a hospital?"

She looked at me, appalled. "That would be cruel!" she whispered.

I began to rebut, but then the neighbor returned with the spoon for us to share and I could not finish my sentence. Instead we sat in the dirt, passing around one utensil, talking of the weather and the size of the peas, complimenting each other on irrelevant notions, ignoring the fact that one woman had escaped from house arrest and the other guarded a nude man chained to her bed.

I have lost all sense of what crazy means.

But I do still recognize courage.

Sometime soon after that escapade, Hermilda showed up at the after-school group, sneaking over intermittently at first, but then becoming a regular attendee. In the beginning she took part in the regular craft class, then escorted me to her home and cooked for me as had been our custom, but one day the soup tasted too delicious not to share, and in the excitement generated by my profuse praise Hermilda agreed to teach the children to make it. Before I left that day, once emotions subsided, she tried to withdraw her commitment, but I held her to it and swore I would come next Wednesday unprepared to teach.

As the week wore on I thought of her and hoped she did not fret too much. When I finally returned she did not immediately appear, but we awaited her patiently, the schoolgirls and I, the boys having left: "Cooking's for girls!" We crowded into the elementary kitchen, a little lean-to apposing the schoolhouse, and sat boisterously on the floor around a firepit used primarily to warm the midmorning milk.

Hermilda arrived late, visibly shaking with fear, her countenance cowed and the vegetables dancing a nervous shuffle in the cradle of her skirt. When her face lifted and she saw us all she yelped, dropped the food, then turned and fled, scuttling back toward her house with frantic steps. I caught up with her quickly though, turned her around, said, "You can do this!" Holding tight to her hand, I coaxed her back.

That first time I provided the commentary, for she could not speak. Nothing more than squeaks and gasps erupted from her whenever she dropped a gourd or the knife, which occurred rather frequently. So I narrated for her nervous, constricted movements, further limited in scope by the group of girls in their flamboyant *traje* swarming around her. Lighting the fire, she set aflame her own hair, and then looked at me with a look of "I am dying here," but someone behind her beat out the burn and I made a joke at my own expense. The laughter helped. I described Hermilda's culinary skill and her cheeks blushed. By plying her with questions, I managed to wrangle from her in the ensuing weeks a few words now and then, until finally one day she spoke without my prodding.

Here I will skip ahead, and you can fill in for yourself the transformation that occurred. I will only say that Hermilda changed. Proof came when she let down the hem of her skirts, for they no longer fell all the way to her ankles, and you may insist it is only that she stood straighter but I will always believe she gained confidence-won height. You must believe me, she grew, she grew! She talked more, too, and laughed from deep within herself. Suddenly she told stories, and then one day she gave advice, which only someone sure of herself can do. At that, I knew it was time for me to go and that the children would be well served in my absence.

I did not cherish the final farewell, and I will tell you what I missed the most in the end: the day's conclusion. The end of the afternoon, when, full of good food and competent instruction, the girls crowded around her, and Hermilda became more glorious in their eyes even than I. I always hung back at that point, stepping a little closer to the door every seventh day, for this was the goal—to leave them to her and disappear. But until I left them to her care for good I savored that last bit of time, when the young girls massed around her and swaddled her in long-overdue adulation.

What a joy it is to see someone become the person a child believes she can be.

10. Hermilda's Story

*B*y the time I met Elena, the me I was in the beginning had almost completely disappeared. I went away for so long I even stopped missing myself. With anyone else who might remember the me of before gone, who will know the way I looked or the way I talked if even I forget? No one! So when I tell you the story of Elena I will also be telling you the story of how I came back to being me and learned to get used to myself all over again.

I had heard all about Elena before I met her. I heard her talking, talking, talking to the children, the teachers, and anyone she passed. She was always talking: "Hello to you! Good day to you! Goodbye until tomorrow!" Not just the people she knew. I could sit in my house and hear her instructions and opinions and ideas from the schoolhouse. Never in my life have I heard any woman talk as much as Elena. She talks like a man! Poor thing. Who will ever marry her? What man wants a wife he has to talk to? The other marital problem I see for her is that on the day she first came to my house to make a proper introduction I got a good look finally at the size of her! She is like a stalk of corn, a piece of maize, a not well-watered one. I keep telling her we have to fatten her up to be more attractive, but she just sips her broth and leaves the wisquil. She is a vegetarian which means she does not eat the meat which is good for the safety, but bad for her blood; it will be weak. What man wants a skinny weak wife? Everyone would just talk behind his back and say he was too much of a sissy to provide good food for her. Not enough of a man to make her fat. Otherwise she could be pretty, but she has too many sticking-out bones so I think it likely she will marry no one. So what a surprise she is still so happy!

That is the thing about her, the confusing thing, because who expects to find happiness in an old unmarried person like her? Happiness is the lucky child's thing, the thing I thought I'd always have because I was a lucky child, but then you grow up and it goes away. These were my thoughts when I met Elena.

When I was the me I used to be, I thought getting married would be the happiest thing. I loved my Papa and thought that to have a man like him all to myself would be the best thing that could happen. I did not like to have to share him with my brothers, my sister, and my mother, but because he loved me the most I did not have to share him often. He let me go to the fields with him and I got to accompany him on the trips he took to the capital and to the market town to sell our food. We also collected firewood together on the mountain. He tied the big loads to his back and the little loads to mine and while I followed him he taught me all the things I know and told me the stories of our ancestors that I still have in my head although there is no one to share them with anymore. My husband does not want my daughter to know them because she is a Ladina and has no need for stories of the Maya, he says. She wears the Ladina clothes and goes to the school where they make you Ladina and my husband says this is a better thing than a Maya and she is lucky to have his strong blood in her instead of my shameful spirit. To know this about my daughter would make my Papa sad I am sure, but I am not my father's daughter anymore. I am my husband's wife, with no other family, and so I do not think much on these thoughts.

To protect me from becoming a Ladina and forgetting who I am and where I come from my Papa did not send me to the school, but instead taught me all the things he knows from his own mind. Not just the stories of our people the Quiché but also the prayers to the maize for the good harvest and the way of reading the clouds to know when to sow and the use of the leaves and the north-facing moss for good health. He taught me not to offend the fire through waste and to respect the sun and because I did so it smiled on us and made our lives good. I was a child and I thought it would last.

In the year of the eclipse, the great battle between good and evil, the government men came to our mountain and said to my father and the other men that the land was not ours to use anymore, but now belonged to a man from the capital, a politician who got our fields as a gift from *el presidente*. "This is not possible," I recall my father saying to them, "for the land is for the nourishment of the people and the good use of the community and therefore can belong to no one man." My father who had never been wrong before was wrong then. The big machines came and they rolled through our *milpa* so that the corn we needed to eat in the winter was destroyed. With the rest of the community we went higher up onto the mountain, but the cold came and the food was scarce.

My father was a proud man who loved the land where his family has lived since the time of the kings, but the land stopped loving him that year when evil won out and the government men sent us away. He buried my brother and he buried my sister before he finally gave up and walked with the rest of us off of the mountain. And here is where the happiness of my life ended and something else began.

Our family's soul got left behind on our mountain; it stayed lodged there in its place in the main post of our house when we moved into a communal hut with ten other families. It had only a covering for the rain, no walls. We slept on the floor beside strangers who also came to pick the coffee on the coast because the mountains were not for the Maya anymore. It might have been like a new different community except we all spoke the different dialects so no one could talk to the others. So in the middle of all these people my family was alone.

Still we worked together because this is what my family did, we protected each other, and we picked the coffee from the sunup to the sundown—even the littlest one who stayed near us and added his tiny harvest to our load. If we picked all day without one break and if I could equal the harvest of half of one adult, there would be enough to weigh in at the end of the day to buy a bread and some beans at the *jefe's* store. My parents let me eat until I was not so hungry and then they ate the rest, but still my father got thin and tired, and it is only because this slowed him down enough for me to keep up that I was there beside him when he fell to the ground and shook, his head hitting my feet, on the day he died. His shaking cracked the branch off a coffee plant, so we did not eat that night because our wages paid for the broken limb and the wasted beans that spilled from his pouch as he died. My father's natural happy spirit shook right out of him that day due to the never-ending sadness brought about by our loss of soul, and although I lived, what little was left of my spirit went with his and I have always felt that we died together that day.

The rest that happened from then on just seems like the ending of my original life, and though it is a terrible thing to think of, because I was already dead I do not remember having any feeling for it.

All my family's money that we had earned and were trying to keep so we could go home after winter paid for the burial. It cost more than we had so even the future's money that we had not yet earned had to get spent and we owed the *jefe* very much work to be paid up fully. But without my father we could not earn as much every day and with some food added in we got further behind so that it seemed we would never pay for having buried our father in the *jefe's* earth. Finally the *jefe* said we used too much space, ate too much food, and did not earn enough so he kicked us out. Because all the money was gone there was none for the bus and we had nowhere to go. We spent the night, my mother and the baby and me, on the road and she tucked her body over us to prevent the dust from sticking to our skin. In the morning she waved for the trucks but everyone passed us by. We got hungry; when my mother's milk dried my baby brother began to cry. He cried until no more tears would come, and it was many days of my mother begging until finally a man stopped in a truck full of other workers going home and said he had room for one, no more, and she looked at the baby and she looked at me, many times back-and-forth, and finally she put her hand on my face and said, "You are twelve; not a child anymore. You must act like a woman now. Be strong."

Then she got on the truck with the baby held tightly in her arms and she went away. I watched after her until there was only dust and shadows on the road. I kept watching, all through the night, in case she returned. But I never saw my family again.

* * *

In all the years I have lived here, in this house, with this husband of mine, since my child was born, the first and only thing that changed was the arrival of Elena. Until she came, every day I got up in the morning and heated the café and wrapped the tamales in *tuza* I collected the day before. During the day while my husband was at work and my daughter was at school and my mother-in-law was on her excursions I did the chores of the house, always the same:

- Feed the chickens; collect any eggs; fix any holes in the fence if an animal got in there; clean any dead chicken carcasses and boil the remaining meat and bones.

- Catch some rainwater to wash the clothes in a bucket; set them to dry on the edge of the roof; mend any holes with my needle; collect the dry clothes and pile them under the bed of the person they belong to.
- Gather up soft leaves or paper trash from the street by the front door; pile these inside the latrine with a rock on top to keep them there for wiping.
- Remember all the things we need from market like gasoline to fill the bottles we light at night and matches and oregano and beans; tell my husband so he can give the money to my mother-in-law so she can buy these things.
- Cut the branches off the trees for firewood with my machete; chop them up small; stock my mother-in-law's kitchen with wood for her and then some little pieces for me too; make her cookfire ready for when she comes home.
- Pick the wisquil from the vine and the squash from the field; sharpen the knife to cut the vegetables; boil the soup; prepare the beans; cook an egg if there is one for dinner.
- Wash the pot and the plates and the knife and fork in the reserved water I didn't use for laundry; clean the rooms of the house; sweep the porch; arrange the belongings that got left by my family in the wrong places.
- And on some days, but not all of them, do some of these things: Put out the rat poison and collect the dead rats; repair the broken tools; heat bathwater over the fire for my husband and daughter and mother-in-law, then wash myself if there is any left; plant vegetable seeds; tie back on the roof sticks that came off in the rain; kill any puppies that got born.

These are all the things that occupied my days. I repeated the same things over and over again; I didn't even think about it. My body just went and did the tasks and sometimes night would come and I wouldn't even realize the day had passed. That is how it was and always had been in my life here until Elena came.

There was just something about her that right from the beginning made me behave differently with her than with my husband or my daughter or my mother-in-law. First, when she just landed right at my house all loud and alert, she startled me so much that I started out more loud and alert too than I would normally be. Second, she has the biggest whitest teeth you have ever seen and all of them are still in her mouth. Her wide smile makes you want to smile back at it. Then I found out she is a vegetarian which makes her unlike other *americanos* who eat children, and I was so surprised and relieved that I forgot very quickly how much she had scared me and I just wanted to learn all about her. She is the first person I have talked to for many years, besides my husband, my daughter, and my mother-in-law. Even those three don't really talk to me, except for my daughter sometimes. So Elena is the most exciting thing that has ever happened in my life for as long as I can remember.

The best thing is that she is kind to me and seems to enjoy my company. I like to listen to her talk when she tells me stories about herself and about the United States. She does not mind when I contradict her— like when she said the streets in the States are paved with tar and I told her that is not correct, that I have heard they are paved with gold. Even if she says she does not agree, she is interested in hearing my own thoughts, and asks me many questions and listens hard to my answers, so I do a lot of thinking when she comes to visit. Also, I learn new things, like how to put my name down on paper and how to knit and to cook by putting a pot inside a pot which she calls baking. Elena teaches me many things, and it made my heart suddenly remember the good feelings it had when my Papa was alive.

My Papa always said, "Do not just accept a thing for what it is but ask, 'Why?'" He said, for an example, that it is not enough to know that a seed put into the earth will grow into a corn stalk. One must know why it becomes a stalk, and how its growth reflects the will of the Mother Earth, and what manner of nurturing through prayer and fondness will encourage the many stalks to grow tall and fruitful and feed the community. He said, "It is the person who does not ask these questions and seek their answers who will have a hungry family." So I was a curious child, and my father showed great patience for my learning.

I remember especially the night my pig—the one I had been given by my father to raise and take care of—disappeared after the birthing and the weaning of the piglets. I asked my father where she went and he replied that with all the new pigs we did not need the grown one anymore, and she got traded for some beans, some sugar, and a hoe. I did not know much of negotiations then and I was very angry, asking, "Why did my own pig have to go away?"

My father did not ignore me or try to change my feeling but only said: "Sometimes we must let go of the things we care for and trust that other things will come in their place. The summer ends so that winter can come, and the old stalk withers so that the new harvest can grow. So it is we must not make ourselves dependent on any one person or thing."

It took me some time to let go of my anger, but in that way I learned to be accepting of the world and to be unafraid of asking my questions.

But then, there was a long time when my questions got put aside, when my father died and my life changed. The man who found me in the road after my mother left bought me a *bolsa* of Coke, and after I drank the whole bag empty fast through the straw he bought me another and also a paper cone of *mariñon* nuts. For this reason, and because there was no reason not to, I accompanied him to his town to become his wife. He paid for the bus fare and his generosity made me grateful, and also for the first time in many days I felt safe.

I know that I misled him, for I did not show my true nature on that trip on the bus. Due to all of the events that had happened and the shock of it all I did not talk and only sat quietly and let him put his hand on me, leading me in all the directions he wanted to go. I showed him respect because he is my elder and he is a man. I hoped my luck and my happiness would return with a husband. That is the last thing I ever really hoped for because soon I learned how things would really be.

As for these things, you already know how they turned out. My husband is mean. Probably because of his meanness he could not find someone who wanted to live with him and so he found someone who needed to: me. He lives with his mother who is old but healthy and is living a very long time, and she hates me and I am scared of her. She can be mean to me right in front of him and it does not matter, they will laugh, but once when she kicked the dog he told her to leave it alone. His house belongs to him and his mother, and I am the thing that is here to keep it neat, collect the water and the eggs, and heat their baths.

At first, when I did not know better, when I did not yet know how it was to be, I asked, "Aren't we going to have a marriage ceremony? When am I to bathe? Where are you going and may I come?" and other questions that did not even seem to me to be big curiosities, but only a way to understand the necessities. On the fourth day when I asked, "Where is the broom?" I only meant to sweep the porch, but my mother-in-law had enough of my questions I guess.

She spun around with her finger pointed in my face and said to her son, "Shut her up!"

"Shut up!" he said to me.

"But I only want to clear the porch for you!" I said.

My mother-in-law kept pointing at me and yelled again, "Shut her up!"

"Shut up!" he said to me again.

I started to say, "I don't understand what is wrong. . . ." but my mother-in-law started to scream and she smacked my husband on the head, one smack to one ear, one smack on the other ear that started to bleed, one smack to the top of his head.

All the while she was yelling, "This is my house and I will be obeyed, you stupid dickless wimp who cannot control the ugly bitch he dragged into my house! Act like a fucking man!"

All this she said while still smacking him, and he turned red, swung back his fist, and the next thing I remember I woke up on the porch floor when it was dark out with the blood all around me, and none of my teeth still in my mouth.

How stupid I was to think when I got on the bus with this man that maybe my father had to die so I could start fresh, so that I could be the new harvest from the death of the old stalk. But on the porch that night, in my blood without my teeth, I realized I was not the new harvest. I was the pig. I traded myself for two *bolsas* of Coke, a paper cone of *mariñones*, and bus fare. So I put the thoughts and teachings of my father far from my mind; I asked no more questions and only did as I was told. That is how I lived until Elena came and resurrected the teachings of my father from the closed place inside me where I hid his memory. Elena with her kindness allowed me to be curious again and to learn. She gave me something to look forward to, and what happened is this: I looked into myself for the first time in a long time and thought, "Where did my happiness go? Who is this stranger that I have become?"

* * *

They say that children are a woman's pride, but what they mean is that many sons are a woman's pride. To have only one child, and for that child to be a daughter, is a shameful thing according to my husband and according to his mother.

The main thing wrong with me is that I did not have any pregnancies for many years. My husband would ride on me every night like a galloping horse and still nothing happened. Every day I prayed for a child so that we could stop making the attempts at pregnancy, because it was an embarrassing action. The little board at the top of our bed pressed right up against the little board at the top of my mother-in-law's bed in our narrow room, so even when it was dark inside and she couldn't see us the movement rattled both the beds and she would sometimes yell, "Hurry up and finish!" or "Enough already!" The nights of the full moon were the most terrible though, because the light shone in and the first time this happened I saw her staring at me with glowing eyes and she yelled, "What are you smiling for?!" even though I never smiled now that I had no teeth and nothing to smile for anyway. After that, whenever there was too much light, I lay on my stomach with my face down so I couldn't see her and let him go in from the back.

I consulted with the midwife many times, and she brought me all the herbs to try and remedies for sterility. I did all the things she said and even more! If she said to mix a handful of the crushed leaves over my soup, I mixed two handfuls for extra effort. I said all the prayers, not only in the morning but also in the night, and gazed for an extra long time at the harvest moon and would ache with the need to urinate all through the night if I had to so as not to disturb the seed he put in me. I wanted a child very much so that someone would love me and so that my husband would not have a reason to turn me out. Any husband, even a bad one, is better than none.

During those years they told me always that I was worthless and that no one ever had a more useless wife, who could not even produce one child for her husband. Even though at the beginning I tried not to listen to their words, it got said so often that finally it just felt like the best way to describe me. When finally, after all that time, I did swell up with a child, I thought it was my chance to finally prove my worth. Even the ripping pain of the birth I anticipated so that finally I could prove my usefulness and capability. It was not an easy birth, with the feet out first, and then it was here. A girl.

The last thing I heard for some time was my husband's response to the news: "¡Qué vida más pisado—ni Dios me quiere!"

I bled too much to ever have any more children, and I think they would have just left me to die, but the midwife insisted on staying and unfortunately made me well again. During that time I only remember hearing my husband's words over and over in my head:

"¡Qué vida más pisado—ni Dios me quiere!"

"¡Qué vida más pisado—ni Dios me quiere!"

"¡Qué vida más pisado—ni Dios me quiere!"

Those words could have come from my own mouth: "Life could not be worse—even God has forsaken me!" and I knew then with certainty that it was my fate not to be good at the important things. This is the me that Elena encountered many years later, full of the shame of my sterility and inabilities, and accustomed to my role as the cleaner of the house.

As I told you before, I found Elena's presence at first to be very exciting. But once I became more accustomed to her visits I began to wonder why it was she continued to visit with me, Hermilda, when surely she might spend her time in a more productive way. I hid this question in me for much time, but finally because she showed great patience for my other curiosities, I decided to ask her about this concern. I still remember how we were on that day: sitting at the table, across from each other, in my corner kitchen with our heads bent down over the knitting yarn as I learned the connection stitch. I took a large breath, closed my eyes, and asked her, "Elena, why do you visit with me?"

She said back to me, "Because you invited me."

So I said back to her: "But from my yard I have heard many children and also their parents invite you to their houses, and you say, 'Thank you,' but do not always have the time to give to them. So I am wondering why you waste your time with me when there are other smarter and better people who would like for you to come to their homes?"

She said my name, then, "Hermilda," but I was still holding my closed eyes facing down, afraid suddenly of her answer. So she said again, "Hermilda," and in her voice my name sounded soft like a quiet song, like the sun from behind a cloud calling to the flower to turn its face. Then she put her hand over my hand and spoke these words, which I have held in my mind forever after: "Of all of the people I have met in my travels, Hermilda, there is none better or smarter than you. You have a good and gracious heart, and I am humbled by the great kindness you have bestowed on me, a stranger. You have a sharp and inquisitive mind, and not only learn quickly, but also have much to teach. You have ready and able hands, and in all you touch demonstrate great skill. I spend my time with you because it is an honor to be counted as your friend."

Who is the person, and when is the last time, that anyone said anything like this to me—to me, Hermilda?

If I did not trust her more than anyone I know, and if I did not see her to be a true and honest person, I would not have believed these words she said. But Elena knew more about the world than anyone I ever met, and so she made me wonder if what I had come to think of me in these years could perhaps be wrong. All through the rest of that night, and all the nights since, I let hers be the voice I hear before I sleep, and also the voice I hear when I rise again. When my husband or my mother-in-law says something cruel I do my best effort to close my ears and I hear instead Elena's words: Gracious heart, Sharp mind, Able hands, Great skill. After some time, it started to work, and in only a short while her words drew back the memory of my father's same words. The two of them together now sing to my heart a new song of me. It was faint at first, but grew louder with each passing day.

So it is that day which now stands out from all others, that moment when she put her hand on my hand, that I can look back on and say, "That is the day I, Hermilda, began to come back to being myself."

* * *

I have been busy making recipes from my own mind. My tongue has a good way of knowing when the tastes go right together, and with a thoughtful consideration of the combinations I can make even the normal foods taste special. The squash is a good ally that will adapt itself to the mixtures of different spices, and the fruits from the trees that I forage up the hill, beyond our field, yield great sweetness when put to the flame. I collect the food very gently and coax out of it with kind talk the best of its flavor. So while I cook I have a conversation with the materials and they most often answer me with a fine taste and it is as if I am not working alone but in friendly company.

I most especially like to do the baking with one pot inside another pot like Elena showed me. I first put the big pot over the flame, and on the inside bottom place three same-sized rocks to balance the other smaller pot inside. The lid goes on the large pot, so that the heat of the fire spins and wraps all around the small pot inside. This is the way to make the breads and the *dulces* that so many others think can only come from the big ovens in the city. The sugar cooked in this way does not bubble or get sticky, but instead floats in the heart of the food and lies on the tongue like a piece of soft melting cotton.

Elena introduced me to this way of cooking after I asked her one day to tell me what she does in her home alone. The week before as I watched her walk away down the road, waving to her back and calling *adios*, I suddenly wondered, "What is she walking to?" It had been so long since I walked down that road myself that I had forgotten its turns and did not know anymore who lived in the houses along its path. From the time of my girlhood, when I watched my mother leave, I have always been the one watching others depart, staring after the empty roads. I finally began to wonder what have I missed out on by always being the one who gets left behind.

I thought to myself, "What might the life of Elena be like when she goes away from me, and what I might be doing down that road right now if I had the life of Elena?" Here is the list I came up with in my head of the things I could do in a house of my own: get a bath with warm water when I wanted (my house would have water that came out of the *pila* warm); sit with the sun on my face for long periods of time; have a servant collect the eggs and pick up the dead rats; leave my hair straight down sometimes instead of always in braids; eat sweet *dulces* at every meal; stay in the bed until the sun rises; whistle with birds. The next time I saw her I asked Elena to tell me of the things she does when she returns home, the enjoyable things, so I could reflect on her list and test it against my own. She said: read books; take a walk; throw a stick for Calixta; write letters to her family; drink cocoa; visit friends; try new recipes.

"Recipes?" I said.

She explained that recipes are instructions for combining food to make something new and delicious. Suddenly she looked around my kitchen and asked, "Do you have any bananas and any flour?" and because I did she taught to me the way of making the wonderful recipe of sweet banana bread. I make it many times each week now, and carry the pieces in my pockets so that I can have a bite of it whenever I want. I make many other recipes too, that I design in my mind, and Elena says they show great accomplishment.

Now that I have this thing of which to be proud, and also have begun to ponder the question of where the road goes as it passes my house, I have decided it is time to make some of my own decisions about where I can go and what I can do with this food I create. When the sneaking out with Elena to my old friend's house was a success, I then tried visiting the school with Elena on Wednesdays. It was all very good and I had the chance to share my skills with the students. At first I worried they would not like me, but what a surprise when they gathered around me and gave me praise when they tasted my food! In spite of my nervousness, it was as Elena said it would be: I was, again, after such a long time without feeling, happy.

What a strange relief to have found I am yet alive; I have not died!

For many weeks after that, I made my plan to preserve the me I have begun to be again. I will say that at the first, the thought of tying up my husband and my mother-in-law, like my friend chained up her husband, and calling them crazy, did appeal to me. But of course there were many problems with that plan, such as catching them and not getting killed while I tried, and although it was fun to think of I did not think of it as the serious thing to do. And although I did not like him, I will say that in those weeks of planning I came to think of my husband as I thought of myself, a prisoner to his own mother who then made me a prisoner to him. Which is why I thought to leave her out of it, and let her believe that nothing had changed, so that she would leave him free to let me be. I thought on my plan for many weeks; when I finally got the courage I needed, it was many more weeks still before the right moment came.

In the end, I only talked to him. Do not forget, though, that it had been some years since we spoke to each other more than a few words, so talking alone was enough of a surprise. I had my speech and I made it just the way I planned, with my face set in just the way I hoped to hold it to hide the fear. Throughout it all I kept my hand with the knife in my pocket in case I needed it, and it gave me strength even though I had no use for it in the end. I waited until my daughter was in school, and my mother-in-law was at the market. My husband returned from the field early to fix the lace in his shoe that I had cut through the night before. When he arrived, and sat on the bed to restring his shoe, here is what I said.

I said: "For many years I have been your wife and I have served you well. I know you do not like me nor think good thoughts of me, nor I of you, and that will never change." (As I had hoped, I shocked him with my speech, and he did not move to strike me in his surprise.)

I continued: "But no more will you tell me what I cannot do and where I cannot go. I will do all of the tasks I have always done, and neither you nor your mother will ever know that anything has changed, but when no one else is around, I will make the decisions for myself of what to do with the time that is mine. And if you think to try and stop me, or to strike me or punish me or keep me from doing these things, I will put poison in your food and murder you dead and your mother with you."

When he did not move to kill me or to respond, I knew he could see the me I was again and that I would be, in small ways, free. So still I do my chores and light my mother-in-law's fire, and I cook the beans and the eggs for my family with the tamales and the tortillas too. But for myself and for my class I make the new recipe inventions. On those days I work extra hard and fast at my other tasks, but this brings me some pleasure for now I do it for my own purposes. My husband still does not talk to me, and that is fine for he does not interest me, and my mother-in-law I no longer let myself hear.

But to the children, my students, I behave like my Papa behaved with me. I may still be my husband's wife, but I am also again my father's daughter and delight in sharing his teachings and his ways. This is the way I bring him back to the world, and also the way that I, Hermilda, return. Though it is perhaps only a small change for you to hear about, I am happy with all that I have gotten back. It is more than I expected, and that is more than enough for me.

11. ELENA'S STORY, SUMMER 1993

I used to think the earth would move when a government crumbled. The animals would run ahead—run for their lives!—and we'd follow the rats to a high place and contemplate jumping. I thought a regime's toppling would raise a mighty dust cloud to enshroud us all and drown us in a sea of disturbed particles. I thought we would all stand still and a part of us never again move from the place we paused when we heard the news; you know where you were, after all, when Kennedy got shot . . . Pearl Harbor bombed . . . the World Trade Centers fell.

Why shouldn't the Richter scale respond to a revolution? How can a despot fall without anyone sensing the reverberation?

But all began normally, let me tell you, just like any other season.

I opened the shutters one morning to a half dozen men peeing on the front wall of my house and an old woman crapping in the street in front of my door, and the only thing that made the morning slightly different from any other is that I recognized only three of them which meant the *feria* had drawn some strangers to town. Overnight the festival and its celebrants overtook Zataque. The town square had cleared of the women who amassed there every morning to share the water pump and gossip. Loose dogs got chased from their habitual beds on the postal steps, and the evangelists with their megaphones and the Mormons with their white shirts decamped their recruitment stations and scurried together out of the way of the workers.

A tent city sprung up in the open plaza in the center of town, a marvel of ingenuity and sheer unbeatable willpower. Rows and rows of booths (built of broken chair parts, firewood, and pieces of wall not entirely necessary to the integrity of one's house) lined the arcade, with rain-sheltering tarps stretched above tethered to the trees, the roofs, and the main electric cord powering the town hall and mayor's office. I worried that a good, strong wind would not only flatten the *feria*, but plunge us all into an ungovernable darkness.

On the heels of the tent city came the carnies, that odd assortment of gypsy folk and little people of the back-alley milieu with their universal siren call, "Step right up!" I wandered among the booths as they began to take shape, and from here and there a midget would try to trade me a pinball for some change or a man with half an arm would wink in my direction and lick his lips dramatically, as if perhaps he thought himself enticing. But generally I found them more amusing than threatening, and with Cali trailing me to snarl at their liberties, I moved freely within the walls of the burgeoning fair.

At one point I sat for hours and watched the construction of the Ferris wheel, which arrived on a flatbed truck in large chunks and was resurrected smack in the center of the main street. It went up in a surprisingly short period of time and stood fully intact except for one missing metal pin that caused the tenth basket to intermittently slip from its moorings and dangle precariously on the descent. Someone found a thick wooden stick that fit precisely in the pin slot, but when I noticed it tended to shift and slide I offered them my hair tie to fasten it in place more securely. So I feel I played an essential part in the grand ceremony that year, for it is entirely possible that my scrunchie prevented anyone from falling from the Ferris wheel to his untimely death above the city.

It took two full days for the town to prepare for the *feria*, and the emotional tenor of the townsfolk escalated in direct proportion to the public land space consumed by the carnival. When the day of the festivity finally rolled around everyone upended a celebratory glass; when the builders took breaks they drowned their thirst; when the revelers arrived, out came the booze to welcome them. So much liquor flowed through the town that week the streets became slippery with overflow. I hated to see the mothers drink with a baby dangling from a breast, but they kept time with all the others in the consumptive orgy, and I admit to losing patience swiftly with these intemperate, if festive, inclinations. One night, starting early and continuing too late, a drunk planted himself beneath my window to serenade the world at large with his plaintive, wailing lament. I stuck cotton in my ears, put my head beneath a pillow, then two, but nothing worked until I threw open the shutters and overturned a frigid bucket of bathwater onto his head, shocking him into silence. But he still did not move!, just sat there wet, and I felt bad briefly for it was a cold, cold night and the water would frost him while

I slept warm in my bed (but the operative word here is slept, slept at last, so my regret disappeared rapidly).

The following morning I awoke to the pummeling of little fists on my bedroom wall, and I rushed outside to find a mass of costumed schoolchildren milling around the owner of the apothecary (the richest man in town) who shouted, "How is it you are not yet awake? We are waiting for you to begin the parade!" They did not stay, but took off as soon as they saw me up.

"Bring your camera," the shopkeeper hollered back over his shoulder as he and the children ran down the street toward a mass of hundreds, or even thousands, of regional spectators and tipsy partiers lining the streets in prolonged anticipation of my tardy arrival. I dressed hastily and we scurried to our places: mine beside the mayor, and Cali's beside me. From our perch on the platform at the bend in the road we could scout the whole retinue of good things to come. Dozens of flatbed trucks borrowed from heaven knows where lined the street, primped with cardboard prop-ups and fabric skirts to represent "A Day at the Beach!" or "The Proud Maya!" Each float brimmed with adolescent girls apparently chosen for their voluptuous nature, costumed lavishly to correspond with the float's general theme, making "A Day at the Beach!" exceedingly popular. Flanking the floats were the bands—but wait, let me not get ahead, let me describe it to you as it began and meandered past.

The mayor, who had already begun drinking—or better stated, perhaps had not yet finished drinking from the night before—slurred his speech and then shot a loaded pistol into the air above the crowd. (Where do these bullets go?, the ones that do not come back down and lodge in someone's head?) The apothecary man pressed play, the tape recorder sent its music through to the bullhorns, the crowd cheered, the children marched, and we were off! First to pass our privileged parade stand were the bawdy boys of Zataque proper, transformed into an organized troupe of trumpeters. Every young man wore well-polished patent leather boots and a red and blue troubadour's suit complete with a gold waist sash and dangling tassels. More impressive, each one raised an actual brass trumpet to his lips in perfect time, and when they sucked in a collective breath as if to regale us the apothecary man pressed another button and the tape recorder sang out a majestic trumpet solo. The boys moved their fingers in time with the rhythm of the song and swelled with pride at the music which they were, in fact, not actually making. Only occasionally did someone accidentally direct air into an instrument and shatter the illusion with an ear-piercing and chagrin-studded screech. Trailing the boys came the young girls of the school, dressed to match in their store-bought color-coordinated cheerleader uni-forms, shaking oversized pom-poms in uncoordinated rapture above their heads.

Interrupted only by the floats and a change of costume, the school-children of the region sauntered past, grouped into unique color schemes and performance themes. All the decorated boys carried instru-ments: either trumpets, trombones, snare drums, or tubas. The girls played cheerleader, majorette, flag corps, or kick line. The apothecary man had the timing down perfectly so that he topped the machinations of the unskilled musicians with professional cover of their chosen instruments, and the parents and neighbors hurrahed as if many long hours of imagined practice had finally paid off in this public perform-ance. Sometimes the children lifted their hands to collectively wave at these family members, a teacher, or myself, and it smacked of surre-alism the first few times this happened, when their hands left the keys and the music continued, but even this anomaly became perfectly ordi-nary rather quickly.

I have always loved a parade.

The spirit of a showman hovers in me. Do not be misled by my dress and my hair which I tried to hide, tucking my slacks into the tops of my socks so no snatch of skin would show and pulling my hair into a tight, contained bun. I only outfitted myself in this way to thwart attention of a sexual nature, which in Guatemala proves dangerous and rather fool-hardy. Attention of any other orientation is never something I shied from. My feet were made to march, my chest to puff out; The Music Man has nothing on me—I am a girl meant to parade.

Sensing that innate nature, within a year of my birth my parents put me in my first procession. Dressing the crib as a meadow with wheels on its bottom and wings on me, Father pushed my newborn sister and me through the neighborhood streets where we won first prize, we baby butterflies in our nest bed, the stars of the annual Halloween parade. From there on out we promenaded in every advertised city parade. My favorite is still Philadelphia's New Year's Mummers Parade, which for years I did not realize involved me only as a spectator. My parents had friends who belonged to the corps and they stopped when they reached us, calling us all into the street with them, where we danced the

215

Mummers' Strut for a block or so down Broad Street, me thinking all the time we played an integral part.

So when an adolescent fake-majorette reached to pet Cali and dropped her baton near me I picked it up, joined the cortege, began a routine reminiscent of the time—before the flute and the marching band, before the pom-poms and the homecoming floats—when I took up twirling as a means to maximize my parade participation. I twirled and kicked and spun in graceless circles, generally making a stunning spectacle of myself, but my saving grace is that I can laugh at myself, too, and did so heartily while the audience squealed. Fancy fingerwork finished, everyone cheered, so I bowed deeply in reverence to their indulgence and rushed back to my seat content at having made their celebration mine also. Perhaps this is why so many took to me so easily: I am a person who will spontaneously join in your parade.

"Get your camera ready," demanded the mayor. "Here comes the best part."

Bringing up the rear, in the anchor position, roared a massive tractor, the type with tires taller than a man and a mean-toothed scooper in which a bear or two, or even three, could comfortably hibernate a full season without ever bumping up against one another. Pointing to this misplaced oddity, the mayor bellowed: "Here is our queen!"

One of the little girls in my Zataque craft class won the May Queen crown, which additionally made her queen of the entire *feria*. Some genetic anomaly made her skin too white, not an albino, but missing pigment just the same, and so she, like I, got loved for her pale skin and voted the queen of every year. There she hung, dangling ten feet in the air from the tractor grill.

She wore a poufy yellow dress, some American child's Easter outfit no doubt, which flounced around her tiny frame, this girlchild queen. What looked to be her father's belt strangled her middle, woven through the metal grating behind her and cinched tight to bind them together. Her little white legs showed all the way to the top, for gravity had pulled her body down and her dress up. One shoe had disappeared, with the left-behind sock threatening to follow. She looked like a bug, a mushed-up plastered-on casualty of too-fast driving, but when she waved, how they applauded!

The mayor halted the tail end of the parade so I could photograph for posterity the queen's suspension. Sadly, the tractor operator became overenthused by this brush with fame and the resulting photo shows only the child's startled head disappearing behind the rapidly rising scooper. This is the only picture we have because it is at that moment that I ran out of film.

I need no picture, though, to take me back. Every carnival barker since calls to me from there, and I could be a million miles from Guatemala but with a dart in my hand I am again popping balloons to win a tiny prize for my neighbor's kids who trailed me through the night. Now when I ride Ferris wheels (although I always skip the tenth basket; it has become a superstition) I look down from the top no matter where I am, and all I can see is Zataque; whatever is truly below me becomes all cracked tile roofs and smoky fires. When I bite into corn on the cob, there I am!, back around a soot-sogged roasting *comal* with the women who pinched me and said: "You are too skinny, nothing but bones! Eat, eat and get fat!, otherwise how will you ever attract a husband?" They put extra butter on my cob and a dash of something flavorful to make me *spicy* (they said with a smirk), and the result is that I can no longer eat corn unless it is drenched in lime and chile powder.

And when I tell children stories now I hold them close, forgetting sometimes that I no longer need to keep them warm.

"Where are your shoes?" I wondered, standing in the circle of my tiny admirers. The nights still fell frosty cold, yet the visiting village children persisted in running around barefoot; this, when I had seen them all wearing shoes during the parade.

They shivered, but the shivering didn't dim their delight. "We don't have shoes," one little girl said.

"I know you didn't have shoes before," I replied, "but I saw you all wearing shoes in the parade today."

"Oh, *seño*," the oldest boy responded, "those are not shoes for wearing. Those are shoes for marching in the parade."

"But shoes are shoes," I theorized, "and it's cold, so why aren't you wearing them?"

"Because if we wore them every day," he said, speaking more loudly and enunciating emphatically, clearly thinking I was a bit dense, "then they would not look good for the parade, and our parents would be embarrassed by us."

Before I could respond, he rushed on. "And we did look good, didn't we?!"

Yes, I said, they did.

And the *feria* was great fun!

Yes, I said, it was.

And there has never been a more exciting festival!

Well, I said, actually . . . there is Easter in Antigua.

"Where is Antigua?" asked a wee boy, and I told them it is right here in their own country, in Guatemala, toward the east.

"Where is east?" asked a girl, and at that I gathered them to me, for this would be a long story. We sat together on the postal steps, removed a touch from the shouts and bells and barks of the festivities. I opened my jacket so as many as possible could squeeze under into the warmth. A few sat on my lap and the rest cuddled up close so we could warm each other, and Cali helped by lying across our outstretched legs and covering up our bare spots with her fur.

"East is where the sun comes from," I began, "and if you look at that mountain over there, in the morning, right when the light starts to show over the top, Antigua is the place the sun rests at just that moment . . . "

* * *

The volcanoes *Agua* and *Fuego* keep blowing their tops and burying Antigua in boiled air and lava every few hundred years. That's why Guatemala City is the capital now, because Antigua can never decide whether to live or die. Rarely is her antipathy more obvious than during Easter week, when all alive collaborate to gloriously document Christ's mournful death, when the streets themselves buzz in animated anticipation of the world's largest funeral.

There is something haunting about a city that keeps reemerging from her own impending doom without taking a single step to prolong her future life. Without rebuilding everyone simply reconvenes, and life progresses gamely amid the most recent ruins. For this reason Antigua strikes a chord in me, plucks the nerves stretched taut between my heart and my stomach, and I resonate with her resolve to get settled with the dole life dishes out. Antigua would not be so beautiful were she not so fleeting, and yet so eternal, did she not press on in spite of hardship, and in this struggle I feel her kin to me. She calls to my soul.

Antigua, too, you must remember, is the place I first awoke in Guatemala, the town to which I came in the night from the plane, and when I saw this country in the daylight for the first time it was from Antigua's doorstep that I took my first look. I found a handmade ladder inside the hotel that morning, and using it, climbed onto the roof where

I stood and looked out onto the life that would soon be mine. Because Antigua is the place from which I first ventured out, returning to her is always a homecoming.

She treats her drifters well.

Antigua is fluent in Spanish and German and English—tinged with British, Irish, and Australian accents—and she is boning up as we speak on the Asian tongues, for we have colonized her into an expatriate outpost. Most, like me, only linger, but others have come and stayed, becoming the anchors of her inhomogeneous lifestyle, pylons toward which the rest of us travelers gravitate for safe, if temporary, mooring. But Americans are her favorite (I say with bias), and proof is that Doña Luisa's is the hub around which she revolves.

Doña Luisa is an American who for all practical purposes is Guatemalan. She owns a restaurant and the heart of every wayward traveler. In her rooms people find not only a hot meal but a boarder to room with, a school to study at, and if you are lost and someone is looking for you, Doña Luisa will feed you ice cream while you wait, for surely this is where the searcher will come first. (And if you have a Cali pup you are traveling with, the dog will eat banana splits beneath the table while you fill up on beans and eggs!)

Here is my advice: If you go there, go for breakfast, because the cinnamon raisin bread is finished baking at 10 AM, and although Doña Luisa has acclimated to Guatemala her recipe is authentic Midwestern American; unless you want to go to the Mennonite bakery on the other end of the country, you cannot get such perfect bread without recrossing the U.S. border. But do not think you will be treated to a taste of home here beyond the bread! Doña Luisa's—and all the rest of Antigua with it—reminds you just a touch of where you've been, but more so of where you are and where you're going. It is only a little bit American and a little bit European, but mostly, proudly, Guatemalan, so that without tearing you from your roots it invites your continued adventuring. Here is where you will dine elbow to elbow with foreigners and natives alike, where the indigenous woman and the British hippie will set out their wares together in friendly sidewalk competition, and neither will the tourists be villainized nor the locals vilified in this most unique of tourist meccas.

This, then, is the perfect place to celebrate Easter. There is synchronicity in the act of honoring Jesus here, a man-God who, like the town, became the stuff of legend for dying a violent, furious death and resurrecting Himself to greater acclaim. So it is that thousands come, and me, too, among those curious flocks, all of us clamoring to see the grand theatre Antigua makes of His suffering.

I chewed my cinnamon bread with its plump, warm raisins, and sat for hours on the sidewalk edge of the street closed to traffic to witness the preparations. *Alfombras*, carpets they are called, materialized on the bumpy stonework roads in a slow and tortured manner, fabricated of dyed sawdust drizzled into prismatic patterns by hundreds of hands gingerly maneuvering amid makeshift horizontal scaffolding. Every citizen competed in twenty-four-hour shifts, sprinkling the colorful wood shavings into designs that had been planned many months in advance: a dove with her olive branch, the scene on Calvary, the opening words to Genesis (and also a big white swan who swam her way in a circular pattern across the street; although I could not trace her to the Bible I liked her best). The workmanship progressed frenetically, for the carpets must finish in time for the first parade, but not so soon that their integrity cannot be guarded and preserved until the precise moment of their holy and predestined destruction. The result is that we tens of thousands of spectators squished ourselves onto the sidewalks, rubbing against each other clumsily in a calculated attempt at passage, terrified of destroying the artistry of murals that stretched for miles (winding through all the main and back streets where the week's processions would wend), careful not to trip and fall where only Christ incarnate is allowed to prostrate himself.

I'm going to trust you know the Jesus story: how He rode proudly into town, got betrayed, judged, thorned and nailed only to come back to life on Easter Sunday. So then you know the order of events. He rode into town in purple, for He is the King of the Jews, and His minions wore purple, too, the color of royalty. It all began at the great cathedral (you are with me, aren't you?, for we have left Jerusalem and are back in Antigua) where the horses and the men gathered inside—all of them, yes, horses in church!—and at the appointed moment, early in the morning on the first day, the priests pulled back the doors and the tribute began. Out galloped horses swaddled in albs, who bore on their backs only the lesser men, for the bravest, strongest, most repentant men carried upon themselves the body of Christ. But ahead of them all strode the priest, with his vestments trailing the ground, and in his arms splayed like God without the cross he swung incense in cradles of gold and his somber face warned: "Repent! Repent! The time is at hand!"

The horsemen, too, the purple prophets, swung their incense, so the myrrh smell confronted me before the men appeared, as did the sound of the funereal band. The music started upbeat on this day of enthusiasm, but cautioned in the long hanging notes of the saxophone that things would turn morbid quickly.

To see the daised processions come down the street each day was to witness the stations of the cross parade before me. The horsemen kept always to the sides, leaving the carpets undisturbed so the priest could be the first to put a foot upon them. He stepped oblivious to the beauty he destroyed, for his mind fell only on the Christ behind him. Christ carved in a sacred wooden altar floated down the street behind the priest.

Every day, each parade, has an altar that defines it (altar is the Spanish word, and I cannot find an appropriate English translation, so do not be confused by your own preconceptions—this is not the simple altar from the front of your church; this is a river barge sans water). On this first day, the altar-barge bore Him home, so I played the part of a loyal believer and welcomed Him back. Tomorrow would be His betrayal and I would be a booing turncoat, the next day His judgment and I a heckling accuser, for the crowd had a large part in the spectacle and I played along heartily. But today I cheered wooden Jesus astride his wooden donkey, His wooden hand waving at me from the wooden altar; tons of wood, hefted to the shoulder, conveyed with crushing agony upon the backs of a few dozen men. One man stood in front and led the charge, rocking his body left and right, the rest rocking at his bidding. With each swoop to the right they took a step in that direction, and with each swoop to the left they took another, so the massive motif swayed with a groaning creaking wail slowly forward. It looked to be torture for the men—how could it be otherwise? (To put it in perspective for you, imagine picking up a Greyhound bus and carrying it above you instead of riding within.) But as I understand it, they vied for months to be the ones suffering, to shoulder the Lord, for in doing so they paid their penance, wiped clean the slate of their souls, bought a year out of purgatory for themselves and their families, too, if they ached enough.

Stress can warp a man's perspective, and for the first time none of those remorseful, violet-clad men looked at me or in any way acknowledged my presence—nor that of the other thousands ganged beside me, screaming. Their sweat-stained suits stuck to them, their teeth clenched and bit out little bits of blood. Their eyes glazed. The wooden edges bore into their collarbones, and my neck ached on their behalf. Some stooped to seek reprieve, leaving the more contrite to stand tall and heft the extra burden, so they were not pained equally and the crowd was thus able to accurately measure the worth of each man.

Between them, the shirkers and the he-men alike, they desecrated the delightful designs underfoot.

Here is where things began to get weird, and weirdest of all, in retrospect, is that the weirdness crept into my life so insidiously that I hardly noticed the change. Here is where the bitterness must have begun, and it is only now as I lay the story out for you that I can trace its inception. When I write it all out like this, chronologically, what strikes me is that I am practically the lamb—I might have joined the parade myself!—who heedlessly followed the Lord right up onto Calvary. What the two of us didn't know, the places where we wandered and the betrayals we closed our eyes to, could kill a person. It got Him. I just barely escaped.

I woke up that night in my hostel room to find an intruder standing over the bed watching me sleep. I awoke face to face with him but not frightened (and that is one of the things that is weird!), only unsettled, and, keeping my wits, I threw back the covers and stood, saying, "Excuse me please," as I stepped around him as if he were merely my roommate, and he let me pass and I left the room. Some American men were staying next door, and they opened their door to me and let me stay there, after they checked and found my room empty with only a broken lock, for the voyeur must have left quickly behind me.

The next day I awoke feeling odd to start with, as you can imagine. Loitering before the next parade began, moving away from the crowd in Roman red and gold, those masses preparing to deceive the One who came to help, I strolled into a jewelry store. They do beautiful things with jade in Antigua, especially at Casa de Jade, where they sculpt little things like stone rings rimmed in gold, but also statues standing regally in the corners. Everything has a polished sheen that I love to touch, and the attendant kindly handed me a green heart pendant which I lifted to rub against my cheek just as the gruesome sound started. I thought at first they planned to brew me some coffee and began to grind me some beans, for this is the only other time I have heard a similar noise, but then one of the lapidaries ran past with a thumb and three fingers, a red bubbling fountain spurting from the fourth space, and I realized the beans had been his bones and the coffee grinder the polisher of the trinkets I fondled in my palm.

I froze. Someone pulled me out of the way in time, so the crazed man did not flatten me as he fled through the door, but still some of his blood got on me, crimson polka dots on my white shirt. I didn't even notice, though, until later that afternoon. Later, when I reached out my arms to snatch the bleeding child, the little boy's blood had already gotten on me too, and by then I couldn't discern anymore whose blood was whose on my wet red sleeves or even whether any of it belonged to me.

It's all flooding back, but this happened first: I left the jade store, disturbed, and found a space to sit on the curb beside a little boy and his father.

The boy could not have been more than five. He wore a blue tattered shirt and his hair had a rumpled, uncared-for look. Nonetheless, he smiled brightly with white straight teeth, for he was a charmer. He had a little stick that he rapped on the curb in time with the drums. Then his twig became a baton and he directed the horsemen to proceed forward quickly for he wanted to see what came behind them. As he turned to look past me down the street his stick grazed the edge of my cheek, which could not be helped for we were sitting so close together. His father, who until that point had utterly ignored him, must have seen him scrape me with the stick and in apology to me, I suppose, punched the child viciously in the back of the neck.

He was a small boy and the father's arms rippled with power, so the blow sent him splaying facedown in the street where a horse reared, as horses will do, in an attempt not to step on and further hurt a fallen child. The father sprang forward off the sidewalk, embedded his hand in his son's hair, ripped his head backward and in doing so sprayed the crowd with blood squirting from a fresh gash on the boy's forehead. "Sit still and shut up," he said with eerie calm as he threw the boy back onto the sidewalk.

Have you ever been in a bad situation, a really bad one? For me it is as if time slows down, and I perceive everything I would have otherwise missed, and what happens in seconds is dragged out to minutes in my mind so that what was actually continuous action becomes a sequence of small vignettes instead. Two policemen stood not ten feet from us that day, close enough for one to have a blood droplet on his shoe, but when I looked at them expectantly they turned their backs to

223

the scene, continuing to laugh and chat together. I looked to the woman who sat beside the father, for she could have been his wife, and to the people gathered behind him who could have been his friends or family, but they had all turned stony stares to the parade, looking ahead and above, but not below. Their immobility said that even if the boy burst into flames right then and there they would not lift a hand to so much as fan themselves. Only the horse wanted to look and turn back, but his rider kicked him hard until he finally paraded forward.

The child tried hard not to cry; I willed him luck and weighed the danger of reaching out and touching him, gently. (I would be no match for the father, who could overpower my skinny girl frame too, otherwise my decisions might have been quicker and easier.) The boy moved before I did, though. The tears overwhelmed him and with an unstifled sob he reached to caress the blackening back of his neck.

"I said sit still!" yelled the father now, and in one action he did these two things: He whacked the boy's arm from his neck with one hand and clenched the child's whole head between the flexed fingers of the other. I looked at the father then, full in the eyes for the first time, and in the direction of his gaze I realized he meant to smash his boy's face onto the edge of the curbstone. No one else moved. No one steadied his hand. Instead the father thrust the child forward onto me when, at the last minute, realizing I was his only hope, I threw my body there where the man meant to split his son's skull on the sidewalk and caught the child hard in my arms.

I tried to jump up fast, to back off, for we had no other option, but the child weighed heavily on my chest and I couldn't get my feet under me fast enough. Expecting a fight, I rolled over onto the boy, thinking that at least then the blows could fall on me, but they didn't come and instead I heard a threatening voice. It spoke in Spanish, but with a British or Australian accent, and when I turned to look a tourist had jumped over the heads of the seated spectators, lifted the father into the air, cuffed him about the neck, and, suspending him overhead, said, "If you touch this boy again, I will KILL you." And he meant it.

We sat together in this way through the rest of the parade: the father, the man, me beside him cradling the boy whose blood and tears dried on my shoulder. We did not speak. When the parade ended, the father stood and so did the child, and the tourist touched me on the arm, a gentle kindred caress but firm, too, in that it said: "Stay behind. It is not safe. I will follow them and keep the watch." I never saw the boy or the father or the man again, and although the Samaritan's intentions were good he no doubt lost them in the crowd, or got shut out by their front door; at some point, even if he kept up an intent vigil, he would have had to turn toward his own home. I was left to wonder endlessly: Did we buy the boy reprieve or make his penance worse? Barter a bloody nose for a broken jaw? Is his beating now worse at the hand of the father doubly inflamed by those (by me!) who failed to hesitate and leapt to the defense of the child who could not be forever defended?

I might have wondered the same for myself. Put together (but who puts things like this together at the time, when they seem to be just odd coincidences strung along indifferently?) the intruder in the room, the chopped-up hand, the bloody beaten boy—they might have been signs. I wonder if, in retrospect, the world was not trying to say to me: "Watch out. Stay aware. The tide is about to turn."

* * *

I got robbed.

Not just someone stole my shirt . . . someone pinched my pots . . . someone used my brush . . . someone took my bed robbed, but *really* robbed. Of the important stuff. My own gullibility let the whole thing happen, too, and that is almost the worst part.

Here are the details in a nutshell: I came in to the capital to sign for some cash, money wired from the States, the end result of almost two years of grant writing that would allow me to turn the schoolchildren's art projects into teacher-training manuals for continued use. I needed two IDs to get the funds, my passport and international driver's license. I would need to hobnob a bit, and brought my best clothes. It was all in my backpack when my backpack got stolen.

I started out vigilant and actually did remain so, as I should have been, paranoid to be carrying thousands of *quetzales* in cash in my bag. Bureaucracy demanded the funds be issued in cash and deposited in my own bank, four hours away by bus. I skimmed a little money to buy passage on a Pullman, figuring this to be more safe than the school buses with the hordes all mashed together. I sat awaiting departure in the furthest corner of the terminal, at the end of a long row of empty seats, where I could scan the whole room and everyone in it alertly. I put the bag on the floor between my legs and wrapped my right ankle twice through the straps so it became an attached extension of my leg. (This description smacks of justification, I am aware, but I beg indulgence because the recollection still smarts—no, I'm lying; the fact is, it continues to infuriate me to this day, which is why I try not to think about it—and I feel so stupid!, I cannot believe I got bamboozled so easily!, and to soothe my ego I remind myself over and over again that really I did everything right.)

The lobby filled up quickly, mostly with indigenous peddlers heading home to the highlands. An older indigenous man with his farmer's hat and his weathered hands sat down in my row of chairs, about five seats away, with a map of Guatemala City upside down in his grip. He held it close to his face, for eyesight diminishes with age, and every few minutes he'd rotate it and try to discern the details, but never wound up with it right side up. He couldn't read. Most indigenous Guatemalans can't—well over 90 percent are illiterate—and even those who do read in Quiché or one of the other twenty-seven or so native languages often cannot read in Spanish. He looked lost and put his head in his hands, embarrassed, dejected.

I know what it is to be alone and frightened in a strange, overwhelming place. I know what it is to be scared in a room full of strangers. I could not help myself. I leaned toward him quietly, so as not to draw any overt attention to his distress, and asked softly, "May I be of some help to you?"

"Please *seño*," he said humbly, "I would very much appreciate if you could tell me, is this the bus to Huehuetenango?"

"No," I said, "this is the bus to Quetzaltenango. The bus direct to Huehue leaves from another station."

"Ay, *fijese*," he moaned, rubbing his forehead with his free hand and shaking the map in the other. "I am only a poor farmer and am lost in this city. This is not the place for me! I must get home," he cried. "Can you tell me how to get home?"

He turned the map so I could see it, his map of the capital, hoping I could point out to him the route to the correct station, but from five seats away I could not discern the tiny type. I shimmied over a seat, carefully, aware to keep my right foot dangling behind me, rooted to the bag. "Turn the map toward me so I can look at it more closely," I said, but the poor shy man only extended his hands with the map a little bit, and I had to lean in further, and one strap slipped from my ankle, but no worries for I had wrapped my ankle through twice and still had hold.

"Okay," I said, after studying the street map for a moment, "you are very close. You need to leave this building and turn to the left, then take a right on . . . " He looked more lost. He did not know right from left. He shook his head and tucked his chin into his chest; the only humane thing was to reassure him with a gentle pat on the knee, so I stretched as far as I could reach, torn between two purposes (do not ask why I did not drag the bag down the row with me; it was heavy, this was a brief interaction, I got lazy . . . I do not know). "Let me explain better," I said, and using my hands tried to point out his route, an action which set me off balance, splayed across the aisle as I now was.

Finally, understanding, he took both my hands in his. "You are a good, kind person," he said. "Thank you, thank you for helping a lost old man. May God bless you." He stood then and backed away from me, holding my gaze the whole way to the door, bowing and thanking me as he shuffled away, then quickly spun and walked out the door in the wrong direction without a backward glance.

Of the entire interaction, that sharp, incongruous end is the only thing that rang false.

I looked down. My bag was gone.

My decorum departed for awhile then, too.

It is a classic dupe—one person distracts, the other pilfers—and I made a pariah of myself trying to undo the offense. I punched through the doors of all the departing buses and yanked every bag from the overhead racks in search of mine. I kicked over all the trashcans and flung about debris. I glared immodestly at the urinating men in the restroom. Then I ran. I ran a few miles through the city, which I could easily do, light and unhindered as I was. I ran toward a safe place, which was all I could do; I had no money, no bus, no taxi, only my feet and they wanted to run.

The city exploded around me. It offered no solace. Horns blared, brakes squealed, people shouted. Their desperate maneuvers and the fumy stench of burning rubber succeeded in compelling me out of the street and onto the sidewalk, where I had just barely hopped when the sideview mirror of a bus whacked me on the head, knocked me to the curb, and returned my senses to me. The city suffered too, and required wise navigation. Riot-geared police crowded the main square, hedging in the student demonstrators and their burning bus. Traffic snarled on the thoroughfare, where some army men surrounded a dead body, rooted through its pockets, smoked its cigarettes. Beggars clutched at my shins, but I had nothing to give them and could sadly, honestly, say so. I ran, ran, ran, choked on exhaust, startled at backfire, tripped in the broken asphalt, and cried my way blurry with shame and loathing.

"What kind of people are you?!" I screamed in disgust just before I fled the bus terminal. "What kind of people are you?!" I roared as I climbed onto a seat back and spun to condemn the crowd. "I am just a girl, alone!" I sobbed. "No different than any of the rest of you! No richer! No different! How could you all just sit there—" and here I began to weep, my whole body shaking at the betrayal, my shoulders convulsed before the stunned yet indifferent audience "—and not make a single move to help me? Is there not even one person among you with the courage to do the thing that is right?" I might have calmed down at that point, exhausted, but they all stopped looking at me right then and averted their eyes. They had done that to me before!, that is how all this started!, that is why the crime worked!, and my rage at their unwillingness to *see* me erupted, compelling my own wrongdoing.

"What kind of people are you?!" I snarled as I stepped to the floor. "Is it any wonder that the world despises and ignores you?" I did not want to leave without hitting someone, and my whole body shook with restraint. "This is a worthless country, and you!—" I said, lunging at the woman beside me, raising my hand as if to hit her, shoving my face up into her face and liking how scared she looked, how much I frightened her "—and you!—" I spun on an old man beside her, pointing my finger in his face, the rest of my hand a fist "—every one of you are worthless, horrid people. You should be ashamed of yourselves!" I screamed. I turned then and ran, as much toward safety as away from them, and further away still from my own worst vision of myself, the me I did not want to be, the me their fire forged and forced upon myself.

The entire incident is regrettable. My behavior made it no better.

I ran to be free of all that Guatemala had brought upon me.

* * *

We were two wounded waifs, me afraid of what staying might do to me, her afraid of what being back would entail. My running brought us together again, for as I bounded through the door of the Peace Corps office that day needing reprieve, running from the robbery, she sat alone on the sofa in the lounge room usually crowded by many. Claire, my first example of what my life here could be, the seasoned Volunteer I got sent to as a trainee—what now, a year and a half ago? She looked too tiny cradled amid the cushions, not the lionized Claire who gave me my first real taste of what living in Guatemala would mean to me. In her home I had had one final week to shed my novitiate skin, decide for sure if I were up to the task of staying, commit myself to going forth on my own. In my memory, in my imaginings, my mentor of a year and a half ago had been elevated to saintly proportions. The frail creature on the couch hardly favored the Claire of my mind's eye.

"You're back," I said, for she had been gone.

"You are still here," she said, for my staying power startled her.

I knew the bones of her story. The fractured word had reached me, on the *chisme* line that carries gossip and worthy news in a splintered fashion across the country, from ear to ear, from home to home.

"You don't look bad," I said, given her circumstances.

"You look terrible," she replied tenderly, noticing mine.

"I got robbed," I answered, and in telling someone I knew, someone who cared for me, my eyes rewelled, and in spite of the now trivial nature of my woes, I wanted to cry again.

"I got raped," she whispered, and the same thing happened. She looked at me through tears, so I went to her and, sitting on the floor by her feet, put my head in her lap, and she touched her dainty hand to my hair, and though it had been many, many months of separate living we found each other again at the necessary moment and clung together. I cried in her lap; she cried on my shoulder.

It is surprising that she recognized me so quickly when I ran into the Peace Corps office that day, for the desperate robbed runner I was hardly resembled the girl Claire must have remembered me being when first we met at her house such a long time ago.

I had my royal blue backpack with me then, not yet broken in, the straps new and crisp and the pockets untested, a different entity altogether than the bag which this year and a half later got stolen. At the beginning, the royal blue backpack and the royal blue sleeping bag, which still smelled new on that long-ago day, complemented each other, and I had chosen to wear the Laura Ashley dress and the matching hair bow for the blue-hued violets that made me an impressive ensemble. I wore mascara still at that point, and some rouge, too, for color, and my lips were yet unchapped, plump and red, healthy. I arrived an unknown, sent to Claire, the veteran Volunteer, for a week of on-site training. I smiled to win her affection as I put my bags in the corner of her bedroom, but she and the two other Volunteers visiting with her, a middle-aged woman and a youngish man, all looked back at me stupidly. They didn't smile in return at first, but neither were they unkind. What were their faces like? What's the best way to describe them? Here it is: They were riveted, like visitors to a park or a zoo where a small caged animal suddenly got loose from its enclosure and wandered into their path, spurring in these onlookers not fear (for the animal stood placidly) but a stare of dumbfounded transfixion at encountering a creature so obviously misplaced.

That is the look I brought to those three.

The ensuing silence almost turned awkward, but then the middle-aged woman said, "Everything about you matches" and I said—

"Yes, thank you"

—realizing only after I graciously accepted her compliment that she had not been complimenting me at all, perhaps the exact opposite, or at best simply stating an observance to fill the void. My ensemble did not impress her, it made her want to laugh.

The three moved a step closer; the youngish man hooked his finger through the strap of my pack and said—again, not a compliment— "Everything you have is new."

I followed his gaze, his darting eyes appraising the difference between my bag and his and that of the other visitor, theirs piled against the wall, bags and belongings I hadn't noticed in the myopic way of a newcomer, so focused on self and fitting in. But in his eyes I noticed finally what he and they had noticed at the beginning: their years-old packs with the broken straps, holes, and homespun fixes. Though Guatemala is hard on a person and harder still on his things, Guatemala did not do all that. Those packs had been on backs years before they got here, bags hiked into forests and other foreign countries, belongings that went camping and on other adventures, bags that found themselves tossed into mud, huddled against by hardy spirits who made good and necessary use of their gear.

My brand-spanking-new backpack practically stood up at that point and shouted, "Ellen has never done those things you have done!" My unused sleeping bag screamed in tandem: "Camping?! Do you think she's been camping?! Only if you consider hooking the trailer up to a water and electricity hitch at the Family Fun Center for the weekend!, swimming in the pool!, taking a trail ride!" Here when I'd spent so much time picking my equipment for its pretty nature, my things sided with the youngish man and middle-aged woman and said aloud what the older Volunteers thought: that I did not belong in this room, in this town, in this country with them. They came prepared, I did not. I couldn't last.

Then the tiniest thing happened to make all the difference. Claire put her arm around my waist and said, "What I wouldn't give for a few new things," making my incompetence feel like privilege. "We must be the same size," she continued. "You'll need something warm and I'd love something pretty, so perhaps we can swap some clothes while you're here." With her words, she dismissed my lack of preparation and found a solution. Nothing much, nothing I imagine she'd remember having done or said of any consequence so as to effect great change. But poof!—there went the spell of my inadequacy in the shadow of her tiny allegiance.

I could give back a bit to her now; we would serve each other well. I ran to the Peace Corps office that day to recover from my theft; the staff fronted me some funds to scrape by on, let me hunt through the lost and found box for some clothes, promised to replace my stolen grant money once I had a police report in hand. Claire stopped at the office on her return from the States, where she'd been evacuated for medical treatment following her violent assault. She needed to go home to her site, but wanted someone to make the trip with her. We fell into the agreement easily: She would stay with me in the capital until I got what I needed, then we would travel together. I would be her safety net and would drop her off on my way back to Zataque.

I got in line at the police station early the next day and again the day after that. The line of people waiting to report their victimhood snaked out the door of the building, down the block, around the corner. I fell in at the end of the line on the first day, and stood there in the sun leaning against the wall, then slid down the wall to the pavement, and finally napped on the sidewalk. I awoke to the doors closing and the people dispelling, so I came back again the next morning and stood in the same place. No one moved. Finally, at midday, I turned to the man before me, exasperated, and said, "I can't believe I've been standing in line for two days just to report a robbery."

"Oh no, *seño*," he replied, "this is not the line for the reporting of crimes."

"Ay, *fíjese*," I cursed, "I've been standing in the wrong line for two days?!"

"Oh, no, *seño*, this is the right line," he said.

231

I looked down at the little man, a bit older than I probably, but substantially shorter, his helpful smile level with my shoulder, and said, "But you just said I am in the wrong line."

"I did not say you are in the wrong line. If you have been robbed, you are in the right line. This is just not the line for the reporting of crimes."

I had to ask him specifically, "What line is this, then?" because he stopped speaking spontaneously and would not continue, as if his statement made perfect sense.

"This is the line to get a ticket that will tell you the date when you can return here to report your crime," he answered.

Oh my God. "I have to come *back* here, some *other* time, to file a report?" I moaned. "I've been waiting in line for two days for a *ticket*?"

"This won't work!" I ranted, "I can't come back here! I don't even live around here!" I got louder, switched to English, shouted to myself. "I can't go home without a report! A report is the only way I'll get the money to go home! I have got to have a report! Going home without a report IS NOT AN OPTION! I need a report!" The dozens of people in line before me, and the few who had subsequently built up behind me, all turned to stare, but the man at my side just shook his head in sympathy, rolled his eyes toward heaven, wrapped his arms around his sweatered belly and rocked himself back-and-forth, slowly, as if to say, "Yes, dear, you are not the first to have been driven mad by the process."

His looking at me like a lunatic shut me up.

"Okay." I said. "Tell me, how long have you been in this line?"

"Me?, only four days, but the man at the front, I think that this is his second week of waiting."

"Okay," I said. "And do you know why that man, who was at the front of the line yesterday, did not go away, but is still at the front of the line today?"

"Oh yes, *seño*. It is because on some days they give out the tickets, and on some days they do not."

Hmm.

"And if that man does get a ticket, telling him when to return and report his crime, do you know what the date on that ticket will be?" I wondered.

"Oh no, *seño*, I am not that smart to know this thing you ask," he grinned humbly.

"Okay, but do you have any ideas—like does he get to come back the next day, or the next week?"

"None of those," he said. "But maybe the next month or the month after that one perhaps."

I smiled back at him. We stood like two smiling fools tipsy on the folly of the situation.

"Okay," I said, just checking for sure, "but when he returns, on the date on his ticket, does he get to go inside then and file his report?"

"Oh no, *seño*, that does not ever happen. He gets to get back in a new line!"

That is when I jumped out of line, and ran back to the hotel where Claire waited for my return.

(Let me just say, there is something glorious about cloistering oneself with a person whose circumstances are substantially more dire than your own, which does not mean I had no sympathy for Claire or that I enjoyed her sorrow—quite the opposite!—but only that her assault softened the edges of my fury at my own predicament. I gauged my perspective, altered my attitude, against the measure of her experience. In tally, she remained significantly worse off than I. This calmed me.)

Claire hovered in that mental place of not really wanting to yet acknowledge she was back in Guatemala, smarting still from her break in the States, and I was in that mental place of wishing myself far away, so we settled on having a homestyle evening out to soothe us both. We planned a movie at the theatre in *Zona 9*, the big cinema with the Hollywood films some months late, but walking there I got a sense that the streets were not for us that night, not a place the two of us should be. There is nothing specific I can put my finger on to say, "Aha!—here is the pulse of my discontent." People were doing all the regular, everyday things. The habited nuns slipped us each a missal, urged us buy a candle, light the flame, erase our sins on the cracked cathedral stairs. The beggar kids lay on the sidewalk, pinching our legs and tugging on our skirt hems as we stepped around them. The hawkers hawked, the sellers sold, the rioters rioted. From the shops radios blared and from the buses exhaust spurted. Lights went on and off as people came and went, darkness fell, and candles burned to save us all.

Nothing unusual, nothing markedly different, only my sense of it, and when we stopped on the corner before crossing, waiting not to be hit, Claire asked me, "Do you still want to see the movie?" proving that she felt it too. I said no and without another word we turned and went in the other direction. Even the new McDonalds where we paused on our retreat, which should have been the capstone to our American evening with its American food, could not hold us, for when we placed our order and the lady at the counter asked, "Eat in or take out?" we said takeout simultaneously without prior coordination, and hurried back to the hotel.

The best thing about hotels in Guatemala is that if you search hard enough there is always roof access, where you can sit in peace above whatever is happening below you. We ate our fries and chewed our burgers there, with only the sky—which could have been the sky above anyplace in the whole world!—over us. With the smell of grease and meat on me, but especially on my fingers, I could bury my face in my hands and remove myself from this place to quietly contemplate a solution to my dilemma. I needed that police report now; without that report I could not replace my money, I could not buy passage home.

Claire sat calmly near me, where our separate thoughts consumed us in the safety of our shared presence, until she broke the silent reverie with a statement:

"It was a policeman."

Saying it deflated her, for as I lifted my face from my palms and watched her through the crevices my splayed fingers made, her bones went limp and she melted onto the shingles until she pliantly lay like a balloon that all the air has abruptly oozed out of.

"It was a policeman," she said again, in a tone which called for a reaction, and though I did not yet know of what we spoke I laid myself beside her, staring up into the black space, as if to say, "I am with you."

When she said it again, for the third time, "It was a policeman," I caught on and knew where we were going. I slowly extended my hand so that it covered hers, wrapping my fingers around her palm, making a nest for her hand to rest in. I could not go all the way there with her; I could not go back or change a thing to keep her safe. So I did all I could do: I held her hand, kept her warm, and anchored her down through this return journey.

It was a policeman. He asked her to step outside of the crowded market, as if he were protecting her from some covert danger, and, turning the empty corner with her, put his gun to her forehead and that is how it happened. On the ground, where the animals fuck.

I kept my hand steady through the whole story, which took concentration, neither grasping her too hard nor failing to hold her strongly

234

enough. When the part came where he shot the gun I did not startle, but kept my hand still and my pulse stable so that with my body, if not my words, she could sense that it did not shock me and I would not question or judge or label, and she could be scared now for my support would be unwavering. We could hold hands on the roof beneath the black, black sky for as long as she needed.

I do not remember moving back inside, but we did, to our own separate beds full of fleas and scabies that would require special creams to rid from our bodies, but that is okay, these are the easy illnesses to eliminate. Fleas only crawl on the surface, scabies only get just under the skin. It is the deeper hurts that a pill or a potion cannot prevent. As I lay there, slapping at the bites and scratching the itches, I remember how I thought, a long time ago, that these situations could not be real. In training, they described the illnesses and the affronts to which we would be subjected, and I thought, as did the rest of us I'm sure, "No way, none of that will ever happen to me!" When the director said, in his portentous voice, as he rattled off the list of things—of horrors!—that might come, "You should know, going in, that we will do everything we can to assist you if you are harmed, but we will not prosecute the offense nor in any way support you if you attempt to do so," I bristled at the aberrational nature of his comments, but let the feeling go because it could never apply to me.

What a shock to be one of the ones of whom he spoke.

Lying in the bed, scratching the fleas, listening to us breathe after the robbery and the rape, trying to hold our lungs to a steady pattern so as not to lose control of other more important things, I let go fully of my contempt for his remark and realized, in fact, that he did know better, right from the beginning. Bad enough to stand in line endlessly to report a theft; imagine waiting post-rape with a bruised and bloody bottom to get a ticket to get back in line to report the offense, perhaps, in the long run, to the cop who committed the crime. When the protector is the perpetrator, what option is prosecution? What recourse exists when gender alone is the consummate weakness?

Our minds meshed, or at least dwelled in the same depths, for it is then that I heard Claire cry, the first tears I knew her to shed that night, for the earlier account had been dry eyed and clinical. I slipped from my bed and silently slid beneath the sheets beside her, and, molding my body alongside hers, held my borrowed sleeve to her wet cheek and gave subtle company to her tears. Whatever hell the world was up to outside and beneath us, we would turn our backs to it and huddle as one.

That is how we slept, together, unmoving, through to morning, and when I awoke the solution had come to me.

Turning the tables could be as simple as turning a trick.

Were I to have wavered, the morning messenger steeled me. A coup had occurred overnight, the president dethroned; by embassy order U.S. citizens had to evacuate the capital.

I moved quickly, used the last of my loaned funds to buy mascara and other makeup, a whole slew of it, washing my hair in the sink and letting it hang down, free and wavy, no bun today. I cut off the length of my borrowed dress and with some thread and a needle took up the hem, and shortened the sleeves, too, so my shoulders would show.

"Don't do it," Claire said as I dolled up that morning, initiating my plan to return to the police station for the report I needed. "This is too risky," she insisted.

"I'll be fine," I said, and I suppose it is because she could not deter me with fear for myself that she said:

"But you have a responsibility as a woman, to other women, not to be what they think we are," and that stopped me, for it is what I had been thinking at first, and it is an argument that on any other day may have dissuaded me, but today, this one time, and only this one time, I had decided to use the system. Not buck it. *Use* it. To my advantage.

"Claire, don't remind me of my responsibility to the world," I countered. "I've been aware of—and met!—that responsibility every day. But today, I'm being responsible to myself. And I am getting the two of us out of this city. Wait here. I'll buy us bus tickets on my way back. Be ready to leave by lunchtime."

Having read this far, you are no longer naïve; have you already guessed how this got resolved? I knew the police chief, could tell who he was by his entourage, had noticed these mornings what time he arrived and so I knew where to be, which door he would use. I stalked him. Kept him always in my sight as he exited the car, climbed the stairs, reached for the knob, and at the last moment threw myself upon his feet, prostrated myself before him, conjured tears. He lifted me up with his hands on my skin and petted my head while I eyed him with meretricious longing and gasped out my lines in a husky, come-hither voice: "Might he help me? . . . I had great need . . . only the strongest

236

and most capable of men would do." The words reeked, but they got me ushered directly into his office as I suspected they would.

He let me put on my song and dance for the whole office crowd, the secretaries and the underlings who cherished their parts of big strong providers to my maiden in distress, but then the chief asked them to clear the room and this is the part I'd been waiting for, knowing it would come, and my heart pumped so hard I heard it in my head, the thump-thump-thump against my dampening skin, but I kept my voice even and my breathing timed, for here came the game I had to win.

"I was hoping we might arrange something privately," I said—and at this he grinned—"a way, perhaps, to hurry the system a bit, whereby I get the report I need, and you receive appropriate thanks for your gracious assistance."

He stood and stepped around his desk at that, clambered over a heap of paperwork by his chair, came at me past the collection of unremitted reports accumulated over the years, thousands and thousands of them, the carbon copies still attached, unfiled, piled in yellowing untouched towers along the walls. With one hand he reached for his belt and with the other he swiped from his desk to the floor the agonized stories of my predecessors, the men who'd been standing in line for weeks before me, but I rose then also and stopped his movement in my grip, saying, "I had something else in mind." Told him I had a friend, we had no plans for the night, did he live in town?, was he free to be entertained? He drew me a map to his house while on the appropriate form I filled in the details of my robbery, which he signed and stamped and from which I tore my official copy before agreeing to the terms by which we'd meet later.

Claire and I were back in our respective homes out west, unmolested, recompensed, hours before the appointed time, long before the chief even began shaving and primping for our spurious soiree.

If you need me to rationalize this for you, and I suppose, in truth, I feel compelled to do so, this is the solution that came to me while I slept, robbed and used beside a rape victim: My sexuality has and will continue to be taken advantage of for someone else's benefit, unless I decide to use it for my own. On reflection, although I do not typically support end-justifies-the-means kinds of rationalizations, this fact cannot be avoided: In the final tally, I got precisely what I wanted from him that day, and he got not one single thing from me.

(Oh, how I wish I could let it go at this! But my conscience nags at me. . . .)

Only on the good days is this the story I stick to: the tale of how one's greatest strength is using whatever meager resources are available. I can spin it a hundred different ways, and I still come out on top. But on the bad days the shame of it gets to me. Those are the days, although I try not to go there often, when I recall the feeling as I left, full of myself and my overt powers, new to the trick of manipulation and high on the giddy rapture of success. It lasted only until I stepped out the door, a mere thirty seconds or less, for in the outside air the glory of my ruse soured in the eyes of all the men, victims too, who maintained their place in line, waited their turn, met the requirements, and did not cheat their way through the door. Whatever swelled in me before I got outside dissipated in front of those men. So full of shame I could not speak, but knowing I could not leave without making even the smallest of reparations, I reached out my hand to the man who had stood in line ahead of me, who stood there still, and he did a thing for which I am grateful. He grasped my hand, pulled my eyes to his, and said with resignation: "*No tengas pena*, 'do not worry.' This is Guatemala. One must do what one must do."

The problem is, I could never adjust to the depravity so lightly. If you must know, it gnaws at me still.

12. Claire's Story

The thing you don't understand at first, right when a crime is committed against you, is how far out into your life the repercussions will keep extending; Ellen and I began to realize this at just about the same time, I think. See, at first you believe that if you can just get away from the scene of the crime you can put it behind you. That's why I ran from the rapist to the bus station, and that's why she ran from the robber to the Peace Corps office. We were both headed in the same direction, suffering under the same false impression: that just the act of removing yourself might be enough to save you and that you would be okay if only you could get away. (And in light of the fact that your ability to escape means you haven't been killed, I guess that theory is true to a limited degree, making you one of the "lucky" ones.) But what you don't realize in that first rush of fleeing a crime is that it is still stalking along right behind you. It is on your mind. It is under your skin. It has become part of you, and it alters everything you see.

I got on the first bus out of town after it happened. After I got raped. There was nothing in between that I can remember, only that he got off me and I got on the bus. It wasn't even a bus that was headed in the right direction, but it was leaving and it was the first to go, so I got on it anyway and changed buses later to get to where I really needed to go. In those first moments, I could only think about getting away, and I would have taken a bus to hell if it had been the first one to pull out of the station. But like I said, no matter how far I got from the town, from the market, from the rapist, from the act, it all stayed with me, and not just because I was sticky and bleeding and my wet clothes kept his smell on me.

Everything I noticed throughout the whole ride was framed by what had just occurred. It was as if I had blinders on to all the regular stuff, and what caught my eyes and mind were only other horrific acts after that. I have no idea if anyone sat next to me while I rode, but I noticed that before we even left town we passed a dead and mashed chicken carcass on the right side of the road. A few miles later, we hit a dog and he went flying, without one of his legs, into the dirt. I remember nothing about the rest of the scenery, but I know that halfway to the capital we passed some vultures eating the stomach out of a dead cow, and once we arrived in the city we got held up in traffic slowly passing the body of a dead woman still pinned under the front tires of a pickup truck. I recall thinking that soon someone would put up a little white cross on the side of the road for her, but I didn't yet realize the size of the one I was to bear. The sun may have been shining, babies may have been born, someone—somewhere—surely must have been falling in love. But to me, from my perspective, it was nothing more than a ruthlessly deadly day.

Other than noticing all the death around me, my only other focus was to get to the Peace Corps office. I knew someone there would help me. It took me seven and a half hours, traveling on two cross-country buses and three city buses, to make the trip. I kept thinking that when I arrived the security cameras, the guards, and the big steel gate would shut everything out and make me safe, but inside there were doctor's visits and questions and probes; the locks I'd been counting on didn't do a thing to prevent me from having to relive it over and over again. When the country director decided to send me home, to medevac me to the States, I agreed because I thought I would be safe there. It wasn't until later that I finally realized that I just took myself with me wherever I went. I could change my surroundings, but I could never seem to leave my experiences behind. Do you see? What he did, when he raped me, was oblige me to travel with him for the rest of my life.

Ellen got stalked in much the same way. When I bumped into her after I arrived back in Guatemala from my stay in the States, when I was sitting in the Peace Corps office trying to figure out how to get back to my site and she came running in after being robbed, there was already an edge to her that was remarkably different from the aura she gave off when we originally met. Talk about first impressions! Truthfully, Ellen was, upon her arrival as a trainee, everything you never expected to see here. I had heard people refer to her when she first showed up in country as The China Doll, but it wasn't until a month or so later that I met her myself. She got sent to me for a week of on-site training and it was hard to believe she had lived through the past month intact. She really was just like a little doll, perfectly done up and dressed up, everything matching, nothing worn-out. Most striking, though, was the look about her. She was so obviously taken with everything and awed by her surroundings, like a little bird that fell from its nest and stared out at the new view through big wide eyes, shocked as all get-out to realize the world consisted of more than a straw and twig aerie. As for me, since I was always the child who insisted on scooping up lost baby birds and trying to return them to their backyard nests, I had an overwhelming urge to protect her as best I could while everyone else quietly placed bets on how long she would last.

I have to admit, she made it an easy game for folks. The first night Ellen stayed at my house, after dinner with some other Volunteers I'd invited over, she excused herself to use the bathroom. Because of the water shortage, I have a sign hanging over my toilet, like most Volunteers who are lucky enough to have toilets, that reads: "If it's yellow, let it mellow. If it's brown, flush it down." So, when she came out of the bathroom and walked over to the *pila* for a bucket of water to flush with, everyone turned to watch her from the kitchen table while someone remarked to her that she should obey the sign and not waste the water unless she took a shit. You know, just offering her some helpful advice. Well, she turned about eighteen shades of red, and finally muttered that she *was* obeying the sign, and walked back to the bathroom with the water bucket. Even after she came back to the table she stayed flushed for a long time, and I couldn't help being as stunned as everyone else to realize how mortified she was to acknowledge she pooped! Everything about her made you think that, as opposed to simply believing her shit smelled like roses (which would have been bad enough), she believed she should have been absolved of the mortal need to shit at all. I was beginning to think her survival through the past month had been a fluke, and surely she wouldn't make it all the way through the rest of the week. I expected her to be one of the dropouts.

The very next day, she practically proved me right. We hitched a ride together out to the edge of a mountain pass about six miles from town. From there, we had to climb down a steep embankment—a crevasse, really—to a village in the valley below. She took one look over the edge and stammered, "We have to go all the way down there?"

Uh-huh, I nodded. There was no road or vehicle that could navigate a drop so steep. To get down there you had to hoof it.

"But how in heaven's name are we going to get back up here once we're down there?" she asked incredulously.

"How do you think we're going to get back up?" I remarked, unable to hide the sarcasm in my voice, and then answered the question myself when she looked at me blankly and shrugged. "We'll climb," I said. Duh.

"Oh, my," Ellen said sweetly. "I don't know if I can do that!"

"Well, if you want to come, and if you want to learn, then you don't really have any choice," I said, hopping down onto the first ledge and turning briefly to see if she was coming with me or staying put.

She stood there for a second like she was considering her options, then took a deep breath, steeled herself, and said, "Okay, then. . . ." right before she jumped off the edge of the cliff behind me. It was hard for her to get down, and even harder to get back up, but despite the fact that the return trip looked like it should have killed her, she never uttered another word of complaint. Now I'll tell you, I've had plenty of trainees come to visit over the years, and I've seen plenty of trainees quit halfway back up that hill. We jokingly refer to it as the testing ground, and trust that it will scare off all the Volunteers-in-training who don't have the mettle to make it all the way. So I should have known then, in the way she plowed right on through, that there was more to her than met the eye. Turns out, there was a strength in her that probably just hadn't ever been truly tested and a stony presence not at all like the moniker she was mistakenly tagged with.

By the next time I ran into her in the Peace Corps office, over one full year later, The China Doll was all but gone. Well, okay, it's not as if Ellen had morphed into a totally different being—there were still things about her that were feminine and tender. She still wore her dresses, worn out and ragged though they had now become, and it was obvious she still took care of herself and tended to her appearance—things a lot of Volunteers just let go over time, thinking they aren't appropriate companions to toughness and endurance. But I'm not talking about appearances; I'm talking about essence. The fragility she arrived with is what had disappeared. Innocence lost is such a coined phrase, but it is exactly what I'm trying to describe. She—we—had grown. Wizened. Which is not a bad thing, entirely, for everyone must eventually mature. But still, it was sort of sad to see how quickly naïveté could get whittled away under the pressure to protect yourself at all costs and at every turn. Bumping into her again in the office, then, was bittersweet. Her wariness was like a mirror reflecting back to me the extent to which things had changed for all of us. Although what happened to me was more violent and I think, in retrospect, that I therefore must have been the more paranoid of the two of us at that point, it really doesn't matter whether you are robbed or raped or mugged or beaten. Victimhood alters you. Just like Guatemala alters you. It gets into your bones. You are never the same, even if you want to be.

I think that must be why everyone so consistently wondered why I didn't quit. Why, after I'd been medevac-ed to the States and had a perfectly plausible reason to stay put there instead of returning to Guatemala, I went back to finish out the last few months of my tour. Like with most things, there is no easy answer, no single Aha! moment that made up my mind for me. Primarily, home just wasn't the safety net I thought it would have been. In fairness, my family did everything they knew to do to be supportive of me, but still they were more awkward and uncomfortable than I was prepared to deal with. I come from good Kentucky farming stock, the type of folks who can chop their arm off in a grainer, retrieve it, and stoically walk alone over two miles for help, but haven't the foggiest idea what to do or say to the daughter, to the sister, who's been raped. Accidents they can handle with aplomb, whereas violations are another thing entirely. An accident can be talked about, turned into family legend, and worn like a badge to be shared with and admired by the rest of the community. A rape, though, is an insult to be hidden at all costs, because while accidents may be acts of fate, rapes are . . . well, to many good Southerners, rapes still too often involve women in short skirts and see-through blouses, doing things that might incite a man inclined to trashy behavior in the first place to behave in even more criminal ways. Not that my family thought I deserved to be raped—quite the opposite, in fact; it broke their hearts. But it wasn't a heartbreak they were prepared to discuss or disclose, and since they didn't know what to do with my problem they mostly ignored it. They behaved as if I had come home on a furlough with a slight cold that with luck would pass quickly while they all attempted to avoid catching it.

When I announced I would be going back to Guatemala, over a pot roast dinner one night after about a month of tiptoeing around what had occurred, the very first thing my father said was, "How can you do this to us?!" Funny thing is, those were the exact first words he said over two years before when I told him I was thinking of joining the Peace Corps to begin with. It didn't hurt me the same way the second time as it did the first; by then I knew it was his own fear speaking and didn't really have anything to do with me. But that's exactly why I couldn't stay, why I had to go back. Because they would never understand that I wasn't doing it to them, that it had nothing to do with them at all. I was doing it for me, as I had a right and a responsibility to do. I had little choice but to leave, just like the proverbial rider had better get right back up on the horse after a fall. Had I stayed, I sensed their anxieties would eventually become mine, and without even realizing what was occurring I would be bound forever to the farmlands of Kentucky, as fenced in by fear of the future's many unknowable possibilities as everyone else seemed to be.

As I saw it, going back was the better—if not the only—option open to me.

* * *

It wasn't as if I didn't have a virtual family waiting for me in Guatemala, people I could go back to who would make me feel as if I were returning home after all. In truth, over the past two years, there were Volunteers I had drawn closer to, and established deeper relationships with, than I had managed to develop with some of my own siblings over the course of my entire life. Which isn't to say I wasn't attached to my brothers and sisters, but instead just indicates the intensity of the bonds that can form between strangers once they're forced together in a foreign country with no one to rely on but each other. Well, okay, I guess it is that way for some siblings in their homeland also, the ones forced to roam the streets together, to protect each other from abuse and neglect, siblings living in horrible circumstances in their own houses who have no choice but to cling to each other for their survival. Viewed in that light, I'm lucky I didn't need my real family that way. But I needed the other Volunteers that way, right from the beginning, before there was even any danger involved. They were people to acclimate with, to speak English to when Spanish words wouldn't come or simply required too much brain energy, someone's hand to hold—figuratively or literally—through the surprise of a culture so different from what is familiar and known to you. They are the people to drink a beer with, who will give you their last twenty *quetzales* to wipe yourself with when there isn't toilet paper and you haven't yet gotten used to the idea of using nothing, and they are also the people who can hear the word RAPE a hundred times without flinching and know you never deserved it, people who don't have any idea what to say, but keep listening anyway without turning away.

Even the Volunteers I wasn't particularly close to due to the limits of geography, personality, or assignment, the ones I had never counted among my close circle of friends—like Ellen!—could come through for you in a vital moment and there would be an instant connection. Not to sound sappy, but it really is a soul mate kind of crowd. Clearly, that doesn't mean everyone liked each other unconditionally or got on marvelously, but I am 100 percent certain that, if necessary, any one of us would have dropped everything at a moment's notice to come to the assistance of even the ones we cared for the least. Maybe that's also why so many Volunteers wind up marrying other Volunteers, because at our core we share something so vital in common—ethics, motives, spirit—that allows us to *know* each other as few other people in our lives can ever really be known.

So you can see the benefit to me of returning to that crowd after my rape. Just by virtue of being there long enough they were all survivors in their own right too, victims of different things that hurt in different ways, but they all chose to stay anyway, to hang in there, to keep trying. They understood my choices because they all knew that had our circumstances been only slightly different, it could have so easily been me listening to their story of assault instead of the other way around. In fact, it *had* been me listening before, because it seems just about everyone has their own story to tell at one point or another, many of which are just as insulting and dark and frightening as mine. We all just kept rotating roles, taking turns between being the storyteller and the comforter as the need arose. Women got raped before me, and women got raped after me. One young girl had lofty plans to visit the Mayan ruins in Tikál and opted, for safety's sake, to spend the money for a plane ticket instead of risking a bus ride through restricted guerrilla-warfare territory, only to wind up dead when her plane crashed into a mountainside. Then there was the guy in Ellen's training group who got kidnapped by road bandits, beaten, tied up, and left for dead in the woods, where he was discovered sometime later.

We got used to talking through such tales. In fact, one of the hardest things about sharing my experience with other Volunteers wasn't the telling, as it had been with my own family, but trying to avoid the feeling of "Why me?" that kept descending upon me, a feeling I didn't want to wallow in, but at the same time found incredibly difficult not to indulge. Because while there were a fair share of tragic stories, more commonplace in Peace Corps lore were the almost mythic stories of tragedy averted.

One afternoon, fishing for conversation in the hotel room where Ellen and I holed up awaiting her police report that would allow her to recoup her lost money and head back to our sites, we somehow wound up discussing college philosophy classes. Ellen said that one thing her experience in Central America had done was inspire her to return to school to take one of those courses someday, for the sole reason that when presented with the proverbial assignment to provide evidence that God existed, she could prove the thesis and ace the class with one concise sentence: "Most Peace Corps Volunteers finish their tours alive and unharmed."

I should say "almost" everyone, but instead I'm going to go out on a limb, ditch the "almost," and just say everyone—every single Volunteer, I'm sure of it—had some kind of a pulled-back-from-the-edge story. For instance, there were the two who were riding on the bus with the drunk driver that went swinging around a curve and right off the edge of the road, over the mountain pass, rolling the whole way down, and they climbed out over the dead bodies with only a sprained wrist and a broken collarbone. There was also the Volunteer whose decision to share her sandwich with a tired man she encountered along a dusty road, who turned out to be a government subversive, resulted in the fire-bombing of not only her house but also the houses of two other local Volunteers—on a night when they had all unexpectedly met at a friend's house for dinner, had too much to drink, and passed out before returning to sure deaths in their respective homes. But one of the best stories was Ellen's. Although she was kind enough not to mention it to me directly in light of my encounter, I had heard it told and retold by others plenty of times before.

She had taken a bus, alone, to the capital, scheduling her trip so she'd arrive well before nightfall. However, due to a flat tire, an engine shortage, or some other minor disaster, the bus pulled into the city well after dark where it finally broke down for good in an unfamiliar part of town. All the riders dispersed quickly, and she was alone, lost, in a wretched, graffitied, deserted sector. So she did what any of us would have done: She walked, fast and upright, down the widest street in the area with hope of soon encountering recognizable turf. Which is just what happened; she found her bearings and only needed to pass through a tunnel under an overpass to be back in a familiar, populated part of the city. Right before she ducked into the tunnel, though, an obviously drunk man slipped out of an alley and began following her. She didn't turn to look, in an effort to avoid a face-to-face encounter with him, but she could see his shadow cast onto the building wall by the streetlight and could hear his footsteps closing in on her. Knowing there was no other way off the street, alone in the middle of the night, she tried not to panic and instead quickened her step and kept hurrying forward. Then, just before stepping into the tunnel, she suddenly heard a second set of footsteps bearing down on her as well. At this point in the story, whoever is retelling it affects a lower voice and leans in close and conspiratorially, insisting that Ellen swears she never saw a shadow belonging to the second pursuer, although those of the drunk man and herself were clearly outlined on the wall. Furthermore, Ellen claims that the sound of those additional footsteps brought to her only an odd sense of peace and a certain knowledge of two things: 1) she would be jumped by the drunk when she entered the tunnel, and 2) she would be perfectly safe. And that is exactly what came to pass. The drunk man lunged and grabbed her around the face and neck at the tunnel entrance, and just as he did his body was ripped up and backward off of her with such force that it caused her to stumble, and the last thing she saw as she ran to safety in the park at the other end of the tunnel was the drunk's body, airborne, soaring over a two-lane highway, and crashing against the wall halfway up the side of the building on the other side of the road.

Ellen is not an overtly religious person, yet I know she refers to that experience as her angel story. Lots of Volunteers have them. Let me say right up front that I don't begrudge them their good fortune. I really don't! I mean, thank God they weren't hurt. But still, stories like that inevitably leave me wondering where my angel was. Where was my force with no shadow, and reassuring footsteps to keep me safe when I needed it? Why was she guarded when I wasn't? If God could send an angel to watch over her, then why not me? Where is the fairness in keeping one person safe, and letting another land in harm's way?

I have always had a strong faith in God; I never before had a reason not to. I went to church every Sunday with my family all throughout my childhood and am one of those rare people who kept going on my own, without fail, once I was living elsewhere. The traditions, the rituals, and the murmuring of the whole congregation as one made me feel safe, as if I were part of something that was bigger and stronger than myself alone. I made my confessions and I lived my life righteously just the way I was taught to do, and I took to heart the sermon about how God does not put before us challenges we cannot handle.

"Of course He doesn't," said the priest when I went to him for counseling the week after arriving back at my parents' home after my rape. "Count your blessings," he said. "At least you're not pregnant."

At least I'm not pregnant?! That's the best he could do?! Of course I wasn't pregnant, because despite everything I believed in I swallowed the morning-after pill they offered me in the nurse's office after they stitched me up, the pill that wasn't even legal yet in the States, but could be gotten in Guatemala, and so then on top of all the other pains I had uncontrollable cramps and more bleeding and the extra guilt of betraying my faith to alleviate my fears. Then the best the priest could offer me was the idea that I was blessed not to be pregnant, as if I should be grateful for having avoided that inconvenience? I would have been grateful not to have had any reason to swallow that pill in the first place, and felt more blessed had I not been raped at all!

So if God couldn't protect me, or wouldn't protect me, then did it really just come down to some random coincidence that put me in the path of harm and allowed other people to escape it? I wondered what would have happened if I had gotten out of bed at seven that morning, like I intended, instead of rolling over with a book and falling back asleep until eight? Would I have missed him at that hour? Would I have finished my shopping and been home making soup before he had a chance to wander around the last booth and spot me haggling over the cost of carrots? Or even if I had slept in, as I did, and arrived only just ahead of him, but paid full price for my vegetables, might I have had those extra few minutes to steal away before he saw me and began to imagine me on the ground beneath him? Or maybe there's nothing I could have done to avoid him; maybe we were fated to meet like a train barreling down on a car stalled at a railway crossing. Is it just plain old bad luck that the man I encountered that morning had seen *Basic Instinct* with Sharon Stone at the local theatre, with subtitles, so he assumed all American women loved to have sex with such ferocity—wherever, whenever—and thought he was doing me a favor, whereas the man who passed me without incident the day before, as I walked alone on a mountain pass, was simply too poor to ever go to the movies and didn't therefore have such a warped impression of what American women might want and what he could take from me? If it is all that random, then what point is there in believing in a God, a God who isn't supposed to present us with challenges we cannot handle, yet abandoned me when I needed Him the most? What in the world could have been the purpose in that?

As much as the image of that man's face, and the feel of him on me, these questions disturbed me and hurt me equally. I couldn't escape my own mind any more than I could escape the rapist! When the priest couldn't help to calm me, when his answers failed, I went to see a shrink.

The shrink was a woman, a rape victim herself, who gathered together other female casualties of various assaults—rape, domestic violence, battery, you name it—in a small room with chairs in a circle from 7-9 PM on Tuesday and Thursday nights in the annex of a suburban Louisville hospital. I was born in that hospital, on the third floor. The support group met in the basement. There was something kind of secret about our little club, something covert about the subterranean door we used to enter and exit through, something clandestine about using the back parking lot instead of strolling in under the "Welcome" sign out front. Clearly, there were women there who still feared for their safety, which made sense; some of them were shuttled over from the shelter where they hid out behind an anonymous address. But there were also women there entirely out of harm's way who still carried their fear in with them on a nightly basis, defined by what had transpired, yet at the same time utterly horrified at the prospect of being recognized, marked, or labeled by others according to what had been done to them. They lived their lives both consumed by the violence and doing everything they could to hide it. Some had been coming for years, twice a week, and still looked as if they had been assaulted yesterday and thought they might be assaulted again tomorrow. Honestly, it is them I have to thank, more than anyone else, for my salvation, because they showed me the difference between living through a rape and surviving one. You could live through a rape and still be perpetually haunted by it, but to survive one you had to decide to live beyond it.

So although it took me a little while to catch on, I finally realized that I wanted to survive. And to survive, I would have to go back to Guatemala. My unfinished goals were back there, and even though I couldn't ever fully escape the effects of what happened to me, I could prevent it from disrupting the context of the rest of my life. I might always see his face in my nightmares, and on the bad nights I might startle too easily and vigilantly recheck the locks on the doors, and the memory of him might always linger on the edge of my thoughts. But I got to decide whether that would remind me of his strength in overpowering me, or whether it would remind me of my own strength in living through it. I wanted to live beyond him. I wanted to survive.

And here's the thing: Once I was able to reframe my experience in that way, I realized that maybe, if I were willing to walk through the front door with my head held high, to park in the front lot and enter beneath the "Welcome" sign just like everyone else, knowing I deserved to be able to do so, some other injured woman might eventually find the courage to follow me in. That is how I discovered purpose in what happened to me. Now, maybe you think I'm just trying too hard to get my head around something that can't be explained, or maybe you believe I'm simply attempting to hold onto the faith that I'm afraid of losing completely, but if those are possibilities then isn't it just as plausible that what happened to me wasn't a failing of faith or circumstance but instead a necessity, so that someday someone else can draw their strength from me?

Short of overanalyzing, let's just say that it's all those things that happened during my medevac, my time away, that allowed me to go back. Sometimes it is only by distancing ourselves from something that we can see it most clearly. That is why I said to Ellen, that day when we reconnected in the office after she'd been robbed, that maybe it was time she thought about heading back to the States for a break. "I don't know how you do it," I told her. "I wouldn't have been able to see this through had I not gone away for awhile."

"I don't know how *you* do it," she replied. "I've begun to think that if I left, I might never find the strength to return."

But she is wrong. In some of us, in her, in me, strength runs deep, and those pools within us, though shallow at times, are reservoirs of resources to be ceaselessly retapped.

* * *

So all that's left to tell you now is how that week together in the capital ended—after the coup started and we got Ellen's police report and her money—and we headed west, taking off for home together on a bus with everyone else who was fleeing the city. That day traveling was the last we spent together, ever. I never saw her again after that.

She had come back from the police station that afternoon with everything we needed, including the bus tickets, and I was too nervous to ask her directly at first how she had accomplished it all. When she took off that morning I wasn't sure how much she would have to sacrifice to ensure our safe return.

"Everything worked out okay?" I asked her as she changed out of her short skirt into traveling clothes, wiping the makeup from her face onto the hem of the discarded dress.

"Yep."

"Are you sure you're all right?" I pressed.

"I'm perfectly fine," she said, scooping up the bag I had packed for her and turning to rush out the door. But then she saw my concern and slowed down for just a minute. "Really, Claire, it all worked out fine; no problems." Then she smiled, a victory smile, and because she was in such an upbeat and uncompromised mood, I found it easy enough to believe her. We raced out of the hotel together, in a hurry to catch the bus.

While all the words I've said to you already, about being strong, about surviving, about living beyond fear are true, you have to remember that at that point it was all still fresh to me, and I can't pretend the chaos in the streets wasn't frightening. Student demonstrators were forming march lines, swamping city vehicles and looting stores, while police in riot gear trampled them under horses' hooves and shot their guns recklessly into the crowd. We could have easily gotten separated as we ran away from the city square by the presidential palace, where things were the most out of control, where people supportive of the old president and people supportive of the new one were closing in on each other, except that at some point Ellen reached back, grabbed hold of my arm, and held me so tightly that two weeks later I could still see the bruised outline of her fingers fading on my forearm. The noise, the gunshots, and the shouting policemen were just too much, too soon, too similar to what had happened to me, so finally I just covered my ears and let her drag me along.

(Remember how I said that when I first met Ellen, I thought she wouldn't have made it through that week of training without my help? Ironically, looking back, I can honestly say that when the tables turned a year and a half later I wouldn't have made it through that week in the capital without her. And if you think about it, if she hadn't been victimized, if she hadn't been robbed, she would have had no reason to go to the office where we bumped into each other. She would have been gone, and I would have been alone. So perhaps there is something to my theory, beyond just desperation, that we are not abandoned to violence but led through it for a greater purpose. Maybe these things do have to happen to line up our paths, so we can be there for one another when we're needed the most. One way or the other, having her there with me helped to redeem my still-shaky faith. When I count my blessings, she is among them.)

We made it to the station, with time to spare, and got on the bus. Leaving the city behind was a relief, and everything progressed normally until, about halfway home, the bus screeched to a halt, and I craned my neck out the window to see what was going on.

"It's a blockade," I said, just as the army soldiers boarded through the front and back doors, barricading the exit and rushing down the aisle. With their wooden batons, they knocked people toward the exit, picking mostly young men, who would be their new military recruits, and us. I couldn't get away from this day that kept replaying my attack, men in uniforms with badges and guns who were supposed to be helpers and were instead assailants! Thank God Ellen knew what had happened to me, so she could understand my panic, and we held hands tightly with our backs against the exterior wall of the bus where the soldier pushed us after ushering everyone outside. The young men who were removed with us were loaded into transport trucks; their fear was actually something you could smell.

The soldier standing over us ordered us to turn over our passports, but Ellen's was gone. It had been in her stolen bag. She didn't have one. "*Fíjese,*" he said. "That is unfortunate. Now you will both have to come with us."

This could not happen to me again! I tightened my grip on her hand and pulled it back; I could not go! But she stepped toward the soldier and said, "I have a note from the chief of police of Guatemala City, ensuring our safe passage." Then she turned to me quickly, and in English whispered, "Everything is okay," prying her hand out of mine to reach into her pocket for a piece of paper. I couldn't figure out what she handed to him—it looked like official police stationery with a map and directions written across the page. "We're expected back at Chief

Ortega de Leon's home this evening," she said coolly, "and I'm sure you don't want to be the one responsible for disrupting his plans."

The soldier studied the paper for a minute but then said: "You're not going to the police chief's house! You're headed in the opposite direction."

She didn't budge. "We're headed home to freshen up and will barely have time to catch the 5:30 Pullman back to the capital as it is!" He hesitated, and you could see he was trying to decide whether to believe her or not. Ellen took full advantage of his doubt. "Truthfully," she said angrily, as if she had the power to do him more damage than he could do to her, "I'm not going to be the one who has to explain this to the chief!" With that, she put her hands on her hips, stared him right in the face, and said, "What is your name?" She asked with such authority that to my great surprise he gave it to her; she reached and plucked a pen right out of his own pocket and scribbled his name on the back of the police letterhead. "And your station number, and direct phone line?" she asked, without even looking up, and he licked his lips nervously but still answered her. She wrote it all down and then said: "Fine! If there are any further delays, I'll have him contact you directly." Then she turned and looked at me with a desperate glance, and pushed me ahead of her back up the stairs of the bus.

We were so close to being back on the bus, almost safe, when the yelling started outside and a different, stronger man's voice commanded us to stop. Obviously, this was the captain in charge, and he berated the younger soldier we'd been talking with before pushing him aside.

"We cannot allow you to travel without a passport," the captain insisted. "You will have to come with us right now. Get off the bus."

Ellen stood between him and me, and my heart sank when she stepped back down to the bottom stair because I thought she had given up and was getting off. If I hadn't been right behind her, too scared to move away, I wouldn't have been able to see or hear what she did next.

All sweetness, she leaned in close to him and said: "Sir, of course you are right. Obviously, I have violated the law by traveling without my passport, but I am also in a terrible predicament, as I have an appointment I cannot miss later today. Given that you are in charge here, I am hoping you will be able to solve my problem for me." With that, she reached into her bra and pulled out a huge wad of cash. I had seen her hide the replacement grant money that the Peace Corps issued her after she turned in the police report; the money was scattered all over her body—in her shoes, socks, underwear—so I knew she had plenty more, but still, the roll she palmed was a sizeable amount. She held it discreetly between her breast and his chest. "I am wondering what the fine for traveling without a passport is," she mused, "and if there isn't a way I could entrust you, given your stature, to take my payment and see that the fine is properly paid off on my behalf." She made a private show of counting her cash, and told him she had 350 *quetzales*. He snickered.

"The fine," he said, "is actually four hundred *quetzales*."

Then she turned to me. "Claire," she said in a lilting voice, "please be kind and lend me fifty *quetzales* so I can pay my fine." Obviously she didn't want him to see all the rest of the money she carried, so I counted out my own money and handed it to her, which she put in his hand, pressed between her two palms.

"Thank you so much," she said to him, as if he truly were doing her a great favor, "for taking care of this on my behalf." She then began to back up, pushing me behind her, smiling sweetly at him all the way. By the time we sat down in our seat the driver, as anxious as everyone else to be gone, gunned the engine and swung the bus back onto the road.

Ellen was sweating profusely and I was just catching my breath when the army contingent disappeared from view out the back window of the bus. "Whew," she finally sighed, with a half smile, an if-I-don't-laugh-I'm-going-to-sob smile, "that was close." Then she tried to give me back the fifty *quetzales*, but I wouldn't take it. Small price to pay. We rode the rest of the way in grateful silence.

I didn't even realize until the bus stopped that we were in my town, and as people unloaded I barely had time to thank her. "Thank *you*," she said right back to me. "It would have been terrible to have had to go through this alone."

It wasn't until the bus drove off with her on it that I had the where-withal to think about anything other than what had just almost happened. As I waved after her, the little bird metaphor that I had associated with her the first time we met came back to me. I had misjudged her gravely, as I think people often misjudged me. Talk about spying a giant hawk from a distance and mistaking it for a hummingbird or some other frail creature. Only in drawing closer could you see the true potential, and I knew now she would make it through her time here just fine, as would I—despite circumstances that so many others thought would break us.

I would have liked to have been around to see the look of surprise on the faces of all the people who dropped out while she persisted. But like I said, I never saw her again. My tour finished shortly after that, hers some time later, and circumstances never again reconnected us. Funny how little time it takes, though, to make such a profound impact in a person's life. Ten minutes behind a market stall with a gun; one month sitting in a circle in a hospital basement. Or two weeks, separated by more than a year in between, to bolster each other's spirits, shoulder each other's loads, and spur each other courageously onward.

13. Elena's Story, Autumn 1993

$\mathcal{T}$he postman suffered the uncertainty many long months until finally he broke.

"Miss Elena," he said, standing beside his bicycle, fingering the nailed-on wooden seat in anxious anticipation of my maybe-really-bad-news response, "what has happened to our Samuel?"

I had no idea to whom he referred, but this is not unusual. "Our Samuel?" I repeated, a question, as in, "You and I, who see each other so rarely, only when you bring me my opened and peered-through letters, we have a mutual Samuel?"

"Yes," he said, leaning against the stone and mud casing of my door. He wore a woolen tam, which he took off, and put the edge in his mouth, biting it like a man preparing to be hurt grievously without the blessing of anesthesia. His old wrinkled face wrinkled worse, for clearly the fate of Samuel tormented him. "Frst hgt schtik," he groaned, but I had to coax him—

"Come now, take the hat out of your mouth, I can't understand these things you are saying"

—before he pulled the soiled fabric from his lips and said emphatically, "First Samuel got sick, then he got sicker, then he went to the hospital . . ." Still, I did not understand anything of which he spoke. I geared up to give him the Scarlet O'Hara stare, the right brow furrowed, the left arched, the look I practiced for months in the bathroom mirror after seeing *Gone With the Wind* for the first time in the sixth grade, but ultimately the postman said, ". . . then Samuel had surgery, and then the telegrams stopped!"

Oh, yes. I finally caught on.

Samuel is code.

Poor old man, fretting all this time. I didn't get it either at first, but at least I only suffered a short time before I figured out the Samuel gig, the pall of his sickness hanging on me just a few days, whereas it had been with the postman for many months. Too much vicarious agony can torture a soul.

Samuel is a ruse.

The Samuel telegrams all arrived within two weeks of each other, toward the end of May, and because the postman had opened and read them all before resealing them with unsticky tape and delivering them to me, he remembered the contents well. First, the note that Samuel was sick, and me wracking my brain wondering, "Do I know a Samuel?" rifling mentally through the endless retinue of extended friends and family, finding no Samuel among them. Then I felt worse!, because clearly this Samuel wanted me to be aware of his illness and yet I could not even think whom he might be. The anxiety built through the week with each new post, for Samuel deteriorated quickly, got rushed to the hospital, underwent emergency surgery, and hung tenuously to life in intensive care.

Samuel is not a real person.

Perhaps this should have occurred to me at the beginning, but I suffered too much with the mystery of his identity to notice until I finally lined up the telegrams all together in a row on the kitchen table to divine their purpose; each was sent by a different person, people whose names I did not recognize. They were important-sounding people, with government-issue names (sometimes it takes surprises like this to remind me that I work for the government, that I am not my own independent entity in Zataquepeque). I got out my embassy notebook and there, after some searching, found all the names in the section on "Internal Threat," meaning attack from within, a coup. We had three coups at the beginning of the summer, three in two weeks, and the lady's name on the first telegram—the message itself being absolutely irrelevant—meant evacuate the capital (which I had done, all on my own, with Claire and my recovered money, without needing to be directed by a surreptitious signature on a coded document). The subsequent signatures meant not to leave my site, to check in by telegraph or telephone to verify my safety, to prepare to flee under cover of night, and finally to ignore all previous telegrams for everything turned out fine and reverted to normal.

It had all ended before I figured out what any of it meant.

The coups passed; I burned the telegrams. The only measurable impact came these months later in the form of this profound and lingering dread which the invented Samuel inspired in the postman.

"Samuel is fine," I said at length, because it seemed both accurate and honest within the confines of this make-believe situation. I added, "Samuel recovered fully, with no visible scars, and in fact hardly remembers anything about what happened."

The postman let loose with a long breath of air, as if he'd been holding it these many months, waiting to exhale.

"Oh, thank goodness," he groaned, exhausted with relief. "Walk with me, we must let people know—we have all been so worried!"

He held my hand in one of his, pushed his bike with the other. We first strolled past the tavern where he spent his weekends, then to the *comedor* where he took his breakfast. We went to all the places where for many months the postman had tormented the assembled townsfolk's ragged nerves with unceasing worry for the health of my imaginary friend. At each door we now paused; the postman raised our clasped fists high in a victory salute, and shouted through the open doorways, "Elena's friend Samuel is recovered!" to which, to a man, the people gathered inside would lift a hand either to heaven or to their hearts and with a collective sigh of pure joy and the sign of the cross, shout to me their encouragement and glee:

"What a blessed relief!"

"Hurray for Samuel; praised be his doctors!"

"Ay, *Dios bendiga*, it is a miracle from God!"

"Long live our friend and *compadre*, the estimable Samuel!"

As the day wore on, in the Latin way, their relief became more palpable, their exuberance more boundless, and their gestures more effusive. By that evening, grown men cried. Chests got pounded, bottles got raised, dogs howled, and children quieted before the profound spell of collective rejoicing. Long into the night, and for many nights thereafter, from the off-canter barroom tables and the dirty ditches, from the unlit street corners and from the faces pressed, regrettably, against the opposite side of my bedroom wall, a lone or accompanied voice would arise in toast, "To Samuel!"

Samuel never went away, as imaginary friends are supposed to do with the passage of time. Samuel stayed with me and consumed the rest. They asked about him always, and guarded his tenuous return to health as if his recovery signified a chance for us all. Do not be fooled into thinking the villagers had no more realistic things on which to pin their worries. Calamity surrounded us. Breast milk dried up and crops withered. It did not rain enough, or it rained so much that houses and bloated beings floated past. Men went to work in the morning and never returned. Lookouts hid in the hills and watched for guerrillas, armies, police and shouted their warnings to an unprepared town. Governments changed hands three times in two weeks. Satraps ruled. Women got violated. Children got taken.

I heard stories of the sweeps. With the civil war over, all should have changed, the massacres should have stopped and the kidnappings ended. Guatemala wanted its aid back from the rest of the world, and its media blitz made everyone else (who did not live there) believe in reform and in newly enacted social justice. They plastered the world and their own people too with propaganda. I have one of the flyers, pressed on me by a camouflaged man with an Uzi, and it reads verbatim, in faltering English:

Do you know that in Guatemala there are places where you are discover new and unforgettable experiences, miscelanous corner of natural atractives, santuary of the mayan breed, where popullation and army work for the defence of the peace. Our compromise, to guarantee the peace and to protectits confort. Guatemala's Army . . . Basic recommendations follow when you are visiting Guatemala.

1. Have an English-Spanish dictionary.
2. Obtain a tourist guide booklet of the country (it can be adquired the Guatemala's institute of tourism—INGUAT).
3. Carry the necessary items for the type of region to visit (according to weather).
4. In case of emergency approach the detachment of army commands. They will be willing to serve you.
5. In case you need any monetary transaction address to Guatemala's bank, 7th Avenue 22-01 Zone 1 or to banks system.
6. In case of robbery, accident or if you need transportation information approach the national police that will be located in different places of the country.

7. In case of accident communicate to the fire department, phone 122.
8. If you wish to communicate to the United States dial 190 direct USA.
9. For information services communicate to phone 124.

Each phone call is free of change.

Everything here is free of change. We know better than to expect otherwise, which is why what happened scared but did not surprise me.

"Elena!" Lucinda screamed, and though I could not see her yet, for I toiled out back, I recognized her voice even at this unaccustomed pitch. She beat upon my door.

"They are coming!" she yelled and lunged at me as I stepped into the street. "The army," she clarified. "They are coming to recruit boys." They are coming, she meant, in their trucks to steal away the sons ages twelve and up, whom mothers might never again behold. People darted frantically around us, but Lucinda held my gaze and stared at me deeply. It is an historic look that has repeated itself too often, passed from woman to woman, from one who must plead to one who has privilege; it is the look of a mother begging, expecting, that her fellow female will behave as one.

"Take my children," Lucinda pleaded, pressing her two boys into my arms. She turned then and fled without pause for she trusted me and knew my heart. She had nothing and therefore no place to hide her children. I would hide them for her.

The army men swept through quickly, one into each home, taking the boys. I stepped back as the stout man in the shiny boots clicked across my stone floor. He went right to the altar room, the room I kept padlocked due to the spooky sensation the relics, artifacts, and statues within inspired in me. "That room is hexed," I said. "You should not enter."

"Open this door," he said, and though I had the key hidden in my hand—the men came upon us so quickly, I had not had time to replace it yet—I acted as if it still hung in the kitchen basket, as if it had been so long since I used it that I forgot the key's precise place.

I pretended to fumble around, looking first in one basket and then the other; when he cleared his throat impatiently I said, pertly, "Here is the key," and extended it to him, not wanting to make the situation worse.

"Open this door," he repeated, but I responded:

"Oh no! I will not open that door, I will not go near that room!" I made myself animated—"Act!" I willed myself. "Act well!"—and let my very real fear creep into my voice. "I have been told that the last person to enter that room choked to death on a chicken bone that very night," I lied, "and before that the mistress, having looked through the open doorway, died in childbirth with her baby stillborn the very next day. The shamans now say that anyone who opens that door will look upon the very face of death, and death itself will haunt him and come for him within that very same week."

His look says he does not believe in shamans, but I suspect this is a false front; he must be a superstitious man. Superstition is the religion every Guatemalan is born to. I press on in my scary voice.

"So open the door yourself," I say, "for you are far braver than I!" Backing up against the wall, covering my eyes with my hands, I say, "I cannot even look, but tell me sir, if it is true, if you see death's face when you open the door."

I feel now a sense of horror at how close we came to getting caught.

He turned the key, pushed on the door, and though I expected the crash it terrified me just the same. I jumped; the soldier jumped. I felt all the blood in my body pound at once on the walls of my heart so hard that it caused me actual pain, but the boys did not scream, bless them, and the soldier ran so fast from my house he didn't even bother to re-lock the door (which to me would be a dumb thing, you know, not even trying to lock death back in, leaving it free to tear after you).

I didn't want to wait long, but only long enough, before going inside the altar room, winding through the statues to the back, helping the boys down from their perch on a gilded edifice. I had lifted them up there, had said, "Trust me, and be quiet, I will keep you safe." On my way back out I had grabbed the life-size plaster Lucifer statue which had at one time likely been part of some religious depiction of the great heated battle for a tormented soul. The archrival, Michael, is in the room too. But it is Lucifer I tugged with all my might, propping him finally beside the door. After exiting I wedged my arm back in and dragged the very edge of the statue into the path of the opening door, so that when pushed against this devil might totter, off balance, and careen toward any person daring to enter. Finally, just as I heard the voice from beyond and the hard rapping that said, "Open up! This house is to be searched," I winked at the boys, a playful, whimsical gesture, so that they might think we were engaged in a game and not a war.

Lucinda's boys hid in my house once more, and with them many other boys, too. I could have hidden a whole village full of teenagers in my altar room from then on, for the unsettling story—which by now must have become old army lore!—kept all subsequent marauders from setting so much as a foot over my threshold. Clearly the mothers knew, that is why they sent their boys to me, but they never spoke to me of these incidents. No lament, no thank you, no acknowledgement of a kind that anyone else might have recognized, for this is a place where the truth is danced around, where so much is bad that the bad stuff does not get discussed.

Instead, the mothers, and the fathers, too, they ask me about Samuel; more so, I noticed, after these misadventures. Samuel is still code, and we all learned to readily decipher his missives.

"I have been thinking about your friend Samuel," someone would say as she passed in the street, and I knew this to mean, "You are in my thoughts and in my prayers, Elena."

"Give my regards to Samuel," meant, "Thank you, Elena, for this thing you have done for my family, this thing of which I am too frightened to speak."

And, "How is Samuel doing?" meant, "What do you think? Are we safe? Will all turn out well?"

I had no choice. Hope required I create a good, safe life for Samuel, for us all.

So it is that not only did Samuel recover, he fell in love and married. Moved to Miami. Everyone begged then for a photo, and at first I did not know what to do, but eventually I passed around a picture from a distant cousin's wedding that I had recently received in the mail. The postman brought it to me. It is a happy picture.

Who is to say the beaming bridegroom is not our Samuel? Who is to say what is truly real? I say, thank God for the subterfuge of our Samuel. He gave to us a good and sheltered subject on which to rest our troubled thoughts.

* * *

Lucinda is the avatar of the long-suffering indigenous woman. Her husband is *un Deseparecido*, a disappeared. He is the word used as a proper noun instead of as a verb, one of the men (for they are always men, these proper nouns, women are not worthy of being disappeared) who joined the resistance or spoke of the resistance or had the bad luck to overhear someone else's talk of the resistance and because these unlucky ones could not get the sound of the conversation out of their ears fast enough they suffered the same fate. They woke up one morning, had some left-over unhot café. They put on the pants they wore yesterday, which are the ones they plan to sleep in tonight. They stepped around the children on the floor and the baby in the hammock, they ate an egg their wives cracked for them, and the rest of yesterday's beans. Had they known better, had they known it to be the last, they might have kissed their wives, but instead they kicked the dog and didn't look back, because why do that?, they would return tonight. Perhaps they met each other on the path, swapped a joke or at least a *buenos días* before they dispersed to their separate plots, to nurse a seed that did not want to grow or repair a terrace that someone's pig dismantled in search of a cabbage. No one will know precisely how the last morning went because they never returned to bear witness, as if the fields swallowed them up and they transformed from farmers into disappeareds under cover of a foggy gray dawn.

The women understand, which is not to say they are not sad, but only to imply they carry on. They get up in the morning, put on the skirts they wore yesterday, which are the ones they plan to sleep in tonight, eat the remaining beans. They feed their children. They find a trade. They do not talk of the Disappeared, except to say that is what happened. It is not safe; they have sons.

There is only one wife I know to have made a fuss, and know is per-haps not the right word, I should say know of. She is a U.S. citizen, mar-ried to a Guatemalan disappeared. She stages hunger strikes in front of the presidential palace, in front of the embassies, on the median strip in the highway. This is a fact: Her husband got his head chopped off by an army leader who trained for this task under the tutelage of the CIA. Lots of hunger got her that news, but it did not get her a body or a trial, an apology or the hope that it would not happen again. It is over ten years since his head and body split, and just this past year I got an e-mail peti-tion to support her most recent campaign. She has started eating again, gone to Harvard Law School in the interim, and now she is suing the U.S. government for complicity and cover-up. I remember her picture from the newspaper way back then, when I lived in Guatemala and she starved herself, her gaunt face with the disappearing eyes glaring from behind the sign she held. I showed the picture to Lucinda, thinking it might give her confidence, that she might empathize with the woman's attempts.

"How sad," Luci said. Just that: How sad.

"What?" I asked, "That's all?"

"What do you expect me to say?" Luci countered, softly. "Do you want me to do this same silly thing? Do you think this is what her husband would want? This does not make anything change except that now she is a sick and too-skinny woman.

"Now we will not talk about this anymore—you take too many risks, Elena," Luci continued. "But first I say one more thing: That is no way to remember him. One must live."

So Luci sold *paches de papa* at the market, potato loaves wrapped in corn husks, a mush of sweet gluten, and in the one she saved for me each week she put a bubbly piece of pork fat, which I slipped out surreptitiously and fed to Cali when Luci looked away. She kept her six kids clothed in an outfit apiece by selling other things. She had a baby by some other man and wore it on her back; the last one, with her husband, demoted to skirt clinging. She drank a lot; an amount I considered to be rather too much, but which she likely believed to be just enough. She endeared herself to me with her *paches* and her sincere smile; I hired her to do my laundry and other chores; she is the only Guatemalan to whom I would entrust my dog.

I don't remember which came first, the laundry or the dog watching, but it is the Cali-sitting in which she delighted.

"La Calixta is a very smart dog!" Luci said initially, using the term everyone tagged Cali with—*la* Calixta, the One and Only. I had just returned from a trip to the capital, had left Cali at home alone for the first time, with Lucinda hired to look in on her.

"I think she's smart," I agreed.

"No, not just smart, very smart," Luci countered.

(Bear in mind, I love my dog; I am *in* love with my dog. I think she is amazing, and quite possibly the smartest animal ever born. But Luci's emphasis led me to wonder what precisely might have taken place in my absence to sway her so quickly to my point of view.)

"Here is something you did not know," Luci continued. "La Calixta speaks English with you, but with me she speaks Spanish! She knows both of our languages, and here is how I know: The first day, when I came over into the yard, she tried to jump on me and I said, 'No!' loudly in Spanish and she stopped! Then I got out her leash and held it in my hand and called, '¡Venga!' and she came and I hooked the leash on her! Can you believe that?" Luci enthused.

I thought, "Believe it?, yes, this isn't a leap, since No! in English, Spanish, Italian, and dozens of other languages is the same word, and when you touch the leash you could be uttering Greek to her but Cali would still come running to be hooked on."

These subtleties escaped Luci though, and her enthusiasm swelled: "She knew what I meant; she speaks two languages! La Calixta is the smartest dog I have ever met!

"I have told everyone that la Calixta, the gringa's dog, is an amazing bilingual animal," Luci continued. "They have all become very excited by this." The discovery of Cali's ability, and the opportunity to share it, flustered Luci still. She ran out of breath and turned bright red.

"And everything went well, in addition to your communications?" I inquired, looking around the yard. "No problems?"

"No problems," Luci said, "no problems."

"But I notice that none of the dog food is eaten. Was she sick?"

"Oh no, seño, not sick, just not hungry."

"Why in four whole days would she not get hungry?"

"She did not get the chance to get hungry. She got very well entertained while you were gone."

"Entertained?"

"Oh yes, everyone in town got very excited to visit with la Calixta once I explained she is an amazing bilingual dog. I thought that it would not be a good idea for everyone to come to your house while you were gone, so I took la Calixta visiting in their houses. We got served breakfast at one house, lunch at some other, and dinner at another house every day. But don't worry—I made sure they fed us good food, not just a plate of beans and eggs, but some meat too because she is a special gringa dog and needs special food."

"And your children? . . ." I wondered.

"They went on the visits with me," she said. "To assist in the care of la Calixta."

Misguided canine behavioral interpretations aside, Luci is one sharp cookie. She got her whole family fed like kings for four days during my absence.

They needed the food.

For an undernourished woman Luci is fat. Big fat. Rolling jiggling pouches of arm-skin fat. Her face is puffed-up steroid-junkie-ish fat, and her swollen ankles bang right into the logs of her legs. Her proportions imply too many carbs but not enough protein: endless tortillas, but no meat. Somehow, though, she gets her vitamin A, because she is not blind; on the contrary, her irises shimmer with the news that somewhere deep within her well-insulated soul springs a reservoir of boundless joy, miraculously shielded from the drying winds of life. Her eyes toss out glitter from behind the folds and crinkles of cheek fat.

It is that brilliance which captured my heart. I loved Lucinda, and loved also how much she loved me back. Every Wednesday laundry day when I awoke and opened my door, without fail I found her sitting on the stoop awaiting me. As the year wore on and the weather turned, the frost setting in and the mornings dawning unbearably cold, I willed myself to wake earlier and earlier to keep her from lingering in the chill of the dark street. But I never beat her to my doorstep, not once; finally I said to her, "Luci, I have been getting up earlier and earlier so you will not have to sit out here in the cold and wait for me, but it is not working."

To that she replied, "Elenita, my dear little Elena, I have been getting up earlier and earlier too so I will always be here when first you open your door."

On Tuesdays I filled the *pila* full before noon, when the water stopped running, so that the next day we could begin the laundry chore with a half reservoir backup supply of day-old water (the crack in the concrete slipping the other half of our surplus to the weeds on the ground). If Luci worked fast and I ran swiftly between her laboring hands and the clotheslines we could begin hanging the first items when the morning mist dried up, finish rinsing my clothes before the water shut off at Wednesday noon, and remove everything from the lines before the midday storm so that the garments would have time to dry a little bit and grow less mold than if put away more thoroughly damp. It took the better part of the day. Luci assumed the hard chores of breaking the icy layer off the top of yesterday's frozen saved water, plunging her hands in and out, rubbing my things on the stone to cleanse them with water and soap as well as blood and snot that got mixed in when she scraped her fingers and sneezed her illnesses upon my apparel. I hung up the cleaned clothes, the wrung-out-tightly-so-Elena's-hands-won't-get-cold-touching-them clothes, on one of the three lines with my mother's clothespins. Between my task, which required less effort than Luci's more taxing ones, I kept her company in the yard, dancing from foot to foot with my chapped finger stubs stuck in my mouth, the only warm place, trying to heat myself up and Luci too, by blowing my warm breath onto her frosting face, not abandoning her to the inhospitable dawn.

She stood the whole time, feet uncovered, in the frigid runoff and told me her life's stories with a smile.

I paid her twenty *quetzales* a load, twice the going rate in penance for her feet, forty *quetzales* on heavy days when we threw in the bedding and the sleeping bag too. On one of those heavy days, early in our relationship, just as she finished the loathsome chore, clothesline #1 broke and dumped half the day's work into the mud of yesterday's rain. She rerinsed and I rehung and just as I fastened the last of the rewashed laundry onto the spare line, clothesline #2 snapped and dropped the remainder of the clean stuff into the puddles. She relaundered it all, alone, while I ran to the hardware store for more rope. I tell you this because when I returned and tried to pay her double for cleaning my clothes twice, she refused the extra money, said it is not my fault the lines broke and that her job was to leave me with clean laundry, that is what I paid her for.

That interaction alone, even barring all the other wonderful things, made her my best friend, and allowed me to freely give of myself to her.

I could do it because she didn't ask, and she would have turned me down had she known what I was doing.

Almost everyone else asked for some tangible material something: money, food, money, possessions, money. You name it, they thought of it, and wanted it plus some money too, please. Oh, what a hard—and perhaps unnavigable—quest for balance this foists upon one. I moved to Guatemala to give, to learn, to share, and be shared with. But all of that has been done ineffectively for too long all throughout the underdeveloped countries of the world. The missionaries (we will get to them later) share all these philosophies that no one wants or needs and with big hearts and sincere intentions trample cultures, paving the path for people like me with cavernous potholes. Then the aid organizations hand out blankets, food, schoolhouses, and dams that no one has learned how to earn for themselves or maintain in the benefactor's absence, so when the aid workers go home satisfied the dams spout holes and the blankets wear out and the Guatemalans shiver as hungry as ever in the cold of night. The problem is, aware now that the world holds better options, many Guatemalans do what these "humanitarian" actions have taught them, the only thing they know to do to change their circumstances: They beg.

And the begging leads to fighting, and then to the atrocities. The only time I ever fully opened my home to more than just one or two people at a time, right before I left Guatemala for good, I invited in a few good friends, coworkers, some teachers and youth leaders, so they could split amongst themselves my meager household possessions—four wood-slat chairs, a small painted table, some baskets, two frying pans. A fistfight erupted. They began arguing about who had been the better friend to me and therefore deserved it all, hating the idea of sharing amongst themselves (which is so strange, because individually I knew them to be generous people). I said, "Please, everyone, pick one thing, there is something for everyone," but two reached for the same chair and it came down on one head. I threw them out then, said, "Fine, if this is the way you treat each other, I will not provide you with cause!" They left with nothing, but did not wind up empty-handed. Later that week someone returned, chopped the locks off my doors, stole all those things I would have gladly given away, plus things that held importance to me that I meant to keep. I got robbed all the time; my homes had been invaded so often over the years that it might have just made more sense to leave the doors unlocked. But this last affront stung most deeply; in all likelihood, a friend did this.

So, you see, too much gets taken and the urge to give is stolen away as well.

I remember once, perhaps I was eight or nine, visiting my uncle's house in Philadelphia with my dad who smoked then, and a homeless man approached us as we stepped from the car and made a simple request, a cigarette, and my father said no. I thought this plain mean, what harm in sharing a cigarette with a man who had nothing? I stood there on the curb and cried as the homeless man shuffled away, with my father trying to explain himself to me, rationalizations I wanted to ignore, about how giving without earning only encourages one to beg, about the distribution of cigarettes from my uncle's porch attracting an unwelcome element. I could not stop my tears, but I did hear what my father said. I wondered what in life bridged this gap between my inclination to share and his wariness to do the same, if someday I might feel that way also. What hard growing-up process could make the crying child become a stony adult?

If one is not careful, two years, two months, and eight days in Guatemala will force that change. It is more than enough time for a naïve, idealistic girl to become a guarded woman. But thank God for

Luci. She accepted my generosity and returned it, always making me glad I had it to give. Because of her, I have it still.

That said, I will share with you the pretexts which governed our relationship. I wanted to help without patronizing, she wanted to return the favor; we needed a handy excuse to do so.

It started with the *wisquil*, an invasive spiny vegetable I detest that climbed its way up my walls and in a final suicidal gesture slung itself underfoot to pierce Cali and me. I complained about it loudly and purposefully in front of Luci one day, smiting its presence and wishing it gone. "My girls can help you with that," Luci said, and later that afternoon the three of walking age appeared to pick it all up and cart it away. A week's worth of soup.

Later I lamented the weeds in my yard, invented a story about the landlord, angry with me for my lack of yard care, and Luci said, "My girls can help you with that, too," so I paid them a day's wage every few weeks for their Sisyphusian labor. It gave me a chance to feed them lunch. ("A worker cannot work adequately if hungry; providing lunch is part of any hiring deal in the States," I said.) I served them a balanced lunch with protein, some carrots for their eyesight, a vitamin drink from my medicine kit (the taste of which I pretended to detest, but the truth is I love Tang, sweet syrupy-goo Tang).

Every day we found a way to make these funny little trades, without admitting outright to our barter. I would slip a sweater over a child's blue-lipped face, pretending I shrunk it and could wear it no more (for I could wear the same sweater every day, I did not really need two). Then the girls would appear with an egg saying their chicken had suddenly laid an extra. I would send a bowl of pasta home with them, insisting I made too much and could eat no more, and the holes in my clothes would suddenly be patched when I pulled them freshly laundered from my basket. Luci's boys missed out on our daily give-and-take, having been apprenticed when they turned ten to the local bus driver so they could learn a trade and maybe one day be something more respectable than just a farmer. Nonetheless, they clearly knew of our unspoken pact, for whenever I rode the buses on which they took the money I paid the regular fare, whereas on other buses I was charged double for being a girl and for being white.

Our collusion brought us together frequently, and Luci often left the girls with me when she returned home at dusk to cook her *paches* and roam the dinnertime streets beseeching, "*Un quetzal por pache, un*

269

quetzal por pache. . . ." On those evenings, the children and I took turns swinging each other in my hammocks beneath the setting sun, or I would sing old camp songs, then play the ditties back on the tape recorder so we could dance a jig together in the dusty yard. Before darkness crept on us we'd race through the cornfield out back, lose each other in the towering stalks, squeal out our names blindly and chase each other over the hummocks. Painted orange-red by the setting sun, we would toss a stick to Cali, and at the behest of a warm breeze might kick up the river water, skirts held knee-high, before we sank to the ground on the slope of a green hill and welcomed night.

This is what I beg you, please remember.

Multiply in your mind the beauty of this evening and spread it out over the course of the years. Do not let the robberies and the rapes and the assaults dull the sound of these children laughing or chill the warmth of their hands slipped into mine. For fear this might happen I avoided telling the truth all these years, and now I am afraid that what I thought might occur has come to pass. The first readers, the ones to whom I have tentatively extended these pages, have begun to say: "Why did you stay in spite of the risks, when you were so often in jeopardy? Your anger, your fear, comes across very clearly in the pages you've written. What in the world possessed you to remain?"

After leaving, I recall that the bad overshadowed the good for far too long, and I can find no way to tell the full truth without letting those sentiments creep back in. I am unsure how to be honest without distorting the truth. I could say that I had made a commitment, and while it is a true statement it is not my full truthful reason, for though loyal I am not averse to a change of heart. No, I stayed because it was not until the very end that the bad weighed so heavily on me, because interspersed among the hard stuff were the rest of my days.

If you can sense my frustration can you not feel the joy, too? Can you not hear my voice with the children laughing, or see my breath mixing with Luci's as we smile together into the cold, fresh dawn? These are the moments that built the days that comprised the most of my Guatemala life. The laughter and the sweet touches floated me over the stormy waves; the women and the girls are the raft I clung to even after the rocks pierced me and with the air draining out slowly I began to sink into the sea. Right through to the final moment when only my head stayed wearily above water, the buoyancy of those days was enough to allow me one last breath to carry me home.

270

I cannot help that in the retelling the fierce storms loom largest and darken the scene, but in truth there were many glorious sunny days in and amongst the showers of rain.

* * *

Would you believe I befriended the Mormons? In theory, it makes no sense. In theory, I judge the Mormons and other missionaries abominable, these present-day Gnostics, with their unctuous manners and immutable teachings. They of the white shirts and the snake oil pamphlets, the Elder-this and the Elder-that, too good to wear the clothes we wear or play in the places the rest of us gather, they cloister themselves on their private basketball courts and walk in pairs, talking only to each other, a coterie nonpareil, refusing to let anyone else call them by name.

But outside the theories and the standards imposed on them by their sect, they are just boys. Young boys. Boys who, despite the rules prohibiting it, would really love a Coke. Boys who, had it been up to them, had they not been programmed toward the mission, would probably be smoking a joint and listening to REM at a frat party somewhere else. Instead, at twenty, they're wandering through Zataquepeque, hunting even more naïve souls.

Though we passed each other many times in the street, averting our eyes so we wouldn't have to acknowledge each other, slicing each other to pieces with biting remarks made behind our backs, it wasn't until one of the festivals that we actually met. It may have been Day of the Devil, when after the day's work is complete the men dress as loathsome spirits and evil personages, parading through the streets with their masks, costumes, and boogeymen cackles, letting the rest of us chase them from town to be rid of these bad influences for another year. Mostly the men dressed as succubae—for it is woman, you know, who fed them the apple and started the whole licentiously evil thing. Prostitutes, sluts, indigenous women dressed as Ladinas (those race betrayers), women with makeup and high heels, working women (dressed as men, egad, in suitlike attire), Rigoberta Menchú.

Rigoberta Menchú is a scary thing indeed, with her I-broke-the-silence book, picking the scabs off Guatemala's sores and letting the whole world gape into the festering wounds. And for God's sake, she's a woman, which is the real rub. An indigenous woman. Talking to presidents, touring the States, getting her picture in newspapers and on

271

magazine covers where only important men's pictures belong. The Rigoberta parade-man, distinguishable by the sign around his neck, "Winner of the Nobel Peace Prize," got pelted with many chase-out-the-devil tomatoes as he and the other amoral elements took their annual cavort through Zataque.

It is either something the Mormons said about Rigoberta, or something they said at the Day of the Dead Festival, that caught my attention.

Don't let the alliterative names confuse you—Day of the Dead is not the same as Day of the Devil; although both are held annually to relieve the year's problems, otherwise they bear little likeness. On Day of the Dead we all parade together, in mourning black, behind a funereal band preceding an empty coffin (unless there is a fresh dead person who needs to be buried, lucky coincidence). The sky always clouds and weeps with the women into their hankies, who sob in three-quarter time cadence with the droning wail of the brass quartet. Men hang heads and children shuffle. With all eyes aimed downward, puffy and red, the parade gets lost, covers the same ground twice or more than twice, until someone reluctantly takes charge and aims the toes of the coffin toward the cemetery on the hill.

On the graves the lugubrious tone changes. Flowers abound, the knell becomes a flourish, children run pell-mell over the dirt covering the decaying remains of their dead relatives. Everyone finds a dearly departed to honor by rolling, reclining, jumping, and climbing on the mounded tombs. Those of us without our own dead person fan out to any bump in the ground, staking claim to any unclaimed pile of dirt. Food is shared, songs are sung. When the sunlight dims the candles burn; those flaming wicks combine with lilies' scent to lift up into the night sky the purgatorial spirits that have waited all year to be released on the Night of All Souls. When the wax melts, the last of the toasts are tossed to the air, and the last of the rum is poured onto the graves, where by morning it will have mixed with alcohol sickness and bladders' overflow to water the bones of last year's living. This counts as the generations' final soiree. In baby-angel, guerrilla-warfare, not-enough-food country, this is as close as one comes to a family reunion.

Now that I've let myself think about it for awhile, I realize it is here that I met the Mormons, who were harassing an old woman curled up in a corpse-created cavity to pass the night. They warned her the time was at hand and her fate that night her own to choose. As she planted lips-to-the-earth kisses above the place her husband's face might rest, they mentioned his spirit and they mentioned hell, but I don't think they mentioned anything more before I grabbed a boy in each hand, and marched the Elders back to my house for a serious talking-to.

I meant to yell at them, but on the way realized they were just boys. They did not know better because they had not seen better, so instead of hollering I gave them some Cokes, and I let them toy with my radio which they are not supposed to do. I cooked them a dinner, wooed them with food, let them pick the music cassettes we listened to while we ate, all forbidden. I asked them what they thought of Clinton, but they only remembered Bush. I told them I was born in Philadelphia and they asked, "Where is that?" So I got out the *Newsweek* magazines and we poured together over all the world news of which they had previously been unaware.

We talked of politics and philosophy, pop culture and history, but when they steered to religion I refused to follow, allowed that they could come over once a week to talk of things otherwise outlawed, listen to music, make some of their own, but that there would be ground rules they needed to follow. No Bibles and first names only.

"And if I hear of any more threats," I threatened, "these dinners are over."

"Threats?" they opened their mouths to say, but I stopped them before we misled each other.

"These people are my friends," I said, gesturing out the door, including even the Zataquepequeans that I disliked in my collection of confidantes for the moment. "I hear all the shit you're feeding everybody."

To their dumbfounded stares I said, "The volcano?"

(An astute studier of body language would have at that point noted the slight expansion of their pupils, the bump . . . bump . . . bump of the veins in their necks, the finger twiddling and the left-leaning eye rolls that meant, "Dang, we're caught; quick, hunt for a plausible excuse.")

"You have got to stop with the exploding volcano, buried in lava bullshit," I insisted.

Santa Maria the mountain, who has not been a truly active volcano for many eons, looms over Zataque, within earshot of my defense of her dormancy. I climbed her once, in a big group, in spite of policy forbidding her bandit-laced assent, and made it to the top without incident to stare down through the clouds at my pea-sized town. While I enjoyed the trip, I don't know that she liked it. Santa Maria conjures an earthquake every once in a while, shakes us all off her like a dog scratching its fleas back into the grass, and with a thunderous toss every now and again reminds us that she is bigger and that we should leave her alone. The little tremors toss us out of bed, kick us around on the floor in the dead of night, rough us up just enough to command respect. The big ripples, when she is truly mad, are a graver affront, calling calamity down upon her violators.

I was in Xela one day, near her nervous foot, when she gave us a boot of 7.1.

Xela is a sort-of big town, second largest in Guatemala, where I went to shop on occasion in the Americanized grocery. I stood scouting cheese when Santa Maria knocked my feet out from beneath me and slammed me flat onto the floor. She batted us shoppers around for a bit then, rifling through the aisles, crashing into all the food shelves and sending them tottering. I stood and fell, stood and fell, stood and fell and ran with all the other captives toward the exit, but the security guards yanked down the metal bars and chained the doors shut with us inside before running to safety in the open air. (To them we were all would-be looters; crime prevention through mass murder.) Instead of risking suffocation in the mob by the barred exit, everyone climbing atop each other in their gang pursuit of nowhere, I repositioned myself in the toilet paper aisle, gauging these to be the softest things that could possibly land on me, hoping the Charmin might save me if the roof caved in.

The Mormons used these near-catastrophes to their advantage. By sharing their self-invented "scientific proof" that Santa Maria planned to explode soon, by citing the "ecobiologist's conclusion" that Santa Maria intended to sear us all and entomb us in a boiling lava pit, they managed to con more than a handful of terrified villagers into conversion and staked claim to their trembling spirits on behalf of the Church of Jesus Christ of Latter-day Saints. The power of the deathbed conversion to right life's wrongs wields strong emotional riptides. Thing is, though, Santa Maria has her sights set on retirement; she grows no Mount St. Helens bulge, emits no telltale steam, and while the earthquakes are definitely her fault at essence they are motivated more by geography than by eruptive intention.

Santa Maria is not going to blow up. Death by lava will never materialize as the Elders promise, but without my help that wisdom would come too late because by then everyone would have turned Mormon.

In exchange for a weekly dinner date, the boys agreed to modify their tactics.

This proceeded fine for some time, and I collected a band of admirers as the duos rotated in and out of Zataque every month or so. Without fail, a meek knock indicated the newcomers' arrival. "We are looking for someone named Ellen," these new two would say. "The Elders sent us."

"Yes," I'd admit, "I'm Ellen. Bill and Bob (or John and Joseph, or Mark and Matthew) told you to find me, right?" With that I'd astonish them right off the bat, illegally using their predecessors' given names, then I'd place my cassettes in the hands of one and an illicit *Newsweek* in the hands of the other, and we would be fast friends before dinner finished cooking. All could have kept going on like that, going well, for some time, except that one of them decided to desecrate the caves.

Indigenous religious ceremonies are usually consummated in caves, hidden from view, outside grabbing range of the church's long arm. They take place on the ground, not on altars, in the open air instead of beneath a gilded dome, with offerings of eggs and sugar instead of the Host; practices with which I empathize, being primarily pantheistic in my own beliefs. Lucinda introduced me to indigenous religious ceremonies after she learned to trust me and convinced others to do the same.

So it is that I slipped into all the indigenous rituals I could get myself invited to. I hitchhiked to the mount in Momostenango and piled stock petals in the four directions for luck. I got my head anointed at the baths in Zunil to increase my intelligence, and paid eight *quetzales* to have a candle lit for my prosperity. It is Maximón, however, who most cleverly captured my affection and colluded, at length, in my plot to quell the Mormons.

During the mass conversion perpetrated by the Spanish missions during the Conquest, when the natives could choose between pledging allegiance to the pope or having their heads lopped off, Maximón rose in popularity as a hybrid cross between classic Catholicism and pure paganism. He is the turncoat Judas with an indigenous twist, aggregate judge, juror, backstabber, executioner, and penalty assessor. All-around bad dude. He is said to roam the streets at night, exacting penance. Still, he is a crepuscular deity with corporeal presence, and families vie furiously for the chance to host him for a year in their homes, where they charge visitors five *quetzales* each to enter his

275

private room and gaze upon his well-dressed, throne-sitting, plastic mannequin personage.

Lighting a five-*quetzales* candle at his feet buys one minimal grace, as evidenced by the hundreds of flames surrounding his seat, set just far back enough not to melt his synthetic toes. But five *quetzales* more buys you the ultimate salvation. For the extra money you can buy Maximón a shot, and the host will tip his chair back so you can pour the liquor down a tube in Maximón's mouth (which exits the tube at his other end, into a bucket beneath a hole in the throne, from which the host refills the shot glass he'll sell to the next ingenuous visitor). The main benefit of this, aside from sharing a drink with Maximón so he will not have to imbibe alone, is that while toasting you can slip into his solid fisted hand a slip of paper imprecating an unfaithful spouse, or begging his intervention in a spurned business venture with a perfidious partner. Then the retribution comes, for prayers to Maximón are specious; one only visits him with devious intent. The business associate might get *gripe*, the nagging kind that lasts for years, or the wife may fall and bloody her nose which will mar her appearance for the rest of her life, or the paramour may with vague provocation topple from his horse, breaking his neck and ending the affair. If these things come to pass, it is surely the work of Maximón.

Revenge-based religion is a concept Guatemala encouraged me to relate to, and let me tell you, I visited Maximón many times in the upcoming days. I got him thoroughly, if figuratively, drunk in hopes he'd exact judgment on those Mormons, against whom my ire irrevocably turned the day Lucinda invited me along to one of her mountainside rituals.

Because Luci doesn't believe in doctors she solicits shamanistic advice when her children turn feverish. Because she doesn't believe in banks, she murmurs incantations to the gods to spare her house from theft when the money's beneath a rock beside the door. Because she doesn't believe in government, she offers small sacrifices to support the everlasting sanctity of her disappeared husband's presumed-dead soul. And on those rare occasions when no one is delirious, depressed, or otherwise disgruntled, she prays that a rich man might find her fanciful or solicits other relatively banal blessings. On the day in question, she desired divine feedback on the sensibility of raising her *pache* price by ten *centavos*, a move I supported in light of her minimal returns, but which she feared would eliminate a few regular customers. We hiked toward the caves together, to let the omnipotents break the impasse.

As we summitted the mountain, Luci tucked into her pocket the boiled egg she would need to dance around three times counterclockwise to summon the gods, and used her free hands to pulverize some "sugar" to sprinkle over her offering when we reached the top.

"I ran out of real sugar," she said, and of course could not buy any, for that would have required dipping into the shaman's fee, "but I think what I'm making will be good enough." While walking, she ground birth control pills (obtained at the local office of Guatemala's Planned Parenthood equivalent) between her thumb and forefinger and sifted the powder into a bag she brought for me to hold.

"You could have asked me for sugar," I said. "I hate to see you waste your birth control pills for things like this."

"Do not have any worries, Elena, there is no problem. I have plenty of pills left for the plants."

"What do you mean, you have plenty of pills for the plants? You do know you're supposed to eat these pills, right?"

"Well, I know," Luci countered, "but why would I do that? It would keep me from getting pregnant!"

"Right! Preventing pregnancy is the point of eating the pills."

"But I like getting pregnant," Luci said, still grinding away at the medicine. "Getting pregnant means that for a year or so I don't menstruate, so for all that time I don't have to wash out my rags. It saves me a lot of time."

She said this as if there could be no more sensible justification for pregnancy. She said this as if a child were not a consequence.

"But Luci," I argued, "being pregnant results in a baby, and then you wind up spending years cleaning their dirty diapers and clothes. You trade one year's work savings for many years of extra laundry."

"Hmm, I hadn't thought of it that way," she said, as if she really hadn't. She paused for a moment on the path, to contemplate the revelation, or so I thought, but then I realized she only stopped to dump another handful of wasted powder into my rapidly-filling plastic bag.

"So, will you think about eating the pills?" I asked her, but she only said—

"Maybe"

—as if to distract me, and I flashed back to the time I mentioned that if she continued to dump her trash in the river, and then collected her drinking water downstream, it was as if, in essence, she drank her trash. "Hmm, I hadn't thought of it that way," she said then too, but nothing changed.

"The thing is, though," she said now, "the plants really like these pills."

"What does that mean," I pressed her, "when you say 'the plants like the pills?'"

"Well, I stick them in the dirt, all the women do it, the pills make the plants grow larger," Luci said.

I imagined the long rows of women outside the family planning office, requesting their six-month supply of birth control, and the pride of the population propagandists, thinking they would soon curb the explosive birthrate in underdeveloped countries. They are, instead, fertilizing plants.

"Nothing I say is going to make you eat those pills, is it?" I asked her, and she said—

"Maybe"

—yet again, and here is the only good thing about discovering the desecrated caves, which we came upon just then in our journey: The violation stopped this futile conversation which at great length would have gone nowhere.

The chicken sacrifices, laid out typically around the firepit, had all been hacked to pieces; had the chickens not already been dead when the slaughter started it would have been a most gruesome murder. As it was, feathers and guts clung randomly to the soot-stained walls of the cave; organ parts that dried and loosed themselves fell with a sickening plop to the dirt floor. The fire had been peed in and stank of ammonia. The candles had been snapped in half, ground underfoot, wedged into a slippery mosaic of wasted piety.

We did not talk to the gods that day, the *pache* price immediately irrelevant. We cleaned for hours. Collected the fowl parts, piled them back together for fear of disposing of someone's prayers. I sent Luci's girls back to my house to collect all my candles, and that night when the electricity failed and I sat in darkness I considered it penalty for my association. I knew who did this. The shocking execrations in English, spray-painted loudly on the walls, which required much pressure on a blackened coal stick to smudge out, marked it as the work of either the Elders or me. I hoped whoever else saw it before we got there knew enough to know I wouldn't dare.

I did not spare the missionaries my fury this time.

I have never again befriended a Mormon.

* * *

I got stalked right out of Guatemala.

In retrospect, it reminds me a bit of the later time when my husband and I got chased from the central square in El Salvador's capital by a group of homeless people, remnants from the U.S.-backed war I assume, based on their half arms and half legs that made it awkward when they chased us, a few falling, some hopping, and though their disabilities made them individually less threatening, as a mob they still moved maliciously. The one man who could keep up with us when we realized the import of sprinting, for he had only lost his mind and not a body part, stopped on the street corner and with both arms raised and his Messiah beard blowing in the traffic exhaust, screamed after our retreating backs as we darted through the cars, "I give you two days to leave El Salvador, two days to leave Central America, two days to leave the continent!"

My husband's broad-shouldered, blond-head-shaved, buzz-cut look must have been like the Marines redescending without warning on their park bench homes, and since the last time this happened the Marines left with their half limbs I cannot fault the cripples for defending their open-air abode and their intact appendages, for routing us out. I appreciate the small victory we handed them. I hope they talk amongst their lost selves and exaggerate the role they each played in securing the downtown park from invaders. Their efforts have amused us many times over in recollection, which is not to minimize their legitimate remonstrance, but only to imply that the beauty of memory is that it is selective, and in this case we have distilled out the rather nervewracking moment when a gang of twenty descended on us over a crest and have turned the threat into a temperature-cooling gauge of anger.

"I am *so* mad at you!" one of us will, on occasion, holler at the other.

And if the person at fault sheepishly asks, "Mad enough to want me to leave the continent?" the offended will typically answer, on reflection—

"No, probably not quite that mad"

—and some of the fury dissipates in the remembrance of that more aggrieved land.

Only the Guatemala stalking isn't funny, not one bit, not even in hindsight.

If you are keeping track, watching the dates as you turn these pages, you know it is almost time for me to leave. Two years is the Peace Corps contract. Two years have come and two years have gone. This is the end of my Guatemala adventure.

There are a few things you should know up front at this point, boundaries of which you must be aware. I may skip over the details of the last weeks here, just tell you what happened but ignore the why, because in truth I do not want to relive those days after spending so much time trying to forget. That is my prerogative, for I hate the sour tone on which it ended. Additionally, I have with due diligence chosen to define my assault as random, when all reality points to the fact that I was clearly targeted. This is a self-serving decision, but one I am not inclined to reconsider for mere storytelling purposes. You see, when one works professionally in the field of psychology, as I have done now for quite awhile, one learns that denial, which the layperson presumes to be an immature response, can actually serve quite well under limited traumatic circumstances.

I am, and prefer to remain, in denial.

I started that way, and perhaps only came to last those full two years with denial as my staunchest ally, so changing my coping style this late in the game would benefit me not one bit. Way back when, at the start of training, when all seventy-some of us were still eager and wide-eyed, a group of Peace Corps officials showed up one day to give us "The Safety Lecture." They spoke of explosive diarrheal ailments, scabies and brain worms, robbers, rapists, and corrupt police, fistfights turned gunfights, and other catastrophes. The escalating fear among us novitiates became a palpable presence in the room until one cohort jumped up from his chair, as angry as he was frightened, and yelled: "Give me a break! If your point is to scare the pants off of us, fine!, you've succeeded. But is this really necessary? I mean, what chance is there that these things will actually happen to any one of us? Maybe one, two percent?"

"Actually," one of the officials said, "there's probably a one to two percent chance that something like this *won't* happen. To each of you."

Of the seventy-some of us who left the room that day, two left on an airplane headed straight back to the States, and the rest left in denial, for that was the only alternative allowing one to stay.

Put in perspective, I'd had a safe two years.

So it is plausible enough to say, when describing how someone or some few came after me right there at the end, that it wasn't personal. It's just that my time was due, my number drawn, meaning that they came after me for no special reason (that I can think of), inspired by no specific affront (I believe), but only because I was there and had been there long enough that it was bound to happen. It had nothing to do with me in particular and was simply a matter of anteing up. I owed. They came to collect.

There were signs I ignored that I would not have ignored just one season back. But you know how it is—in the end, focus is easy enough to lose. I had a packet of graduate school applications stuffed in the embassy pouch, sent off to destinations across the States, and my thoughts so teemed with imaginings of my next adventure that my future dreams squeezed out space in my mind for the here and now. I had a plane ticket in my hands, and it kept my hands too well occupied. I let things go too far before I fled, because I had stopped paying attention to Guatemala.

That is never a smart thing to do.

Talk about missing the writing on the wall.

Literally. Someone wrote on the wall, in what looked to be blood, or tomato sauce, or a specimen of rather rare red paint. Loosely translated (which is all one could do, given that the spelling and the grammar displayed such insubstantial scholastic experience) it read, "Gringa bitch, I'll fuck you or I'll kill you." I did not take it as personally as I should have, quickly relegating it to the status of a mere biased, bigoted reference to my minority status. My ennui left me vulnerable. Taken together with the smashed locks; the machete stabbed through the back door; the kitchen knives lifted from their jelly jar and joined by the paring knife, the Swiss Army knife, and my own small machete (indeed, the only knife they failed to find being the butcher knife I kept beneath my pillow) all impaled in a line across my kitchen table one afternoon—well, I cannot blame you if you think I should have seen it coming.

In my defense, I will ask, what would you have me do? Go to the police? They would not care. Ask for a town reassignment, for a month? What nonsense! Even going to the director of the umbrella organization within which I worked in Zataque proved fruitless: Only a short time earlier a USAID rep had contacted me to let me know that on that director's recent trip to the States for some sort of governmental training he had been accused of rape and deported back to Zataque and me. Fat chance he'd help me now; hell, I wondered if he wasn't the one coming after me. So I did what one does in these circumstances: I mentioned the threats to a few friends, asked them to keep their eyes open, but moreover I fortified my meager resources. The butcher knife under the pillow cozied up with a lead pipe beneath the bed. A two-by-four buttressed the door, claiming its willingness to solidly hit the side of a head if need be.

I was an invincible twenty-four. No one could actually hurt me. Thus armed in denial and a few token weapons, I ignored the escalation.

I brushed my teeth like always that night, without water, and spit the spume into the bushes. I peed off the end of my porch, hot steam onto the froth, for the latrine lurked too far away in the dark; at night I always peed off the porch; I may have been heedless, but never stupid. Cali peed beside me. She could hold it through the rest of night, but I would get up once more after barricading us in the bedroom. Smart enough never to leave before day returned, I squatted over the pee bucket, a yellow plastic pot for nighttime emissions. In truth, I believe that after slipping back into bed that evening I would have slept through the whole rest of the night, and maybe even through his entry and his rampant intentions, except that Cali woke me.

She stood on the bed. Straddled my body with hers, back feet planted on either side of my head, front feet down around my knees facing the door, me on my back looking up at her belly, flea-bitten and scabby, but hard, tense, and ready to leap. She growled low and long. A menace.

Beyond her augurous growl I heard his footsteps, slow and deliberate, striking the patio stones ruthlessly, with intent, moving toward me.

To recount it as it occurred is an impossibility, for I do not know if the assault lasted a minute or an hour or a day. What I know is that from the moment I opened my eyes beneath my dog to the moment I felt safe enough to close them again I changed, my mind and my spirit senesced, and my perspective could never again aim straight without deflecting off the minute or the hour or the day of that night. What occurred, essentially, is nothing, but it made all the difference. One does not almost slip into a cavernous abyss without forever after being wary of the edge.

What I can tell you is that his footsteps, more than anything else, gutted me

ka-boom   (pause pause) (they echoed)

ka-boom   (pause pause)

the heel first the toe next in the dark no sense of sight no smell no touch just the sound

ka-boom   (pause)

ka-boom   (pause)

that picked up speed the closer he came

ka-boom   ka-boom   ka-boom

before he touched me he almost killed me the KA-BOOMS louder louder slipped under the door slammed on me stole my air sat on me caved me in weighed on me too heavy and the only lucid thing I remember thinking is: "I can't breathe"

KA-BOOM KA-BOOM KA-BOOM

and so prepared, the knife under my head, the pipe beneath my bed, a full young set of lungs to scream with, I did nothing except this: I whispered out loud, so I could hear and direct myself, "Breathe!" and I sucked in oxygen in time not to faint. This is the sum total of my effort to defend myself, the fear an embolus that burst in my brain and left me a hardened corpse.

From the perspective of now I can say that if the ties that bound me to Guatemala had been real threads, each KA-BOOMing step scissored them to shreds. I know I said just a little bit ago that the attack wasn't personal, which I maintain in my mind to this day it wasn't, but that's the me now speaking, not the me then. This is many years later, so it's easy from here to say it wasn't personal (because what a waste does it make of my efforts if in the end they wanted to beat me, rape me, and chase me off?) but in the moment it was a betrayal, as if I committed myself to that land and in return she sent this evil to my door, as if we'd been lovers and she held up the asp to my breast, which I could not forgive although it got scared off and I did, in fact, survive it.

When he smashed through the door the betrayals multiplied: The two-by-four betrayed me as he betrayed me as the neighbors betrayed me (sleeping warm in their beds while the horror transpired) as I betrayed myself, worst of all, by doing nothing but gurgling for air.

But Cali, she did not betray me. Never. Not once.

How does one describe the sound of their fight? To call them growls or snarls or groans or any of the words my mind can wrap around their ululations is not to touch the noise of that night. It ravaged the room. Wood snapping, claws scratching, biting grasping punching slashing little whispers

"breathe, breathe"

I can only describe the sounds for my eyes refused to move as did the rest of me, staring straight up at the docile roof, a piece of rust on the tin where the rain might come through, that should get fixed, one might get wet, while Calixta fought at my heels for my life

"breathe, breathe"

subtle sounds below the ruckus, divots dug in the floor, hard-scrabble scraping, splinters fracturing crumbling grinding, ping-ping-ping of the hinge on the floor, There goes the door!, another thing I should have fixed, those hinges loose in the adobe mud brick that's not like wood not easy to rescrew hinges into

"breathe, breathe"

battering rams, creaking groaning wood stressed, pummeling, rhythmic SMASH SMASH SMASH

"breathe, breathe"

then quiet but for the growl that started the whole thing, her little caisson body holding up the broken door. Growling, ceaseless growling, backing up growling; while door parts thudded to the floor in pieces, Cali stood there just watching out. Only then did I remember to breathe without thinking. I sat straight up, a flashlight in one hand, a butcher knife in the other, aiming the light out the doorway into the dark void where the dog stared and glared and snarled.

That's it.

That's how it ended for me. That is how I left.

Battered-resilient. Loved-despised. Exhausted-fulfilled. Older. Altered.

Ready to go.

14. Lucinda's Story

Oh, there you are! I thought maybe you were out, or that you could not hear me knocking. I just wanted to say hello; I am Elena's friend Lucinda. I heard that you had moved in and thought maybe you would have some news from Elena. Elena. You do not know her? Oh, that is too bad. She is the other gringa, the one who lived here in this house before you. You would have liked her. When I heard that the same organization that sent her here sent you, I thought that maybe you were her friend and she would have told you that I did her laundry. I am very good at laundry and can help you if you want, and I also sell paches de papa—*here, take this one for free. If you like it, you can buy more from me later. I can bring you some every night if you want. Elena liked my* paches *and so did her dog. They used to share them! Elena would eat the corn part and la Calixta would eat the pork. Do you have a dog? Oh, well, in case you decide to get one you should know that I can also take care of dogs—Elena let me take care of la Calixta all the time when she had to go to the capital. Oh, okay, I guess I can come in. That would be nice. That way we can get to know each other better and I can tell you, if you want, about Elena. Well okay, yes, thank you, I'll have a glass with you. Just one, while we talk.*

I loved Elena. I loved Elena like she was a daughter to me, and all the time she was here I tried my best to take care of her and la Calixta. I was hoping that even when her time to stay here was done she might not have to leave, but then the evil men scared her and she had to go. I think it is for the envy that they did that. When the envy gets in evil people they will do terrible things, and that is why it is not good to have anything more than what your neighbors have. Remember that!

Because I was here in Elena's house all the time I knew that she did not have too many more things than most of the neighbors, but nobody else knew that, and they probably thought she had more different things because she is a gringa. They sometimes talked about her big house and her big dog and her bicycle that she rode and her special hair and thought that meant that she was more important than them. But Elena didn't act more important than anyone and never tried to do things to fill anyone up with envy. Maybe it would have been different if the others knew that this big house of hers was mostly empty. It is too bad that they did not know her like I did.

I spent every Wednesday pleasantly with Elena doing her laundry. I always tried to tell her to leave me to do the job, but she liked to stay out here with me and take a part in helping. For such a tiny person she could carry heavy loads to the clotheslines, and my girls and I would laugh while we washed and say that it looked like just a pile of clothing was wandering through the yard with two little twig things poking out at the bottom for legs! It took longer than normal to do Elena's laundry, because I always had to watch her when she threw the washed laundry up over her head and shoulders and walked without being able to see well into the yard to hang it up. I would always have to yell for her to step more to the left or right to avoid any rain puddles, otherwise she would have stepped right into them while carrying a heavy load, which could have given her either the coughing illness or malaria. For a very smart gringa with many years of school, she does not know much about catching illnesses.

Elena got sick with some regularity. I was always warning her that there are certain things you cannot do if you want to stay healthy. I told her very carefully that she needed to avoid cold air whenever her body was hot, never leaving the house at night after cooking the meal, and still one day I heard from the women at the market and the women doing the wash at the community *pila* that Elena had been seen the night before running through the streets in the dark with la Calixta and breaking into a church! When I went to see her about this, what did she have? *Gripe!* She had bad *gripe* with a throat that made her talk scratchy and a fever that you could feel giving off heat even before putting a hand on her head. Oh, that Elena! I told her again that going out at night for any reason, even to break into a church, will make a woman ill. Though she argued that she was not breaking into a church, only trying to get an amplifying speaker removed from her roof so she could sleep, I told her

286

it did not matter because the result was still that she got the *gripe*. Elena then said that she had the *gripe* before she went to the church, so there!, and I said that of course she did, because it was also reported around town that she was seen pedaling her bike through the street during a rainstorm, fast enough to make a person sweat, another thing I warned her not to do to avoid illness.

Just as I was reminding her only to bicycle on sunny days without putting out too much exertion, she ran off toward the latrine. I ran out there too, yelling through the closed door, "Elena, do you have diarrhea?"

"Yes!"

"I am thinking now that instead it could be the bad air from the latrine that is giving you this illness. I have told you before that latrines are dangerously full of bad air—you should go to the bathroom in the cornfield where the air is better!"

"Luci, the latrine is not making me sick."

"Are you vomiting?"

"Yes."

"Are you hungry?"

"No!"

"Than it is not *gripe* or effects of bad air after all! You have all the symptoms of fright sickness!"

"No, Luci, I don't think that's what this is."

"Have you been frightened recently, Elena?"

"I am frightened right now. This conversation is frightening me."

"No, no. Be serious! Did a spirit frighten you?"

"Luci, let me tell you what is frightening about my illness. I not only have a cold, I think I also have worms again. And the frightening thing about that is, the only way to get worms is by eating someone's shit. Want to talk about frightening? How in the world did someone's shit get in my mouth?"

"Oh, that is the stupidest thing I have ever heard! You are a smart girl, why would you think you ate shit? Listen to me, the other night when you were running through the streets late at night, did you see a woman dressed all in white with one human leg and one turkey leg?"

(Now Elena pushed open the door, even though she was still sitting on the latrine.)

"A *turkey* leg?"

"Or a pig leg. Think about it. It would have been a beautiful woman with either the leg of a turkey or the leg of a pig."

Elena stared at me for a while before she said anything again.

"Yes, Luci, that must be exactly what is wrong with me. I don't have a stomachache or a cold. No, what happened is that I bumped into a very attractive half turkey, half pig lady in the street on my way to church the other night."

"I knew it! You met la Llorona!"

Elena pulled the latrine door closed again then, and though I waited a long time she did not come out and she would not answer any more questions either, so finally I went home.

The next day I took the milk money for the week and paid the shaman to break the evil spell of la Llorona on Elena. After he said the prayer and sang the chants, I went home to make dinner, and the girls said Elena had come by to say she was going to the hospital for worm medicine. This was the worst thing that could happen! Quickly, because there was not any extra time, I took out the money I was saving to buy shoes for the littlest one, and the four girls and I got on a bus to go after her. My boys work on the buses, so the driver of the bus knew them and was therefore kind to me. He let me off right in front of the hospital and I told the girls to wait on the grass outside and made them hold hands. I whispered in the ear of my oldest that hospitals are very dangerous places and that she should protect the younger ones in case anything happened. Then I said a prayer and I went in.

All the money I have spent on prayers for all the many years helped to bring me good luck, because I found Elena sitting on a chair right inside the front door. She turned her head and saw me when I ran through the door, all frightened and out of breath, and she said, "What are you doing here?"

"I have come to rescue you!"

"Luci, I'm fine. I've just come for some medicine."

"Okay, now get up. We have to leave right away! People die here!"

"Luci, I'm not dying, I'm just getting worm medicine."

"When my sister's husband had a problem with his appendix he went to the hospital, too, and then when we went to get him he was dead."

"Well, that's probably because his appendix burst."

"His appendix did not burst at home, only at the hospital! It was because of going to the hospital! So, get up now! We have to get out of here! And tell me, did la Llorona touch you?"

288

"What?"

"Elena, think! La Llorona, the woman in white with the turkey leg that you saw the other night? Did she touch you?"

"Luci, I didn't really see any woman. I was being . . . what's the word? How do you say in Spanish: not really honest in an effort to be funny and sort-of mean at the same time?"

"I don't know any word like that. Just answer me. Did la Llorona touch you?"

"There wasn't a Llorona!"

"So she didn't touch you?"

"No, Luci, I haven't been touched by a Llorona."

"Okay, good, than maybe you won't die right now. Maybe we have time to get you out of here still."

Just then a beautiful woman dressed all in white walked right up to us and I screamed! Elena whispered, "Luci, it is not a Llorona, look at her legs." I saw with relief that her legs were both human and she handed Elena a bottle of pills and told her she could go, so I pulled Elena outside as fast as I could.

Because we were already in the city together, Elena thought we should go have some ice cream, and took us all to a place where we sat on very tall chairs with no backs that spun around. Elena took two of her pills and said it should make her feel better, but I told her that the doctor only supplied the remedy, and that it was the shaman I saw earlier that day whose prayers would make it work. We ate two balls of chocolate ice cream each, and then Elena walked us to a special private school where she had a friend who let us into the yard, where there were many things for the girls to play with—things to swing back-and-forth on, and things to climb up and slide down. Elena went on the sliding thing with the three older girls and I sat on the swinging thing for a little while holding the baby, but it was hard to fit in and pinched my thighs. So then I just sat on a regular chair without swinging or spinning around and watched them, thinking it is a good thing we saved Elena from the hospital and that it is good that we were all there to keep each other safe.

I know that Elena liked to make her eyes roll around in her head when I asked her all of my questions about her health, and that she liked to think she had plain simple colds that she got from nowhere, but there is no such thing as just a cold from nowhere. There is a reason for everything, and it is our job to figure out what the reason is. Everything has a reason, although it is often not completely our fault. If a child gets sick, it is probably because a *duende* came and played with her toys in the night, which is not the child's fault except that she should have not left the toys outside where *duendes* wander. If the porch falls off of your house, like the porch fell off of my first house, the one I had with my husband, it does not mean the construction was bad, but maybe just that the wood was cut in the waxing moon and therefore rotted too quickly. If a person drowns, that is witchcraft—and all you have to do is figure out how to stop the spell and the bad things will stop happening to you!

I have thought a lot about the reasons for all the things that have happened. Not just the bad things, but the good things too. I have thought a lot about the reason Elena came to Zataquepeque. I think that maybe, in the time that was left for them, the great spirits thought that my girls could use the extra love, because there is only me to love my children, and one person to love six children does not seem like enough. That is what made me the most sad when Elena left, to think that I was the only person left again in our town who loved my children. But while she was here, Elena loved them. She loved my children well.

What? Their father? Oh, he did love them too, but he has been gone for many years. Probably . . . well, I think that probably, yes, probably he is dead. It is hard to know for sure, because—have you not heard of the Disappeared? Oh. It is okay, I had to tell Elena too. Someday, later, you can remind me and I will tell you. But tonight let's just have happy stories. You should tell me a happy story about the United States! Maybe we can have just one more small drink while you talk, and then I should finish selling these paches. *But tomorrow night I will come back with some more, okay?, just for you, and then we can decide when you want me to do your laundry.*

* * *

Welcome home! Your trip was good? Yes, the house was fine. I checked on it every day, no problems. Here is your key. No, I cannot stay, I am on my way up the mountain to chop some wood for dinner. Well, yes, you can come if you want, if you will not be troubled by the long walk. It will give us plenty of time to catch up, and . . . Really? Now? No, you are right, I said I would tell you, so I will. It is something you need to know anyway, now that we are friends. Maybe though, now that I think about it, we should have a quick drink first, before our long walk. Do you have any Gallo beer here?

290

The dream came back to haunt my sleep again, immediately before Elena's attack, and then again it found me on the night before the accident. Every time it is almost the same, but not exactly, but also not different enough to help me figure out what to do to avoid the terrible things that happen next.

I am standing in a field. There is a hoe beside me working alone to till the earth (something I have always believed that hoes could do). I point to a dark storm cloud coming and tell the hoe to hurry or it will get wet and rust and be ruined, but all of my words only make it move more slowly. When the first raindrop hits it, a big raindrop like a bucket of water dumped down on it, the hoe dissolves into a hole in the ground and out of the hole climbs a *duende* dressed all in black. He is a little man of a height no higher than my knee and he tugs an old black horse out of the hole in the earth at the end of a short rope. He asks me to lift him up so he can braid the horse's mane before the lightning strikes, but when I bend to lift him I notice he is wearing no shoes and has six toes on each of his feet. I say that I cannot help a six-toed man and, anyway, I need to borrow his horse's skull to put on a stake in the field to scare off the coyotes that have appeared on the edge of the clearing. The storm cloud is coming closer and the buckets of raindrops are falling and the wild dogs are all suddenly racing toward me when a lightning bolt shoots down and chops off the horse's head. I catch it in my arms and it spurts pools of blood all around me. Then the blood becomes a river, drowning the screaming *duende* and covering up the still-twitching legs of the headless horse, and I grow taller and taller so that even though everything I know is carried away I am still there, alone, unharmed.

The night before Elena's attack the horse's mane was already braided when it climbed out of the earth, and in the morning when I arrived at her house, can you guess what? She had her hair tied in a long braid hanging down her back! I only thought about this similarity later though, not then, so that is my mistake. On the night before the accident I saw hands reaching for help from under the river of blood and being more alert this time I made sure to avoid rushing water all the next day, forgetting that there are other things that can cover people up and cut off their air.

But the first time the dream came it was just this way I described it. It came to me the first time after spending the day before in that very same field, the field from the dream, with my husband. It was the last time that I ever saw him but I didn't know that then.

My husband burned and cleared our field in March, before the rains came. During the time he prepared our land for the planting, I took the money we had saved—about two weeks' food money—and bought for us some good planting advice. Everyone knows you must be very careful to start planting the maize on a good day, not a bad day, and finish it on another good day, otherwise you will be fearful all throughout the harvest that the ears will not yield sufficiently. It is not as important that the beans and *chilacayote* squash go into the ground on the special days, but for the price I paid the shaman was also able to advise us of a week when all the days were good with no signs pointing to days of bad omen. It was a week that would also allow us to harvest under the full moon, guaranteeing us enough produce to feed our whole family for the rest of the year. With such good advice, what could go wrong? So on the day that was the last day I would see him, my husband and I went together to our *manzana*, full of hope and thoughts of our coming good fortune.

We went to the field together in the custom of all husbands and wives, to make the ritual of the planting. We placed a candle in the dirt and knelt before it, with the tools of my husband laid out beside us. We touched our hands to the earth in a gentle manner to soothe the soil, and spoke together these words of blessing and request for our crops:

"*Dios Mundo*, guardian of the earth, and Father Paxil, owner of the maize, hear our prayers. Jesus Cristo and the Day That Is Today, hear us also and watch over our small piece of land that is all we have to offer to you. Hear our prayer that our gifts and our labors will be received and reward us with maybe a thousand *chilacayotes*. Let the weight of our beans number in the many hundreds. Watch that the snakes do not bite us and keep the sharp sticks from lodging in our feet while we work. Make our labors go fast and stretch the hands and the feet of your stalks high to the sky and deep to the earth. May the great rains wait so you are not drowned, and may your hands and feet not be broken by the swirling winds. If our harvest is large, keep our neighbors from envying against us. If we should need help to reap, may you make our field appear small so other laborers will be eager to help us. Pardon us *Dios Mundo*, pardon us Father Paxil, pardon us Jesus Cristo and Day That Is Today for our large request and thank you for sending the sun to shine your favor upon us."

Then my husband took up his tools and I went home, and we left the candle to burn and dissolve into the ground in the field. Though I have tried hard all the time since to remember the exact hour he got home that night, his last night, and to remember what he wore and what we talked about, I cannot make my mind bring back to me those last hours together. I want to be able to say: "He was wearing his favorite red shirt that I mended on Tuesday"—or—"For his dinner I made a fresh tortilla and a hot pot of café"—or—"Before he fell asleep I wished him a good night and patted his hand." These are the things I need to remember! But I cannot recall if I mended his favorite shirt or not, and though I looked all through the small pile of clothes still I could not say for sure which shirt it was he became disappeared in. I cannot recall if I made him fresh food or if the last meal my husband ate from my hand was old and cold and not to his liking. I cannot hear the last words I spoke to him, nor do I remember if I touched him in a loving manner or instead forgot to touch him at all. My mind is not my friend in this cause, and has never allowed me the small joy I have always longed for of remembering the last of him.

It is just like this: The day after we went to the field together he went back to the field alone, and never returned, and now my memory too is slipping away. My husband used to say this is how it was too for him when he tried to think of his father. His father died a brave death, the death of a revolutionary, during the occupation of the Spanish embassy. My husband could have died there too that day, except that his father would not let him go along. I was pregnant with our first child then, and my father-in-law knew there could be danger, and said that enough children had already been orphaned so that his own about-to-be-born grandchild did not need to be added to the count. My husband was angry, but his father was very firm. Though my father-in-law's action saved my husband that day, the fire that killed him burned always after in his son. I am certain it is the secret things my husband did after that to avenge his father, the things he thought I did not know about that wives always know about, that made the government make him a disappeared.

I knew he went to the secret meetings. I shared his bed! I know the symptoms of a husband who cannot eat because he is sick in his stomach; this is different from a husband who says he cannot eat because he is sick, but in truth cannot eat because of his nerves. I am the woman who washed this man's clothes for ten years, so I knew the smell of sweat from fear and the smell of sweat from him carrying a heavy load were not the same odors. He could make up stories for his absences, but I knew the nature of what he hid from me. He was no more than a few hours late that night, and I knew already he was a disappeared.

293

I did not make inquiries to the police, or even to his *compañeros*, for how was I to know who he thought was the trusted friend, but instead might be the betrayer? But the worst of what I had to do afterward was tell the lies about their father to my children. I did not do it easily. But I know what happens to a son when his father is murdered, the thoughts that cannot leave his head and the senseless revenge he will yearn to seek! So I told them he left us for another family, and made up stories of other sons that he loved more. As the left-behind women of the disappeared, these are the too-hard choices that are forced to be ours. I turned my dead husband, that man I loved, into someone his very own children hate, because it was all I could think to do to save their lives.

Okay. There! Now we are done with that story. All this talking and walking has made me more thirsty. Are you thirsty also? We should have another drink now. Another Gallo beer would taste good. I, um, uh-oh, where is my money? . . . I had some money here in my pocket . . . do you have any money? A few coins? I can repay you soon, when I sell some paches, I can give . . . Oh, good, thank you.

* * *

Tell me again when you have to leave to return to the states. That is not for a long time, right? Oh, good, because it will be terrible when you go. No, it will! It was terrible when Elena left and before you got here. Everything was different before she arrived and then it got worse when she left, but it is a little bit happy again now that you are here. These two months that you have been here have been full of better days! And if we keep thinking on good things, and not on the sad things that might come, it will keep us happy no matter what. So today let us just think and talk of good things so we can smile.

One of my happiest days ever was a day right before Elena left. We had a special day just us together, because Elena was done with her teaching at the school so she had the whole day just to spend with me and the girls. She came to my house in the morning with a blanket and two pair of shoes and some dresses and shirts, because she said that there is too much customs tax to take clothing back into the States and it would be helpful for her if she could just leave the clothes she was not wearing here with us. I had the baby outside with me where I was cooking beans for us on the fire next to the pig pen, but the older girls were inside watching the soap operas from Mexico on the *tele* and I told Elena just to take the clothes in and see who they fit. I could see them jumping around on the beds trying on Elena's clothes, and finally they called me in to show me how some of the clothes fit each of them so I said fine, if it would be helpful to Elena, we could keep the clothing. Even though the girls wore their *traje* during the day I thought it would be a shame to waste Elena's clothes, so I told them that at night or on the especially cold days they could wear her things over the top or underneath for extra warmth.

Then we all stayed inside, the four girls and Elena and me, working to spread the blanket she brought over the three beds. It felt even more crowded than at night, with the six of us crawling on the pushed-together beds. Our hands and knees kept bumping into each other and crashing into the walls while we tried to move the pile of clean clothes and then the pile of dirty clothes from one corner of the bed to the other, so we could spread out the blanket under it. Finally after some time and a lot of laughing—especially when Elena tried to stand and say Ta-Da!, and hit her head on the roof which made us all laugh more—we were ready to test the blanket. Elena unplugged the *tele* from the cord that hung down through the roof, and attached instead the plug from the blanket. She made us all lie down together as if we were asleep on the top of the blanket and said that with patience we would feel something soon, and then it was hot! It was a hot blanket for keeping warm at night! I thought this was too good of a thing for Elena not to keep, but she said that hot blankets are illegal in the United States so it would have to get dumped in the river with the other trash if we did not want it. So in order not to waste it we kept Elena's blanket.

For a long time we curled together that day on the hot blanket and ate beans and watched the Mexican shows on the *tele*. How good and warm it was inside the room of our house that day! The girls combed Elena's hair and made pretty designs with it, and Elena gave everyone what she called a rubbing of the neck to help bring on relaxation. We were lazy do nothings! We passed all of the day like Mayan princesses!

Only when we were too hungry to keep lying there did we get up, and I patted out the tortillas while the girls and Elena went up the mountain road to bring back more wood for the fire. They came back shortly, except Elena stopped by her house first because . . . because she needed water. Ay, *Dios*, I forgot she did that. She had to stop by her house to refill her container of water. Ay, *Dios*. I almost forgot that is how it started. That is the day Elena gave the men her water! That is why the girls came home alone that night, and it is why they went back up later, because of Elena.

What about the girls? What are you asking . . . what do you mean when you say, "Who are the girls?" I do not understand . . . you are saying, all this time, you do not know about the girls?! You have not heard? No one has told you?! All this time you have thought I only had the one baby daughter and two boys? Ay, Dios, *how could nobody have said anything? Just, um, just—just wait. Wait, okay?*

Okay, I am back. I had to go to the store for a minute. I just went for a minute to get us a little drink to share. Do you want a—oh, okay, well, I will just have a little sip myself then, just a few little sips. No, I am fine. Don't look at me—I am not crying! I am fine! Everything is fine! I just need my handkerchief. Where is my handkerchief? Hold this bottle so I can blow my nose. I just cannot believe no one has told you this story. Okay, wait . . . I will tell you. Give me the bottle back for a minute. Then I will tell you. Just one more sip, that is all.

In all those days of that horrible week, there are really only two of the days that I remember clearly and the rest I cannot remember at all. I remember the day it happened. I remember that day too clearly—too much about it is stuck in my head. I remember the temperature of the water on my hands when I looked up, and the rumbling sound of the truck in the valley below, and . . .

I remember more than I want to remember.

But the funeral was nice. I can say with certainty that it was the nicest funeral we have ever had in Zataque. I think that every person who lived in town came, and even the people from the other villages. Some people even came on buses from Xela, important men like the mayor and even the commander of the army detachment who stood up and talked. Although I did not speak to them myself it was very impressive to everyone that such esteemed men were there. Afterward, the truck company put on a very good wake in the municipal building, with all the food paid for and all the bottles of liquor given out for free, and it seemed like everyone had a good time.

It was honorable of the man from the truck company to take care of all those things for me. Late in the evening of the day of the accident the owner of the company came to my house and said he could not make enough apologies for what had happened, and he brought me *aguardiente* to calm my pain that we drank together. He said not to worry, that he would take care of my family. He said he would pay for the funeral and the wake, and to help ease my pain and make my life simpler he would give me two hundred fifty *quetzales* for the life of each child. I was in shock and said thank you, and he had some ink for me to put the print of my thumb on the paper where he wrote down our arrangement. I never saw him or anyone else from the truck company again after that, and the road still has not been finished and probably never will be, but he was an honest man, because he gave all the food and the liquor for the wake like he said he would and the next day three beautiful white coffins were delivered to my yard. Not just plain wood coffins like other people get either, but painted white ones, with metal hinges and locks so that the lids could lift up and down and would not need to get nailed shut. And the best part is that on the top of each coffin, in many lovely colors, were pictures of angels going through the clouds and some letters that spelled out: Eternal Slumber.

If they could have seen them, if they had not been dead, I think the girls would have liked their coffins very much.

It all started because on the day of the accident the girls were missing Elena very much. I made them help me carry all the laundry to the community *pila*, but they were so full of sadness that they were no real help to me with the washing. So I said that if they wanted to feel better, they should do something to remind them of Elena, maybe something Elena would do if she were still here, and I think the idea came to all of us at the same time to take some water up to the workmen on the road. From the town center we could see the men working up on the hill, and they had just all sat down to take a break when we arrived at the *pila*. The girls were with Elena when she had shared her water with the thirsty workmen the week before, and today was an even warmer day. We had a jug with us and water from the community spigot, so it seemed like a perfect idea. I tied the baby to my back so they could move more quickly, and then the three girls ran up the hill balancing the jug of water between them. When they got around the bend I could see them through the tree line, and the littlest one waved to me while the older two poured the water from the jug into the men's cups.

I returned to my washing. The water was not as cold as normal so I turned to splash a little on the baby's face to make her laugh when the unusual rumble started and my heart paused. Then suddenly it was like the wave of bloody water from my dream was swirling all around me and I was spinning, spinning, seeing everything. All of the women spun their heads to the hill and their smiles and their tired looks of hard scrubbing all changed to big wide eyes and screaming mouths. The noise rumbled louder and louder, but even so I could hear the man's screaming scared voice yell: "Look out! There are no brakes!" But I did not see him jump from the cab of the gravel-filled dump truck because my eyes spun to my girls, who were further down on the road by then, almost out of my sight. I saw my oldest daughter, my favorite sweet girl born to me after the boys, when I wanted a girl so badly, the one who would only put on her shoes if I tied them for her even years after she could do it herself, who crawled out of bed while the others slept to talk to me as I cooked, curled in a little round ball by the fire sucking, always sucking, on the edge of her hair—I saw her see the truck coming and I saw her fear splash on her face. I do not know how I saw it from so far away but I did, I saw it, and that brave girl of mine, in that last moment, she reached and scooped her sisters into her skirt, their tiny faces pressed into her waist, so they would not see what she saw, so she could protect them at least from the knowing, and in that last second, that very last second, she turned her face to me with eyes like MOMMA HELP ME and we looked at each other over the houses and over the trees and over the road, the way she looked at me when she was born with her eyes locked tight to my own eyes, this daughter of my own body, and I raised my hand to reach for her and she lifted her hand to reach for me— and then the wheel hit them and the truck lifted up into the air and the gravel came down over them and my daughters were gone.

When I woke up back in my own house, where they carried me, I said to the women gathered there, "Maybe it wasn't them!" (From so far away, maybe I had mistaken the sight of some other children for my children!)

But they said it was them.

I said, "I must go to them, then!" (Hurt children need their mother!)

But they said there was nothing anyone could do.

I said, "Maybe the truck missed them!" (They could have leapt free at the last minute!)

But they said the men were digging through the rock and had found a sweater.

I said, "Everyone wears sweaters, not just my children!"

But they handed me Elena's sweater, the one with the hood that she used to wear tied tight over her head, to warm her ears. The sweater my middle daughter liked so much, the one she had refused to take off ever since Elena pulled it over her head a week ago. The one with the pocket where she would hide her hands and a baby kitten that mewed all night pressed against her belly. The white sweater with letters that say UNIVERSITY OF ALABAMA across the front. The sweater that used to be white is now turned dark red over the place where my little one's heart used to be, and the right arm is even more red at the spot where her tiny elbow was once warmly tucked. The stains have not come out. There was also a big fresh tear in the shoulder by the neck that I have since mended, and gravel dust on all the sides that I have carefully washed off. With my hands on the sweater, that is how I knew it was true that my three daughters were dead. Alive they never would have let it go, this sweater I am wearing now, this ruined sweater of Elena's that is all I have left of my daughters to hold.

There, that is enough! I am done. I do not want to think any more about this right now, okay? We should put our minds somewhere else. Not everything is all bad. It is not! My sons are learning a good trade and my baby girl is still here with me and we can take care of each other. I even have almost one thousand quetzales*! Almost one thousand* quetzales *is the most money I have ever had! I could do so many things with it like ride on the buses with my sons anytime I want to and not even have to sell any more* paches. *Or I could still sell the* paches *but not have to raise up the price and instead buy a bigger* tele *for watching better shows and get some more* huipiles*! I could have a different* huipil *for all of the days of the week! So could my daughters—uh—I mean my daughter. The one who is left. Okay, so that is what I will think about. I will get everything straightened out. I will start right now, in this room, I will straighten it up! Will you help me pick these bottles up? Then in the morning I will make the plans for our new kind of life. My life with my one daughter who is left and my two sons. I will think of only good thoughts tomorrow after I have had some sleep. Oh, wait!—is that bottle empty? Do not throw that out yet. It looks like there is a little bit left in there. I should probably just finish that. So that we don't waste. Can you pass that bottle to me?*

Epilogue to Elena's Story

*I*t is not likely my life will allow me to return to Guatemala as anything but a tourist next time around.

I have not been back since I left, but I know what it has been like for others. They returned a stranger to most. Few recognized them, their friends all grown, moved around. They had no role but that of observer, so they could only watch and not be included. For me, it will never again be like the time the villagers begged me to get pregnant for them, *por favor*, so our town could have its own white baby: not *my* baby but *ours*. If I go back, no group will still think of me as one of their own; I will not be a part of us, I will be separate, they will be them. I will only be a passer-through, which I guess I was the first time, too, but we could pretend more easily then. I had a house and I had keys and that gave me roots, shallow though they were. Tourists never stay, not even in imaginings. They are always Ellen, never Elena.

My bond with Guatemala unraveled in those last few weeks, tore clear through that last night. The invader did me a favor, though; he filled me with fury and fear and a righteous indignation which swifted me home without regret. It is always easier to leave behind something you hate than it is to shun something you love. My anger served me well; it moved me forward, which is the way it must be. Life goes on.

So perhaps you think I am glad to be gone, and have with deliberate intent determined to stay away. If this is the case, you could not be more wrong. Time has softened and tempered my thoughts of her. Guatemala gave to me more than she took, and I would live it all over again, no second thoughts. If I got to repeat my life, rearrange, subtract, add in any experience I wanted, no question I'd keep the Guatemala years. Without a single change that time would be resurrected in the sequel, just the way it was. Guatemala made me *me*, and if she hurt me, the cicatrix is too much a part of who I am to ever relieve myself of it. It is what makes me most proud. It is my battle wound, my numbered tattoo, my Purple Heart that says I *thrived*.

For Volunteers, there is a debriefing which occurs in the country of service before one returns home. It gives us a chance to say those things that cannot be left unsaid. It is our forever goodbye. Of the seventy or so of us who started together, only about twenty remained at the end. There is a look we all wore, an eager-to-leave-yet-sad-to-go stare that burned in some eyes and only glinted in others, for we all had our own separate experiences and left in different states of mind. We were a gaunt lot, I myself weighing only ninety-some diseased pounds, but we were strong, the ones hardened by trials who did not wilt or snap or wear too thin, the tough ones.

"I have to tell you something," my dear friend Zac announced to the group of us, just before we parted (Zac who walked with me into this journey, and would walk with me all the way out). "I used to think of myself as a liberated man who respected women, and recognized their strengths. But I have never in my life known what it was to *truly* respect a woman until I came here, and saw what the women in this group have had to tolerate over the past two years. If there were things that were hard for us men to adapt to and deal with while we've been here, I know they would have been twice as hard had we been female.

"So I want you women to know," he continued without pause, "that I am awed by the strength and the fortitude you have demonstrated. I have no higher respect for anyone than I have for all of you right now." To a man, the others agreed.

Afterward, to me, privately, Zac said, "I need to apologize," but his apology, meant to compliment me, had to betray the insult first. "We all thought you'd fail."

There it was. "I know," I said, "it's okay . . ."

He interrupted me, saying, "No, it's not. Because here's the thing: Of everyone here, of everyone I know, you turned out to be the toughest of all."

So there is the ending I choose to remember.

And I am humble enough to recognize that if I did not fail, it is for being supported, subtly and overtly, with force and with tenderness, with kindness and with love and with a foreign brand of fury, by women who came so close and yet occupy a space a world away.

I will go back to Guatemala one day, as a visitor, yes, but with other purpose, and it will not be the mountains or the rivers that call me there.

I will go back to find the child Alma grown and to touch Rosa's hand again. I will go back to find the part of Guatemala I have stored in me that no years nor distance can ever deplete; I will go back and I will find the *me* that still lives in her villages, the girl I was and the woman I became in the folds of her hills. When I am reunited with Lucinda I will be reunited with something blooming in myself and will, in that moment, be filled with joy. I do not need to be recognized by others, nor welcomed indefinitely, for I will go back only to honor those women, my own self included, who made me who I am and whose essence I carry deeply and forever within me.

They are, in part, who I am, and to this day, even this far away, when I breathe in, I smell the subtle scent of them. When my heart beats the blood, I feel within it the strength of their pulse. And when I exhale, the breath of Guatemala lingers for a moment on the skin of my lips.

All these years later, I can taste her still.

ACKNOWLEDGEMENTS

*W*ith heartfelt gratitude, I extend my most sincere thanks to the following people:

The many friends and family who kindly read through drafts and offered their encouragement and feedback over and over again. Most especially, I am indebted to Wendy Lawton and Janice and David Kaminsky, who inevitably found all the nagging little parts that bothered me, too, and with kindness held me accountable for going back and fixing them.

My parents, Guy and Katie Urbani, for their unflagging lifelong encouragement. But most specifically, in regard to this project, my mother, to whom I read every paragraph long distance over the telephone as I wrote it. Her relentless insistence that it was the most captivating paragraph ever written—Fitzgerald and Hemingway be damned!—gave me the gumption to sit back down and keep writing.

My 10th grade English teacher, Dr. Elizabeth Tarner, who so emphatically insisted I had a way with words that I wound up believing her. My thanks are long overdue for her easy assurances which have, in many ways, influenced my life's direction. Every student should be so lucky.

My son, Elijah, whose threats of a too-imminent arrival resulted in third trimester bed rest, giving me the time I needed to finish the last three chapters. In the horse race between belly and brain, the book beat the baby by barely a nose.

Finally, because I have no right to end this without finishing her story for you, you should know that Cali came home to America with me on December 23, 1993 and lived a good and well-loved life until she died in my arms on January 27, 1999. To adequately describe how profoundly blessed I am to have journeyed through seven years of life with her, there are no words.